The Language of the Body

The Language of the Body

ORIGINALLY PUBLISHED AS

Physical Dynamics of Character Structure

ALEXANDER LOWEN, M.D.

COLLIER BOOKS

A Division of Macmillan Publishing Co., Inc.

NEW YORK

COLLIER MACMILLAN PUBLISHERS

LONDON

Macmillan Publishing Co., Inc.
866 Third Avenue, New York, N.Y. 10022
Collier Macmillan Canada, Ltd.

Library of Congress Catalog Card Number: 58-5661

First Collier Books Edition 1971
Seventh Printing 1976

THE LANGUAGE OF THE BODY was
originally published in a hardcover edition by
Grune and Stratton, Inc. under the title PHYSICAL
DYNAMICS OF CHARACTER STRUCTURE
and is reprinted by arrangement.

Printed in the United States of America

To Leslie, my wife,
who has been a never failing
inspiration to me

Contents

Preface

The movements of expression in the face and body . . . serve as the first means of communication between the mother and her infant. . . . The movements of expression give vividness and energy to our spoken words. They reveal the thoughts and intentions of others more truly than do words, which may be falsified. . . . The free expression by outward signs of an emotion intensifies it. On the other hand, the repression as far as this is possible, of all outward signs softens our emotions. He who gives way to violent gestures will increase his rage; he who does not control the signs of fear will experience fear in a greater degree; and he who remains passive when overwhelmed with grief loses his best chance of recovering elasticity of mind.

CHARLES DARWIN, 1872
*The Expression of Emotion
in Man and Animals*

We are witnessing today an attack upon psychoanalysis from psychiatrists and others who do not deny its basic principles. The criticism stems rather from disappointment with the results of psychoanalytic therapy. For even if one leaves aside the serious problems of cost, time and inconvenience, the hoped-for changes in personality, feeling and behavior frequently do not materialize. True, many patients are helped; some are improved. But the number of patients who spend years in analysis or go from one analyst to another without any significant change in their misery, their dissatisfaction, or their real problems is alarming.

Just the other day, I was consulted by a young woman who had spent four years in analysis and more than one year in another form of therapy. Her comment about these previous experiences is typical.

"The thing I went for wasn't really changed. I always felt that my capacity for feeling was greater than what I experienced. While analysis helped me to understand many things, I did not feel more. In this I was disappointed."

In the face of this situation the reaction from analytic psychiatrists is mixed. Some offer more elaborate formulations while others plead for simple common sense. Unfortunately, neither one of these approaches offers a solution to the problem. Nor can one blame Freud that the great insights he offered the world have proved relatively ineffective in overcoming the severe emotional disturbances from which many individuals suffer. Freud, himself did not hold out this promise. He knew the limitations of his technique.

The situation in which psychoanalysis finds itself today is like that of any other young medical discipline. Can one compare the results achieved by surgery now with those of one hundred years ago? Improvement results from changes in techniques, from a better comprehension of the problem and from heightened skills. If the analysts of our day are to be blamed for the present situation it is only because of their reluctance to modify their traditional procedures.

The history of psychoanalysis is not devoid of experimenters and thinkers. While most have devoted themselves to minor extensions of theory, several, notably Ferenczi and Wilhelm Reich, introduced important innovations in technical procedures. Ferenczi's "activity technique" or "analysis from below" attempted to deal with the difficult character problems which even then defied the psychoanalytic method. Reich's contributions we shall discuss more fully in the course of this study.

The problem which psychoanalysis faces arises from the fact that the analyst deals with body sensations and body feelings on a verbal and mental level, for the subject matter of analysis is the feeling and behavior of the individual. His ideas, fantasies and dreams are explored only as a means to comprehend and reach the feelings and to influence the behavior. Can we not conceive the possibility that there are other ways and means to change feelings and actions? In a letter to W. Fleiss in 1899, Freud revealed his constant interest in this question.

"From time to time I visualize a second part of the method of treatment—provoking patients' feelings as well as their ideas, as if that were quite indispensable."

If Freud failed to devise a method of treatment which would carry out this idea, that failure can be ascribed to the difficulty inherent in the body-mind relationship. So long as the concept of body-mind duality influences one's thinking, that difficulty is insuperable. We can surmise that Freud struggled with this problem all his life. Out of that struggle came the clear formulations which constitute ego psychology. But the same problem confronts the analysts of today as sharply as it did Freud.

It is not my intention in this preface to suggest the answer to this big question. Rather I would like to explain the thesis which underlies this study and which points the way to the solution of this problem. Analysts are aware of the identity of many somatic processes with psychological phenomena. The field of psychosomatic medicine is full of such references. Implied in this identity is the concept that the living organism expresses itself in movement more clearly than in words. But not alone in movement! In pose in posture, in attitude and in every gesture, the organism speaks a language which antedates and transcends its verbal expression. Further there are a number of specific studies which correlate the body structure and physique with emotional attitudes. These can be made as much subject to the analytic technique as dreams, slips of the tongue and the results of free association.

If body structure and temperament are related, as anyone who studies human nature can determine, the question then is: Can one change the character of an individual without some change in the body structure and in its functional motility? Conversely, if one can change the structure and improve its motility can we not effectuate those changes in temperament which the patient demands?

In his emotional expression, the individual is a unity. It is not the mind which becomes angry nor the body which strikes. It is the individual who expresses himself. So we study how a specific individual expresses himself, what is the range of his emotions and what are his limits. It is a study of the motility of the organism for the emotion is based on an ability "to move out."

Here is a clue to the relative failure of psychoanalysis. *It helps comparatively little to understand why one behaves as one does.* The individual afraid to dive into the water may know very well that he won't be hurt. We must understand and learn to overcome the fear of movement.

If the determinants of personality and character are physically structured, must not the therapeutic endeavor equally be physically oriented? Knowledge is but the prelude to action. To be more effective, the analytic therapy should provide for both understanding and movement within the therapeutic situation. The principles of theory and technique which form the framework of this new approach constitute what we call Bioenergetic Analysis and Therapy.

The one man primarily responsible for enlarging and extending the scope of the analytic technique to include the physical expression and activity of the patient was Wilhelm Reich. Much as one may disagree with Reich's later work, this development constitutes one of the major contributions to psychiatry. My indebtedness to Wilhelm Reich, who was my teacher, is expressed by ample references to his ideas in this volume. On the other hand, bioenergetic therapy is independent of Reich and his followers and differs from Reich's theories and techniques in many important aspects—some of which are set forth in this book.

It may be interesting to point out the differences between bioenergetic therapy and the traditional psychoanalytic techniques. First and foremost, the study of the patient is unitary. The bioenergetic therapist analyzes not only the psychological problem of the patient as will every analyst, but also the physical expression of that problem as it is manifested in the body structure and movement of the patient. Second, the technique involves a systematic attempt to release the physical tension which is found in chronically contracted and spastic muscles. Third, the relationship between therapist and patient has an added dimension to that found in psychoanalysis. Since the work is done on a physical level in addition to the analysis on a verbal level, the resulting activity involves the analyst more deeply than do the conventional techniques.

What about transference and counter-transference in such a situation? They are the bridge across which ideas and feelings flow between two individuals. In bioenergetic therapy, the physical contact brings both transference and counter-transference more sharply into focus. This facilitates the affective side of the analytic work. It demands, however, a greater ability on the part of the analyst to handle the resulting emotional tensions. If this ability is lacking, the analyst has not completed his own preparation for the task. Only with humility and candor dare one come face to face with the great wells of feeling which lie at the core of human beings.

This volume makes no pretense to be a complete presentation of the theories and techniques of bioenergetic analysis and therapy. The field is as vast as the subject of life itself. As an introduction to the subject, it should bridge the gap between psychoanalysis and the concept of a physical approach to emotional disorders. Further studies are in progress on both the theoretical and practical aspects of this work.

I should like to express my gratitude to my associate, Dr. John C. Pierrakos, U.S.N.R., whose collaboration in the formulation of the ideas contained in this volume was invaluable, and to Dr. Joel Shor for his patient and critical study of the manuscript. Also, I would like to express my appreciation to the members of the seminar on the dynamics of character structure whose suggestions and criticisms sharpened my ideas. My thanks are due to Miss Dora Akchim who graciously typed the manuscript of this book.

ALEXANDER LOWEN

New York City

Part One

1

Development of Analytic Techniques

The history of the development of analytic concepts and techniques is the story of therapeutic failures. This is true in every field of scientific endeavor; psychiatry and its related disciplines are no exceptions. Every advance is achieved through the recognition of a problem which previous methods of thinking and treatment failed to comprehend and resolve.

The very origin of psychoanalysis was in such a situation. We are familiar with the fact that Freud was interested in neurology and nervous diseases for a long time before he created the method of research and treatment for which he is known. The specific problem to which his attention was directed at the turning point in his career was the problem of hysteria. Previously, Freud had devoted himself "to physical therapy, and had felt absolutely helpless after the disappointing results experienced with Erb's 'electrotherapy.'" He then turned, as we know, to the use of hypnosis and especially to "treatment by suggestion during deep hypnosis" which he learned from Liebault and Bernheim. Freud later stated that he was not happy with this system of treatment in which, frequently, the hypnotist became angry because the patient "resisted" his suggestions. But Freud was also well acquainted with other therapeutic procedures for treating hysterias.

3

In the article which he published with Breuer, "On The Psychical Mechanism of Hysterical Phenomena," Freud (1893, p. 24) laid the basis for the scientific study of mental phenomena. True, the method he employed was hypnosis, but the analytic approach was substituted for the direct suggestion. It is described as follows: "and under hypnosis to arouse recollections relating to the time when the symptom first appeared."

Hypnosis had its limitations. First, not every patient could be hypnotized. Second, Freud did not like to reduce the patient's consciousness. As his insights progressed, Freud substituted free association for hypnosis as a way to the unconscious and later supplemented it with the interpretation of dreams as a source of knowledge about the unconscious.

These new techniques made possible further comprehension of the dynamics of psychic functioning. They revealed two phenomena which were concealed by the use of hypnosis. In 1914 (p. 298), in the article "On The History of the Psychoanalytic Movement," Freud wrote that "the theory of psychoanalysis is an attempt to account for two observed facts that strike one conspicuously and unexpectedly whenever an attempt is made to trace the symptoms of a neurotic back to their sources in his past life: the facts of transference and resistance." The method of psychoanalysis, therefore, "began with the new technique that dispenses with hypnosis."

The importance of the phenomena of transference and resistance to the analytic concept is such that Freud (1914, p. 291) could say "Any line of investigation, no matter what its direction, which recognizes these two facts and takes them as the starting point of its work may call itself psychoanalysis, though it arrives at results other than my own." We would be justified at this point in seeking a definition of these terms and a further statement of how they are handled in the therapeutic situation.

In a lecture on psychotherapy, Freud (1904b, p. 261) had defined resistance as follows: "The discovery of the unconscious and the introduction of it into consciousness is performed in the face of a continuous *resistance* on the part of the patient. The process of bringing this unconscious material to light is associated with 'pain' (unlust), and because of this pain the patient again and again rejects it." At this time, Freud considered psychoanalysis as a process of re-education in which the physician persuaded the patient to overcome the resistance and accept the repressed material.

If we ask about the nature of this pain (unlust) we find that it is the expression of a physical as well as psychical process. In one article, "Freud's Psycho-Analytic Method," (1904a, p. 267) the experience of a repressed memory is described as a feeling of "actual discomfort." Freud had observed that the patient was uneasy, that he moved restlessly and showed signs of more or less disturbance.

In a lecture delivered in 1910 (p. 286), Freud spoke of the curative method of psychoanalysis as being based upon two approaches. One is the interpretation: "We give the patient the conscious idea of what he may expect to find, and the similarity of this with the repressed unconscious one leads him to come upon the latter himself." The second, "more powerful one [lies] in the use of the 'transference.'" We shall examine the problem of the transference more closely later. It is interesting to note, however, that as early as 1910 (p. 288), Freud described the therapeutic task in terms of resistance analysis. "Now, however, our work is aimed directly at finding out and overcoming the resistances." And in an article on dream interpretation (1912b, p. 306) he said, "it is of the greatest importance for the cure that the analyst should always be aware of what is chiefly occupying the surface of the patient's mind at the moment, that he should know just what complexes and resistances are active and what conscious reaction to them will govern the patient's behavior."

Though we are no nearer to a full understanding of the nature of the resistance, it is opportune to study the problem of transference, for we shall see that the two, resistance and transference, form two aspects of a single function. In his discussion of "The Dynamics of Transference," Freud (1921a, pp. 312, 314) started with a basic assumption derived from his years of analytic experience. That is, "that every human being has acquired . . . a special individuality in the exercise of his capacity to love—that is, in the conditions he sets up for loving, in the impulses he gratifies by it, and in the aims he sets out to achieve in it." But in analytic therapy the transference to the physician is marked by an excess; that is, it "is effected not merely by the conscious ideas and expectations of the patient, but also by those that are under suppression, or unconscious." In addition, it develops during the analysis that the "transference provides the strongest resistance to the cure." The answer to this problem provided Freud with an understanding of the dynamics of the transference.

Freud (1912a, p. 319) distinguished two aspects of transference: positive transference and negative transference, separating "the transfer of affectionate feeling from that of hostile feeling." Positive transference showed both a conscious element and an unconscious element rooted in erotic desire. It became obvious, then, that it was the negative transference and the unconscious erotic component of the positive transference which constituted the resistance. The conscious element of the positive transference became the vehicle for the therapeutic suggestion. So far so good, but what is the origin and function of the negative transference? In contrast to the negative transference, the erotic element of the positive transference can be more easily "raised" and resolved.

Before proceeding further, it is well to discuss the means Freud used to overcome the "resistances." The treatment began with the patient committed to the fundamental rule; that is, to say everything that came into his mind without exercising any conscious choice over the material. Under such circumstances, a resistance may manifest itself in the cessation of flow of ideas or associations. Rarely, it may be expressed in the refusal to accept an interpretation. In both situations, experience showed Freud that the patient had made a transfer onto the person of the physician of some part of the material of the "pathogenic complex" which he either withheld from expression or "defended with the utmost obstinacy." These are the negative forces which the analyst can counter with the true positive transference and the patient's hope for cure. The conflicts which arise are then fought out on the field of transference and duplicate those in the emotional life of the patient.

The ambivalence which manifests itself in the transference has characterized the behavior of the patient since early childhood. How is it then, we may ask, that the analyst can upset an equilibrium which though neurotic, has maintained itself during the past life of the patient? If we consider this question seriously, we will realize that there are two factors operating in a psychoanalysis which can shift the balance of forces in favor of a resolution of the conflict. The first is the sympathetic understanding of the patient by the analyst. Despite the fact that the patient may "see" the analyst as a father image or other familial figure, it is contrary to the reality of the situation. The analyst is understanding where the true parent was not, sympathetic where the parent was intolerant, and accepting where the parent was rejecting. As a general attitude, however, these qualities would not be very effective. They derive their power from the fact that the analyst is regarded as being the protagonist of sexual pleasure. It is his affirmative attitude towards sexuality which forms the bridge to the unconscious of the patient. He is at the same time the representative of the sexual instinct as he is, by virtue of the negative transference, responsible for its suppression.

We cannot over-emphasize the importance of Freud's positive attitude towards sexuality as a therapeutic weapon in the early days of psychoanalytic therapy. One must recall the moral atmosphere between 1892 and 1912 to appreciate the full force of his position. In a time when the open discussion of sex among individuals was almost im-

possible Freud's candor and honesty on this subject facilitated the breakthrough of the suppressed sexual drive with
its accompanying images and affect. An interpretation
which today might be accepted as a matter of course in
those years provoked strong resistance and deep yearning.
As the lid was removed from the boiling pot, steam began
to escape. And even in these sophisticated days a valid
interpretation of the sexual dreams and fantasies has potent force. On the other hand this sophistication in analytic and sexual thinking has robbed the analytic interpretation of the power it once had. We are all familiar with
the patient who goes from one analyst to another and who
knows "all about" his Oedipus complex and his incestuous
feelings for his mother.

The transference was and still is based upon the projection onto the person of the analyst of suppressed sexual
desires and fears. Freud (1914, p. 383) was very much
aware of this when he discussed the problem of trans-
ference-love. With a rich background of experience Freud
analyzed the problem clearly and showed how it was to be
handled. One remark is very apt. "I would state as a fundamental principle that the patient's desire and longing
are to be allowed to remain, to serve as driving forces for
the work and for the changes to be wrought." Yet it is not
only in the case of the female patient that the transference
carries the sexual desires and hopes. The male patient,
too, comes with his hopes of increased sexual potency
which he expects the analyst to provide through the technique of the therapy. Here, too, the promise held out by
the positive attitude towards sexuality is the magnet which
draws out the unconscious thoughts.

It is also important to bear in mind that the technique of
resistance and transference analysis found its greatest effectiveness in the treatment of the hysterias, the obsessive-compulsive neuroses, and those emotional disturbances
in which symptom formation was the main element. These
are the problems which confronted Freud in the earlier
years and which are characterized by a dominance of the
conflict on the genital level. Other problems were encoun-

tered which were less amenable to this technique. The problems of masochism, mania and depression, and the psychoses were posed originally as disturbances of the genital function. It soon became apparent, however that the genital problem merely reflected a deeper conflict which had its origin in the pre-oedipal years of the patient's life. Against these deep-rooted disturbances the technique of resistance analysis exploiting the sexual transference made slow and little progress.

With the advent of new and younger analysts, the traditional psychoanalytic technique was modified to meet these more difficult cases. Foremost among these early innovators was Ferenczi with his "activity techniques." We know that Ferenczi's ideas brought him into frequent conflict with Freud who resisted any change in the traditional method of psychoanalysis. However, Ferenczi maintained his allegiance to Freud and to his basic psychoanalytic concepts even though his experiences impelled him to modify in some important respects the therapeutic techniques. The recent publication in English of Ferenczi's papers enables us to properly evaluate his contribution to analytic technique.

As we read Ferenczi's articles and lectures we are impressed with his interest in his patients and in the technical problems of the therapeutic procedure. In her introductory note to his publications, Clara Thompson (1950) says of Ferenczi that "to the end of his life [he] tirelessly sought improvements in technique designed to produce more effective therapy." As early as 1909, in the article "Introjection and Transference," Ferenczi revealed how penetrating was his insight into the therapeutic relationship. Then, in 1920, Ferenczi delivered an address on the development of an active therapy in psychoanalysis.

In this article, as in preceding ones, Ferenczi (1921, p. 199) showed that while ostensibly the analyst adopts a passive attitude during the treatment, his activity is merely held in abeyance until a resistance appears. Communicating an interpretation is in itself an active interference with the patient's psychic activity; it turns the thoughts in a given direction and facilitates the appearance of ideas that otherwise would have been prevented by the resistance from becoming conscious. And one cannot deny that the obligation to follow the fundamental rule is enforced by the analyst in an active if indirect way. Ferenczi (1921, p. 200) clearly pointed out that there has never been a question but that the analyst is active in the therapy. It is different with respect to the patient. "Analysis demands no activities from the patient except punctual appearance at the hours of treatment." But exceptions were soon made in the case of some patients with phobias and others with compulsive symptoms. Freud, himself, had already recognized this.

Ferenczi (1921, pp. 189–198) now proposed to introduce a technique in which "certain tasks in addition to the fundamental rule" are imposed upon the patient. Previously he had described a case in which he had demanded from the patient a "renunciation of certain hitherto unnoticed pleasurable activities" with the result that "the progress of the analysis was visibly accelerated." This case, reported in "Technical Difficulties in the Analysis of a Case of Hysteria," shows a brilliant analysis of the dynamics of the hysterical character structure.

What activities did Ferenczi (1919, pp. 203, 206, 207) demand of his patients? In one exciting case, he required the patient to be a chanteuse, conduct an orchestra and play the piano. In another, the command to write poetical ideas on paper revealed a strong masculinity complex. Symptoms which Ferenczi forbade included the "need of urination immediately before or after the analytic session, a feeling of sickness during the session, unseemly wriggling, plucking at and stroking the face, the hands or other parts of the body, etc." More important, however, than the specific technique is the principle which underlies the "activity" concept. For, as we shall see, the principle was greatly extended by Ferenczi's pupil, Wilhelm Reich. Ferenczi's remarks are, therefore, illuminating:

"The fact that the expressions of emotion or motor actions forced from the patients evoke secondarily memories from the unconscious rests partly on the reciprocity of affect and idea emphasized by Freud in *tramdeutung*. The awakening of a memory can—as in catharsis—bring an emotional reaction with it, but an activity exacted when the patient, or an emotion set at freedom, can equally well expose the repressed ideas associated with such processes. Of course the doctor must have some notion about which affects or actions need reproducing" (1919a, p. 216).

In a later paper, Ferenczi (1923, p. 226) discussed some contraindication to the "active" psychoanalytic technique. At the same time he extended the activity concept. Again a quote is revealing. "I have since then learnt that it is sometimes useful to advise *relaxation exercises*, and that with this kind of relaxation one can overcome the psychical inhibitions and resistances to association." Ferenczi's attention to muscular activity and bodily expression is noted constantly throughout his papers. There is the interesting article on "Thinking and Muscle Innervation" in which the parallelism and similarity of the two processes is analyzed. In a footnote to another article Ferenczi (1925a, p. 286) stated, "There seems to be a certain relation between the capacity in general for relaxation of the musculature and for free association." One further aspect of this kind of analytic technique is given in the observation, "Speaking generally, the methods tend to convince patients that they are able to stand more 'pain,' indeed that they can exploit this 'pain' to extract further pleasure gain; and from this there arises a certain feeling of freedom and self-assurance which is conspicuously absent in the neurotic" (1925, p. 267).

Since it is not my purpose to elucidate Ferenczi's concepts but rather to study his methods as part of the historical development of analytic techniques I must forego further quotes from his most interesting observations. At this point, where we leave Ferenczi (1925b, p. 288) he has extended the analytic concept greatly. The "purely passive association technique [which] starts from whichever psychic superficies is present and works back to the preconscious cachexes of unconscious material might be described as 'analysis from above,' to distinguish it from the 'active' method which I should like to call 'analysis from below.' "

At the time that Ferenczi extended the scope of the analytic procedure other analysts were studying and classifying patterns of behavior. This took the form of character types of which the foremost exponent was Abraham. Prior to this, analysis was mostly symptom analysis. The analyst made a pact with the patient's ego that the character would be spared in return for a resolution of the symptom. Of course the analyst was aware of the patient's character and had to reckon with it while the patient was being gradually prepared to accept painful pieces of insight. But the attack upon the character itself did not come until Reich published his article on "Character Analysis" in 1929.

Character problems are distinguished from neurotic symptoms in that with them the "insight into the illness is lacking." Ferenczi (1925b, p. 291) compared the character to a "private psychosis endured, nay acknowledged by the narcissitic ego whose modification is chiefly resisted by the ego itself." It is precisely in the character disturbances that Ferenczi found the greatest value and usefulness of his activity technique. Where the ego is part and parcel of the very structure which constitutes the basic problem, "analysis from below" can circumvent the defense which the ego erects against an attack upon itself. We shall have the opportunity in subsequent chapters to study how character analysis forms a bridge between ego psychology above and the somatic tensions and disturbances below.

Despite the advances made by Ferenczi, Abraham and Reich, the problems of the emotionally disturbed individual were far from quick solution. Further advances in methodology were needed. The concepts and procedures of the "activity" technique, i.e., of "analysis from below" or a somatic approach, had to be more extensively worked out. The character itself, which is fundamentally a gestalt way of understanding behavior, was not yet fully understood dynamically or genetically. The bridge could not be completed until both the psychic and the somatic functions were comprehended in terms of a unitary system. The functions of the libido as a psychic energy had to be correlated with energy processes on the somatic level. The task was substantially completed in the psychological realm with Freud's publication of *The Ego and the Id* and his preceding study, *Beyond the Pleasure Principle*. Some modifications could be expected but the major relationships and forces were described.

The breakthrough into the somatic field came through the further work of Reich. In 1927 Reich, one of the leaders of the school of younger analysts, published a significant study. It was *The Function of the Orgasm*. In it Reich propounded the theory that the orgasm serves the function of discharging the excess energy of the organism. If that discharge is blocked or insufficient, anxiety develops. It may be possible for some individuals to work off the excess energy through muscular exertion and for others to decrease the anxiety by limiting the production of energy, but such solutions disturb the natural function of the organism directly on the physical level. At the same time, of course, they decrease the possibility of pleasure which alone guarantees the emotional well-being of the individual. Without this concept of the genital function, the comprehension of the dynamics of the emotions in the somatic realm is well nigh impossible.

In the English edition of *The Function of the Orgasm*, Reich (1942, p. 239) relates the treatment of a case of passive homosexuality in 1933. The resistance which was especially strong was "manifested in an extreme attitude of stiffness of the neck [stiff necked]." When the resistance gave way there was a violent negative reaction: "The color of his face kept changing rapidly from white to yellow or blue; the skin was mottled and of various tints; he had severe pains in the neck and occiput; the heart beat was rapid, he had diarrhea, felt worn out and seemed to have lost hold." Reich (1942, p. 240) commented that when "the muscles of the neck relaxed, powerful impulses broke through." From a multitude of such facts Reich deduced that emotional energy which could be expressed sexually, or as anger or anxiety was "bound by chronic muscular tensions."

Ferenczi had made similar observations, especially with respect to the tension of the sphincter muscles, the anus, the urethra and the glottis. He had shown the relation of "tics" to displaced sexual energy and he was aware of muscular attitudes. Ferenczi failed, however, to draw the theoretical conclusions from these observations in terms of the relation of muscle tension to psychic function in general. This Reich did in the concept that the character and the muscular attitude were "functionally identical," that is, they served the same function energetically. In a practical way, this provided a more comprehensive method of therapy in which "analysis from above" was combined with "analysis from below." Reich (1942, p. 241) states, "When a character inhibition would fail to respond to psychic influencing, I would work at the corresponding somatic attitude. Conversely, when a disturbing muscular attitude proved difficult of access, I would work on its characterological expression and thus loosen it up."

The great contributions to the analytic understanding of man have always proceeded from clinical observations. Improvements in technique lead to modifications of theory, innovations in technique to extensions of theory. Reich's formulation of the functional identity of muscular tension and emotional block was one of the great insights developed in the course of the analytic therapy of emotional disturbances. It opened the door to a new field of analytic investigation and Reich was the first to explore its possibilities. In *The Function of the Orgasm* and in *Character Analysis* (third edition), Reich set forth the first results of this new method of treatment and investigation.

It is important to bear in mind that the muscular rigidity is not just the "result" of the process of repression. Where the psychic disturbance contains the meaning or purpose of the repression, the muscular rigidity explains the manner and is the mechanism of the repression. Since the two are immediately linked in the functional unity of emotional expression, one observes constantly how the "dissolution of a muscular rigidity not only liberates vegetative energy, but, in addition, also brings back into memory the very infantile situation in which the repression had taken effect" (1942, p. 267). The term "neurosis" can be extended to signify a chronic disturbance of the natural motility of the organism. From this it follows, too, that the neurosis is identical with a decrease or limitation of aggression, the latter word being used in its natural sense of "to move to."

The character of the individual as it is manifested in his typical pattern of behavior is also portrayed on the somatic level by the form and movement of the body. The sum total of the muscular tensions seen as a gestalt, that is, as a unity, the manner of moving and acting constitutes the "body expression" of the organism. The body expression is the somatic view of the typical emotional expression which is seen on the psychic level as "character." It is no longer necessary to depend on dreams or the technique of free association to disclose the unconscious impulses and their equally unconscious resistances. Not that such techniques have no proper place but a more direct approach to this problem is provided by the attack upon the block in motility or the muscular rigidity itself. All of this and more Reich elaborated. It is our purpose to fill in the gaps and extend the theory and practice. Reich (1942, p. 269), himself, pointed to the necessity of further work along this line when he said, "The dissolution of the muscular spasms follows a law which cannot as yet be completely formulated."

A major technical advance which emerged from the observations and thinking which produced the above formulations was the use of respiration in the therapeutic procedure. Analysis on the somatic level had revealed that patients hold their breath and pull in their belly to suppress anxiety and other sensations. One finds that it is a fairly universal practice. It can easily be observed in children and also in adults. In situations which are experienced as frightening or painful, one sucks in the breath, contracts the diaphragm and tightens the abdominal muscles. Release of the tension results in a sigh. If this becomes a chronic pattern, the chest is held high in the inspiratory position, respiration is shallow and the belly is hard. The decrease in respiration diminishes the intake of oxygen and reduces the production of energy through metabolism. The final result is a loss of affect and a lowering of the emotional tone.

It is in line with Ferenczi's concept of "activity" to ask a patient to breathe easily and naturally during the therapeutic procedure. Of course, like all activity procedures, the application is individual; it depends on the particular patient and his situation. It constitutes, however, a basic procedure. In addition, other suggestions for activity or restraint are used, all of which are designed to bring the patient into contact with or to awareness of a lack of motility or a muscular rigidity. The dissolution of the rigidity then is obtained through the patient's conscious control of the muscular tension and of the emotional impulse blocked by the spastic condition. Movement and expression are the tools of all analytic procedures and these are supplemented where necessary by direct work upon the muscular rigidity.

It is important to recognize the power inherent in these procedures. In this technique, one deals not only with the "derivatives of the unconscious" but with the unconscious mechanism of repression itself. In this way it is possible to bring affects to consciousness with an intensity which is impossible on the verbal level. Ferenczi was aware of the limitations of the ordinary analytic procedures. In "Psychoanalysis of Sexual Habits" (1925b, p. 287) he wrote: "Communication between conscious and unconscious comes about as Freud tells us, 'by the interposition of preconscious links.' Now of course that applies only to unconscious presentations; in the case of unconscious inner trends which 'behave like the repressed,' that is to say, do not get through to consciousness either as emotions or sensations, interpolation of preconscious links will not bring them into consciousness. For example, unconscious inner 'pain' sensations 'can develop driving force without attracting the ego's attention to the compulsion. Only resistance to the compulsion, a blocking of the discharge-reaction, can bring this "Something Else" into consciousness in the form of 'pain.' " The quotes in Ferenczi's observation are from Freud's *The Ego and the Id*.

Reich's description of specific muscle tensions and of their role both as defense mechanisms and as the expression of secondary, derivative drives is valuable reading for any person who wishes to comprehend the dynamics of the body expression. On the other hand since our orientation is somewhat different, though deriving from Reich's basic concepts, and since our technique is correspondingly altered, it is unnecessary to elaborate on his observations or theories.

If the functional unity of the character and the pattern of muscular rigidity is recognized, it then becomes important to find their common root principle. This turns out to be the concept of energy processes.

In the psychic realm, the processes of structuring which go to make up the neurotic equilibrium can only be understood by reference to a "displaceable energy" which Freud called the libido. When one observes physical motility, on the other hand, one is in direct contact with a manifestation of physical energy. It is a basic physical law that all movement is an energy phenomenon. When a patient strikes with his arms an analysis of the movement would reveal the underlying energy process. It is not possible to jump unless energy is brought down into the legs and feet and discharged into the ground. Here again we have reference to basic physical laws: movement involves the discharge of energy and action equals reaction. We act upon the ground in an energetic way and it reacts to lift us upward. While we do not ordinarily think of our movements in this way, such thinking is necessary when one wants to comprehend the dynamics of movement. We should know, too, what the nature of this energy is at work in the human body. How is it related to the psychic energy called libido?

If we are to avoid becoming mystical, we must regard the concept of energy as a physical phenomenon, that is, capable of being measured. We must also follow the physical law that all energy is interchangeable and we must assume, in harmony with modern doctrines in physics, that all forms of energy can be and eventually will be reduced to a common denominator. It is not important at this point to know the final form of this basic energy. We work with the hypothesis that there is one fundamental energy in the human body whether it manifests itself in psychic phenomena or in somatic motion. This energy we call simply "bioenergy." Psychic processes as well as somatic processes are determined by the operation of this bioenergy. All living processes can be reduced to manifestations of this bioenergy.

Such a unitary concept, while in the back of the mind of every analyst, is not immediately practical in analytic therapy. The analytically oriented therapist approaches his patient from the outside. His contact is always from the surface inwards, and deep as he may penetrate into the inner life and deep-seated biological processes, the surface phenomena is never ignored or overlooked. For the problem of the patient as he presents himself to therapy is based upon a difficulty in his relationship to the external world—to people, to reality. In this aspect of his individuality, the patient presents not the unity of the bioenergetic process seen, for example, in the protozoa, but the dichotomy which expresses itself in a body-mind relationship where each sphere is acting upon and reacting with the other. Thus, for the purpose of analytic therapy, a dualistic approach such as characterized Freud's thinking is indispensable. In the next chapter, where this relationship of the mind to the body is more fully explored, our point of view will be dualistic. On the superficial level, a unity is also possible in terms of function and this unitary function which bridges psyche and soma is the character.

2

Somatic Aspect of Ego Psychology

Although psychoanalysis is regarded as a discipline limited to the study of psychic problems, it had its origin in the problems of disturbed somatic functioning, the etiology of which could not be ascribed to organic damage. These problems comprised a group which included hysteria, anxiety neurosis, neurasthenia and obsessive-compulsive behavior. Hysteria was defined by Freud (1894b, p. 65) as the "capacity for conversion . . . the psychophysical capacity to transmute large quantities of excitation into somatic innervation." For all the many years of psychoanalytic study of hysteria, the mechanism whereby this conversion or transmutation takes place has never been fully elucidated. The solution was not possible until Reich formulated the basic law of emotional life; that is, the unity and antithesis of psychosomatic functioning.

If Freud abandoned the attempt to comprehend the neurosis on both the psychic and the somatic level, he never lost sight of the underlying body processes. The remark that the ego is "first and foremost a body ego" indicates this interest (1950c, p. 31). Ferenczi, much more than Freud, tried to correlate biological processes with psychic phenomena. The positive results led him to develop an "active" therapy on the somatic level to complement the analytic work in the psychic realm. In 1925, in the paper entitled "Contra-indications to the 'Active' Psychoanalytic Technique," Ferenczi (1925a, p. 229) seriously questioned the intellectual approach in analysis. "It shows in that along the path of intelligence, which is a function of the ego, really nothing in the way of conviction can occur." Although this is admitted by all analysts today, the way to conviction via immediate body sensation is known to very few analytic psychiatrists. It is the purpose of this book to extend the principle of "analysis from below" and to make available to analytic therapists an understanding of the dynamic somatic processes which underlie the psychic phenomena observed in analysis.

Before it was possible to establish the interrelationship between mind and body processes, the mechanics of the system which alone can comprehend and portray relationships must have been known. It is the paradox of knowledge that the means of knowing must be employed to comprehend the phenomena of knowing. We can be quite sure that Freud was not unaware that psychoanalysis had eventually to be grounded in biology to achieve the scientific status he desired for it. If then he limited psychoanalysis to the study of psychic phenomena it must be because he felt that our knowledge of psychic processes was not sufficiently secure to attempt to bridge the two realms of human functioning. It is to his great merit that he did succeed in constructing a framework of psychic functioning which could serve as the springboard for the leap into biology. For us today a thorough understanding of ego psychology is indispensable to the comprehension of character and the dynamics of a bioenergetic therapy.

In 1923 Freud published a detailed study of the ego and the id. Since then little has been changed in his basic concepts. They will form the basis for our present review. At the outset, however, it must be recognized that the expressions used in psychoanalysis describe mental phenomena. We shall see, however, that the mental interpretation of perceptions, feelings or needs is somewhat confusing and one must supplement the psychic concept with physical actions to give them an appearance of reality.

The concept of the ego is fundamental to analytic thinking. The word "ego" is not an English translation of the German *Das Ich* which Freud used and which the French translate as *le moi*. The correct English word is "The I." We must bear in mind, therefore, that the ego is used as a synonym for the self in the subjective sense. Here, again, the difficulty of knowing the self through the self is apparent. Yet this is the only way, for the ego is the first thing we encounter as we turn inward upon ourselves.

Freud (1950b, p. 15) described the ego well: ". . . in every individual there is a coherent organization of mental processes which we call his ego. This ego includes consciousness and it controls the approaches to motility, i.e., to the discharge of excitations into the external world; it is this institution in the mind which regulates all its own constituent processes, and which goes to sleep at night though even then it continues to exercise a censorship upon dreams." Yet even in such a clear statement some confusion is evident. It is not easy to reconcile the statement that the ego "goes to sleep at night" with its description as an "organization of mental processes." Should we not say that it is rather the person who goes to sleep and not his ego, though the latter is involved in this total function as are the senses and the musculature. With the decrease in activity there is a concomitant decrease in the excitation of the total organism, one result of which is the dimming or extinction of the ego.

There is a valid basis to compare the ego in at least one of its aspects to an electric bulb, for the intelligence is a light. While we attribute the darkness to the extinction of the light in the bulb, we are still aware that it is the cessation of the electric current which is responsible for the darkness. Is not sleep similar? When the excitation quiets down, the light which is the ego dims or goes out.

It is important for practical purposes that we make this distinction as to the basic nature of sleep. Shall we tell our patients who suffer from insomnia to stop thinking? Or, shall we not seek the cause of their inability to stop their conscious mental activity in the persistence of somatic tension and excitation? In his early days Freud recognized that the best inducement to sleep was satisfactory sexual activity. Today we know that the orgasm serves to discharge energy or tension and thereby to facilitate sleep. It is not that the ego refuses to go to sleep; it cannot be dimmed so long as persistent somatic excitation flows into the mental apparatus. The opposite direction of flow, that is, downward, brings this excitation to the organs of discharge, the genitals.

But the ego is more than the light in the darkness of unconscious activity. It controls the approach to motility, or, more properly, it controls motility. Within limits, the ego can release an action or hold it back until conditions are opportune. It can inhibit actions and even repress them beyond consciousness. In this function it resembles the electronic devices which regulate rail traffic and which may replace the train dispatcher and the red, green and yellow light signals. The train may be fully charged with steam or diesel power and ready to roll, but no movement will occur until the signal is given that the track ahead is clear. The ego is like a light which is turned both outward and inward. Outward it searches the environment through the senses; inwardly it comprises a set of signals which govern the outgoing impulses. In addition we know that it has the inherent power to adjust impulses to reality similar to the function of the electronic regulators.

Freud (1950b, pp. 16, 17) knew these relationships well in the psychic realm. "From the ego proceed the repressions, too, by means of which an attempt is made to cut off certain trends in the mind not merely from consciousness but also from their other forms of manifestation and activity." The resistance which the patient shows in analysis can be only the manifest expression of the red light of repression. We can certainly go along with Freud in regarding the repressed and its manifestation in resistance, both unconscious, as part of the ego which then includes both conscious and subconscious elements. But we must make one important distinction. The ego can include only those unconscious elements—fears, impulses, sensations—which were once conscious and then repressed. The problem of developmental failure or arrest is outside the scope of ego psychology. The individual who as a child or infant had never consciously experienced certain sensations cannot acquire them through analysis. Where a person has suffered from a lack of feelings of security in early life what is needed in the therapy is not only analysis but the opportunity and the means to acquire that security in the present. Analysis cannot restore to a chicken its lost ability to fly. Only within the framework of analytic ego psychology is it correct to derive the neurosis from "the antithesis between the organized ego and what is repressed and dissociated from it."

We learn next from Freud that the ego is topographically located at the surface of the mental apparatus where it is in proximity to the external world. This position corresponds to the required function of perception. The ego lights up and perceives the external reality as well as being conscious of internal reality—the needs, impulses and fears; in other words, the sensations of the organism. But we must agree with Freud (1950b, p. 24) when he says that, "Whereas the relation between external perceptions and the ego is quite perspicuous, that between internal perceptions and the ego requires special investigation."

Of this second relationship Freud (1950b, p. 25) remarks, "sensations and feelings only become conscious through reaching the system Perception; if the way forward is barred, they do not come into being as sensations, although the undetermined element corresponding to them is the same as if they did." We can distinguish, therefore, between the internal event (an undetermined quantitative element) and the phenomenon of its perception by which it is given qualitative significance, that is, brought into relation with external reality. It is precisely this "undetermined element" which is the subject of all so-called "active" techniques.

The ego has as its nucleus the system of perception and

embraces the conscious, but this should be extended to include all that was once conscious—the repressed unconscious and the preconscious. The ego as a psychic phenomenon is the perceiving system together with all its perceptions both past and present. Freud follows Groddeck in admitting that the function of the ego is "essentially passive." This conclusion is inevitable in the case of those who identify the self with the system of perception; those who find the "I" in the mind. It is the basis of all bioenergetic techniques that the "I" includes not only the perceptions but also those internal forces, Freud's "undetermined elements," which give rise to perceptions. When the identity of the self is with the feeling, of which the perception is but a part, the individual does not regard his ego as being purely a mental phenomenon. In such individuals perception is merely one component of conscious action.

Freud was not unaware of the difficulties that arise if the ego is regarded only as a psychic process. The main difficulty is the absence of all quantitative factors. In therapeutic work one is obliged to think quantitatively. It is not uncommon today to hear a patient remark that he feels his ego to be "weak." More commonly, the complaint is of a lack of feeling of the self. Observation of these patients reveals a lack of intensity in the feeling tone, and what is more important, a lack of forcefulness in action and expression. It would be a mistake in such cases to place the problem in the system of perception. A strong ego is a sign of emotional health but it can coexist with a severe neurosis if its energy is mostly used for repression.

"It seems that another factor, besides the influence of the system perception, has been at work in bringing about the formation of the ego and its differentiation from the id." Freud (1950b, p. 31) used this remark to introduce a statement which pointed the way to biology: "The ego is first and foremost a body-ego." He elaborated this to say further that "the ego is ultimately derived from bodily sensations, chiefly from those springing from the surface of the body." It shall be our purpose in the latter half of this chapter to analyze those body processes which constitute "that other factor." We shall see that this other factor is not body sensation, for that involves perception, but the deeper process of impulse formation in the organism.

Before we proceed further it is well to consider the relations of the ego to the other subdivisions of the mental faculty. The largest part of the function of the organism is unconscious. This, too, has a representation in the mind; in fact, the greater portion of the nervous system is concerned with bodily activities of which we are completely unaware. Posture, which one takes for granted, involves the control of motility to a very high degree. Consciousness can be extended into this realm but only to a small extent. That part of the mind which is in the same relationship to these involuntary processes as the ego is to voluntary activity, Freud called the "id." Freud did not so define the id. But such a definition follows from his remarks by extension from biology to psychology.

"The ego is not sharply differentiated from the id, its lower portion merges into it." In fact the ego is the part of the id "which has been modified by the direct influence of the world acting through the perception-conscious system" (1950b, pp. 28–29). The analogy which is useful in showing this relationship is the tree. The ego can be compared to the trunk and branches, the id to the roots. The demarcation occurs when the tree emerges from the earth into the light of day.

Indian thinking sees the same relationship in the body itself. Compare the following remark in Erich Neumann's (1954, p. 25) *The Origins and History of Consciousness.* "The diaphragm is supposed to correspond to the earth's surface, and development beyond this zone is coordinated with the 'rising sun,' the state of consciousness that has begun to leave behind the unconscious and all ties with it."

Certainly it is a distortion of Freud's concepts to describe the id as the inherited reservoir of chaotic, instinctual demands which are not yet in harmony with each other nor with the facts of external reality. Neither a tree nor a newborn infant presents a picture of chaos. Extended practical experience with self-demand feeding and self-regulation shows that the newborn infant, not long in contact with the world and without much ego, is endowed with a harmony of instinctual demands most conducive to survival and growth. The chaos which characterizes the instinctual life of most children and adults is produced by outside forces which disturb this harmony.

It is more correct to say as Freud (1950b, p. 29) does that the "ego has the task of bringing the influence of the external world to bear upon the id and its tendencies and endeavors to substitute the reality principle for the pleasure principle which reigns supreme in the id. In the ego perception plays the part which in the id devolves upon instinct." No one who has studied the embryonic development of an egg into a mature organism can help but marvel at a process which passes human understanding. Compared to the unconscious work of coordinating the billions of cells, the myriad tissues and the many organs of a human being, the faculties of reason and imagination seem small and insignificant. And even they have evolved out of the great unconscious as has the flower that blooms on the bush.

The mind is as active in these unconscious activities as it is in the conscious ones. Yet to speak of unconscious feelings, unconscious thoughts, or unconscious fantasies involves an evident contradiction in expression. We saw earlier that the concept of feeling applies only when perception of an internal event occurs. Prior to that time we have only a movement (undetermined element) which lacks a qualitative character—a possible feeling not a latent one. On the other hand there are movements within an organism which are prevented from reaching consciousness and perception by the economic factors of repression and resistance. These are latent and capable of becoming conscious if, through analysis, the restrictive forces are eliminated. The difference is based upon the fact that the second category of unconscious activity *was once conscious*. This is implied in the concept of repression. There is still a third category of unconscious activity, one which is incapable of becoming conscious. This includes the activity of the deep organ systems of the body: the kidney, the liver, the blood vessels, etc. Not all unconscious activity is subject to the dynamics of analytic therapy.

For purposes of analytic thinking one should subdivide unconscious activity into three categories. The deepest layer of the unconscious concerns activities which never become conscious. There can be no argument against this statement as it applies to the deep organ systems. A second category concerns activity which could become conscious but never did. An example of this are postural activities which become set at an early age precluding awareness of a more integrated function. The child who learns to walk at a time when the muscles are not strong enough nor coordinated enough for such activity develops severe tensions in the quadriceps femoris and tensor fascia lata muscles to give it support. This will happen if an infant is left alone for it will make some move to get up and go toward its mother. The tension of these muscle groups will give the leg the rigidity needed for support but at the expense of natural balance and grace. Where one attempts to induce relaxation of these muscles one meets with a resistance that is proportional to the falling anxiety present. It is significant that children who are carried by their mothers for years, as are the American Indians, lack this falling anxiety. But, and this is important, there has never been any repression of the natural movements and sensations—graceful, swinging and pleasurable. These never developed.

The last category then includes the repressed unconscious. We can say that "hard" eyes were once consciously hateful, that a tight jaw expresses unconscious biting impulses, and that tight adductor muscles in the thighs represent the suppression of genital sensation. We cannot say that weak eyes hold back unconscious hate.

As the ego is differentiated from the id, so the superego

crystallizes out of the ego. This concept of the superego is one of the most complex in analytic psychology. It would seem that we should be able to explain human behavior in terms of the functions of the id and the ego. Actually, in each individual, behavior is determined by id forces under control of the reality function of the ego which itself has been modified by the development of an ego ideal or superego.

There is no question as to the role of the superego. In the mental sphere it exerts a censoring function upon thoughts and actions which is distinct from and opposed to the reality function of the ego. Against the perceptual reality of the ego it opposes a reality derived from the person's earliest experiences and represents the code of behavior enforced by the parents. The superego comes into being as an ego defense formation which becomes crystallized and structured early in life. If it no longer fulfills that function vis-à-vis the external world, it is only because that early environment has changed. Its persistence is based upon the fact that it becomes structured as an unconscious limitation of motility which the organism dares not transcend. The superego, then, is a part of the ego which has become unconscious and which uses ego energies to block id impulses in a manner which impoverishes and limits the ego.

Let us summarize our knowledge of the psychic functions at this point. The id represents those psychic processes of which we are unconscious. They can be divided into three categories: those relating to organ activities of which we cannot be conscious, those pertaining to activities of which we are ordinarily unconscious but which by an effort can be raised to consciousness, and those which represent the repressed unconscious. The ego represents psychic processes of which we are conscious because they concern activities which relate us to the external world. From this analysis, one can derive a basic law. An activity becomes conscious as it impinges upon the surface of the body for only thus can it come into relation with the external world. The superego is a psychic process which can prevent an activity from becoming conscious, that is, from reaching the surface of the body. There are other psychic processes which, for the moment, we will ignore. These are the creative or synthetic ego functions.

To comprehend the somatic basis of ego psychology we must consider quantitative factors. In the realm of the soma things are what they seem and energies can be measured quantitatively in terms of the movements they produce. Do we not measure all physical energies in terms of the work they accomplish? We begin with the observation that the ego as a psychic phenomenon is fundamentally a perceptual process. True, the ego as we know it in civilized man is more than perception. It is a perception of perception, a consciousness of consciousness, a self-consciousness. But this second floor is erected upon a first floor in which consciousness is basically perception. In this first stage one should ask—What is being perceived?

The answer to this question is relatively simple. What is perceived is a movement—a movement of the organism which may or may not manifest itself as a displacement in space. This does not mean that everything which moves can be or is perceived. Movement occurs in sleep and also on the unconscious level. We do not ordinarily perceive the movement of our intestines or of the heart. But where there is no movement there is no perception. Movement precedes perception. In the evolution of living structures as well as in the ontological development of the individual, consciousness is a late comer. It arises after life begins and disappears before death. All perception is, therefore, the perception of the movements of the organism, either internally or vis-à-vis the external world. When our own individual movements cease, as at death, perception of external reality ceases.

Ordinarily we are only aware of the gross movements of the body. With attention we can sense the finer movements. Generally if we wish to feel a part of our body we move it. It is not necessary that the movement be a voluntary one, but it is necessary that some motion occur in the part if perception is to be possible. For example, most people do not feel their backs, not even while lying on their back on a couch. This is a common experience in therapeutic sessions. If, now, one blows lightly against the nape of the neck, a wave of excitation can be seen to move upward into the scalp and downward over the back producing gooseflesh and the erection of hairs. The back will then be felt, experienced or perceived. We describe this awareness of the part as "having contact" with it. Contact with a part of the body which is not perceived can be established by increasing the motility of that part. There is a quantitative factor here: the intensity of the movement bears a relation to the quality of the perception. For the present it suffices to say that all sensation, all perception, is dependent on movement.

What determines which movements are perceived, that is, reach consciousness, and which are not? We have Freud's observation that the ego is derived from body sensation, springing chiefly from the surface of the body. Experiments have confirmed the fact that sensation occurs when an internal movement reaches the surface of the body and of the mind where the system perception-conscious is located. I will later refer to Reich's experiments on the subject but there is much clinical observation to support this thesis. It explains why deep organ pain is always perceived as an irradiation on the surface of the body. We know that sensitive instruments such as the electrocardiograph and the electroencephalograph can pick up from the body surface minute differences of electrical potential which translate underlying activity. Perception is a matter of degree, a function of the intensity of the charge at the surface.

The ego is a surface phenomenon, both psychically and somatically. The system perception-conscious lies at the surface of the cerebral cortex. This enables us to comprehend Freud's statement that the ego is the projection of a surface onto a surface. The id, on the other hand is related to processes which occur in the depths below the surface. Here again, the description of id processes as being in the depths applies both to the somatic processes and to the psychic representation of these processes. These latter have their main centers in the regions of the nervous system which lie below the cerebral cortex: the hind-brain, the midbrain and the diencephalon. We can show the somatic aspects of these psychic layers in a simple diagram (Fig. 1) in which the total organism is represented as a sphere, somewhat in the form of a single cell. The center is represented by a nucleus which is the energy source of all movements. An impulse is represented as an energy movement from the center to the periphery.

In Figure 1, the ego corresponds to the surface of the organism, the id to the center and to processes below the surface. Such a schema applies only to the simplest forms of life. In higher organisms, the ego is not only perceptual but also controls the approach to motility. The figure does not provide for such an ego function since there is no way in which an impulse can be prevented from reaching the surface. In the higher organisms there is a layer below the surface which is, in man, to some extent, under the control of the ego. We would expect, therefore, to find a projection of it on the surface of the cerebral cortex. These requirements are met with in the voluntary muscular system of the higher organisms. If, now, we insert this system below the surface, we can show the somatic basis for the structure of the psychic functions.

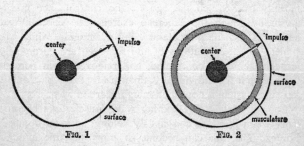

FIG. 1   FIG. 2

In Figure 2, the impulse activates the muscular system before it reaches the surface. The muscular system has a twofold function. Ordinarily, we think of the muscular system as the motor apparatus of the larger organisms. And so it is. But the muscles can hold back movements as well as execute them. One has only to think of such a muscle as the sphincter of the anus to realize how important this function is. Consider the case of an individual who is charged with rage and yet must hold back the impulse to strike. His fists are clenched, his arms are tense and his shoulders are drawn and held back to restrain the impulse. In this process of restraint, the ego as a psychic process prevents the release of the impulse to the surface, that is, to the external world, by maintaining the state of muscular contraction. In this we see the ego in its role of controlling the approach to motility.

We know that a portion of the ego has differentiated to become an unconscious censor of our actions. It will determine what impulses are to be permitted expression and which ones are to be inhibited. But while the superego is a category of psychic processes, it acts to control impulses through the muscular apparatus. In what way, then, does the superego differ from the ego? If an impulse is restrained because it is inappropriate to a situation, the action is conscious, ego controlled and in line with the reality principle. The inhibitions imposed by the superego are unconscious and have nothing to do with the reality of the present day situation. They represent a limitation of motility over which the ego has no control. The mechanism by which the superego exercises its control over actions is also the musculature. But the muscles which are subject to the inhibitions of the superego are chronically tense, chronically contracted, and removed from perception, so that the individual is unaware that this part of his muscular system is nonfunctioning in certain ways.

Let me explain this another way. Muscles can become tense when they are consciously holding back an impulse. For example, one can become so angry that the muscles ache from holding back the impulse. In this case one feels the tension in the muscles. But muscles can be tense and the person unaware of the tension. Here, too, an impulse is being restrained but the restraint is unconscious. This is a superego phenomenon. Just as on the psychic level the superego prevents certain thoughts from reaching consciousness, so on the biological level, spastic, chronically contracted muscles prevent certain impulses from reaching the surface. These muscles are thus removed from conscious control and their function is repressed. It would follow that one could determine the nature of the superego from an analysis of the state of tension in the muscular system. The method and technique of such analytic procedures will be elaborated in the later parts of this book. At this point one can say simply that the pattern of muscular tension determines the expression of the individual and this expression is related to this character structure.

In this presentation, the mind and the body are viewed dualistically. Each is regarded as a separate entity which parallels and interacts with the other. Every action is seen as taking place on two levels—somatic and psychic—at the same time. One can relate the organization of mental processes to a corresponding organization of processes in the body. The concepts of ego, id and superego have very definite counterparts in the somatic sphere. The correspondence goes even deeper than this. Center, direction and periphery can be identified with another set of ideas which Freud developed from his study of psychic phenomena. In his analysis of the instinct Freud postulated that every instinct has a source, an aim and an object. This is an analysis of an instinctual action as it is manifested in the psyche. Without going into a long discussion about the nature of the instinct, we can describe it as an impulsive action which has not been modified by learning or experience. Few such actions persist into adult life. Since the modification occurs at the surface, every action is primarily impulsive and basically instinctual. Now our analysis of the impulse shows that it, too, has a source, an aim and an object. The source is the energy center of the organism in the depths of its id processes. The aim corresponds to the biological direction of which we shall learn more later. The object is that stimulus in the external world which, acting upon the surface (ego), causes the impulse to arise. Only the object is under control of the ego. Source, strength and direction are id phenomena.

We make no pretense that the dualistic approach is the complete answer to the body-mind relationship. Those who are familiar with Reich's work know that his concept of the unity and antithesis of biological functions encompasses this dualism at the same time that it provides unity on a deeper level. In the treatment of the emotional problems of the human organism, the approach from the surface imposes a dualistic viewpoint. To facilitate our thinking about this relationship, I would like to introduce two figures which show different attitudes toward the problem.

In the Chinese symbol of the Yin and the Yang (Fig. 3), the *t'ai chi* is a container of opposites. These opposites have been interpreted as black and white, day and night, heaven and earth, male and female. We can add the opposites, body and mind.

The whole is the cosmos, the macrocosm and microcosm which is the individual life. It is composed of two perfectly equal halves which lie in close contact with each other. These halves are subject to various interpretation, all of which fit the symbol. What impresses us in this symbol is the roundness, the lack of interaction, the unchanging and static quality of the design. It is an expression of Eastern philosophy in which the concept of change and progress is relatively unimportant.

Contrast this symbol with the Hebrew *Star of David* (Fig. 4) in which the same two elements are shown in a different relationship. The equal halves are subject to the same interpretations as before: day and night, heaven and earth, male and female—mind and body.

In this symbol, however, we are impressed by the interpenetration of the opposites. This represents a dynamic quality. The six points show a reaching out, a breaking through the container. The whole figure is angular and lacks the round smoothness of its Eastern counterpart. This concept of interaction of opposites underlies the principle of change and progress. It is not surprising, therefore, that the history of Western thought has its origin in the Judaic-Grecian tradition of conflict.

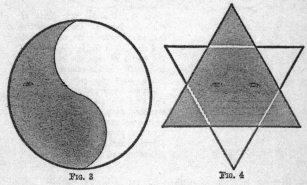

FIG. 3   FIG. 4

It is possible to show the dynamic interaction of opposing forces in still other ways. The more emphasis we place upon the concept of force and the less we put upon structure, the more open does the symbol become.

Figure 5 shows two opposites which may also be interpreted as light and darkness, heaven and earth, male and female, or mind and body. The superimposition of two forces is a concept taken from Reich's work. It is an even more dynamic interpretation than the Hebrew symbol, for interpenetration is replaced by interaction in movement. While it is more dynamic, it lacks the sense of boundary or surface which is related to the ego.

We cannot leave the subject of ego psychology without a discussion of the creative side of the ego function. In Chapter 1 we mentioned that the unity of the opposites was manifested on the surface as a unity of function. Despite the interaction in the depths, the personality is an

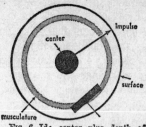

Fig. 5

Fig. 6. Id: center plus depth of organism. Ego: surface plus control over voluntary musculature. The depth and strength of the ego depend upon the degree of conscious control and coordination of the voluntary musculature. Superego: muscle functions which are frozen and inhibited. These are chronically contracted and spastic muscles (block *in* figure) which are beyond conscious control. Character: resultant physical expression of the organism. Ego Ideal: desired physical expression and motility.

entity—a whole. If this unity of the personality is destroyed, we speak of a "split" personality. Psychiatry recognizes this splitting as due to a weakness or disintegration of the ego. But we shall have the occasion to study the problem of schizophrenia in the final chapters of this book. Let us now see if we can understand how the ego functions as an integrative and organizing force.

Again we must look at the psychic aspect of the problem first. Freud, who was dualistic in his thinking, recognized the opposites in human functioning early. In his attempt to comprehend the basic conflicts in the psyche, Freud postulated many pairs of antithetical tendencies. To mention a few, there was the opposition of hunger to sex, of object libido to narcissistic libido, of the ego to sexuality. Finally, in 1920, Freud reduced all forces to two great principles: a life force, *Eros* (sexuality) and a death principle, *Thanatos* (destruction). Such a statement is not far removed from the basic principles which governed man's earliest thinking. Again, the opposites which can join the series: light and dark, heaven and earth, male and female, mind and body—sexuality and destruction.

But Freud went further. Based upon his studies of the neuroses, he recognized that in man the unity of these basic opposites was destroyed. Speaking of these forces as instinctual tendencies, Freud (1950b, p. 80) pointed out that partial or complete defusion occurs. Where the ego functions to maintain the unity of the organism, the superego operates to split that unity. "The super ego arises, as we know, from the identification with the father regarded as a model. Every such identification is in the nature of a desexualization, or even a sublimation. It now seems as though when a transformation of this kind takes place, there occurs at the same time an instinctual defusion."

This defusion of basic instinctual tendencies Freud regarded as the price of civilized existence. The father in Freud's statement is the bearer of cultural demands. Out of a basic split in the personality arises those schisms which characterize civilized man: good and evil, God and devil, culture and nature, etc. Of course, the severity of the split or defusion depends upon individual factors in the family constellation of the growing child, but we can assume that no civilized human being is free from some effects of this problem.

Nothing is more disturbing to the personality than the defusion of its component tendencies or the split in its feelings. Since it is a split in the ego, it is tantamount to an open split in the surface of the body. The ego hastens to repair the defect just as the tissues strive to heal and cover any breach in the skin. But this is not an ordinary wound. A foreign agent has been introduced into the personality structure (the internalization of the parental authority) and this foreign body cannot be removed. The ego is helpless in the face of its superego. It must reconstruct a new pattern of behavior in which the prohibitions of the superego are not challenged. This new pattern of behavior constitutes its personal Weltaunschung, a conscious ideal in which opposing tendencies are re-fused according to the demands of the environment.

This formation of a conscious ego ideal takes place as the child emerges out of its oedipal period. It derives its values by conscious identification with loved figures, older siblings, admired playmates and respected teachers. By means of this ego ideal, the instincts are re-fused "on a higher level." It is this new construction which represents the higher nature of man and not the superego. This conscious ego ideal as opposed to the unconscious superego seems to take definite form at the age when permanent teeth erupt. From then on throughout life it is constantly being evaluated and modified.

If the degree of defusion is too great to be bridged by a conscious effort, or, stated conversely, if the ego is too weak to unite the opposing tendencies, the ego will eliminate the more disturbing element from its ego ideal formation. This compares with the process whereby the child who suffers from severe crossing of the eyes will simply discard the use of one eye. Generally it is the aggressive tendencies which are not allowed conscious participation in the determination of action.

The ego and its derivatives, superego and ego ideal, are subject to the impact of new experiences in the life of the individual. No emotional growth would be possible if these new experiences could not be integrated into existing systems. To accomplish this the ego must open up its barriers to allow experience in just as it must lower them to allow impulses out. The bigger the experience, the greater the opening must be. This is not a question of flexibility or adaptability for these involve no change. Literally, an ego must allow itself to be overwhelmed by each new vital experience so that a new ego will arise in which that experience is properly integrated. But this is only possible where the ego extends in depth. Where the ego is fighting to maintain itself against the superego below, no major growth is possible.

It would be interesting to develop our thinking along these lines but, unfortunately, the subject exceeds the limits of this present undertaking. I shall reserve it, therefore, for another study.

Can we show the somatic counterpart of these principles? I believe we can if we use the diagram developed earlier (Fig. 6).

The ego is a growing force. It grows in strength as well as in coordination and adaptability. Anyone who has observed young children in their physical play cannot help but be impressed by their almost conscious endeavor to develop their physical skill and strength. How excited they are when they learn to swim, to write, to play a musical instrument, etc.! But this growth and development of muscular control and coordination is not limited to children. All through life we strive to increase our coordination in the various activities which interest us. And while there may be a falling off of pure physical strength in middle age, the ability to develop and execute finer movements continues until very late in life. This may explain why the ego becomes stronger with advancing years in most individuals.

This growth of the ego can take place only within the limits imposed by the superego. Many persons, for example, never learn to dance because of the disturbance in the motility of their legs due to early and severe toilet training. Or what is more severe, the ability to speak in public may be greatly handicapped by throat tensions. The problem of the superego and its limitation of motility can be approached via the psyche or the soma. The latter offers a more direct answer to the disturbance which, however, cannot be removed except through an analytic procedure. The problem is to bring to ego consciousness that which has been repressed by the superego.

Bioenergetic therapy combines the activity principle on the somatic level with the analytic procedure on the psychic level. The patient gains new experiences in motility which are then integrated into the ego. The unity of the method is assured by attention to the character which expresses both the psychic and somatic aspects of the personality. Before we study the application of this technique, more must be known about the dynamic energy processes in the organism.

3

The Pleasure Principle

All analytic therapies function within the framework of what is known as the reality principle, that is, the ability of an organism to tolerate pain or unpleasure for the sake of a greater pleasure expected in the future. It is this which makes it possible for a patient to support the painful procedures of the analytic therapy itself. But while we recognize the validity and operation of this principle, we are in the dark so far as knowledge of its underlying mechanisms are concerned. We shall attempt to discover and elucidate some of these mechanisms in Chapter 4 but before we do so we must recognize that the reality principle derives from and is a modification of a more basic general principle which governs the thinking and behavior of organisms. This is *the pleasure principle*.

In his study of unconscious mental processes, Freud found that they followed a law which differed from that governing conscious mental activities. Freud (1911, p. 14) considered these unconscious processes "to be older, primary processes, the residues of a phase of development in which they were the only kind of mental processes." These primary processes obeyed a tendency which he called "the pleasure-pain principle." Simply defined, this means that the organism seeks pleasure and avoids unpleasure or pain. Later, Freud (1950a, p. 2) elaborated this principle

41

by relating "unpleasure to an increase in the quantity of
excitation and pleasure to a diminution." We can simplify
this statement by substituting the word tension for excitation, so that unpleasure or pain is related to an increase,
pleasure to a decrease of tension.

On the psychic level we have few means of deepening
our understanding of this principle. One can add that tension arises as a result of needs, the satisfaction of which
leads to pleasure. But we have not advanced our insight.
Tension is itself a need, just as a need is a tension. Clarification must therefore be sought on the biological level.

In 1934 Reich did a series of experiments at the University of Oslo which had specific bearing on this problem. The details of the procedures are available in Reich's
The Function of the Orgasm, so I shall limit myself here
to a statement of the main observations and conclusions.

It had been shown previously that the electric potential
at the surface of the skin changed with the emotions. This
was the so-called "psychogalvanic phenomenon." Reich's
experiments were designed to determine what happened
in sexual excitation and how this was related to the perception of pleasure. Oscillographic recordings were made
of the skin potential at the erogenous zones under conditions of pleasurable and unpleasurable stimulation. Reich
(1942, p. 335) found at each zone—at the lips, the nipple, the palm of the hand, etc.—that the perception of
pleasure corresponded with a sharp increase of the skin
potential at these areas as recorded on an oscillograph located in another room. On the other hand pressure or
fright produced a marked decrease in skin potential. Further, the "psychic intensity of the pleasure sensation corresponds to the quantity of the bioelectric potential." We
thus have experimental confirmation of Freud's thesis that
the ego in its perceptive function is primarily a phenomenon of the surface of the body. At the same time it is the
projection of the surface phenomenon onto the appropriate area of the brain which makes perception as a conscious process possible. We now have two closely inter-

woven events in the function of perception: projection
onto the surface of the body and projection of the surface
onto another surface.

To comprehend these two phenomena as the unitary
expression of the total organism, which it is, we have recourse to Reich's formulation of the basic law of biological
functioning: the unity and antithesis of vegetative life.
Two functions dominate the vegetative life of the organism, expansion and contraction. They have their identity
in the common function of pulsation which is one of the
qualities of all living organisms. In the somatic realm, as
Reich showed, expansion and contraction occur as a physiological process correlated with the activities of the sympathetic and parasympathetic nervous systems and with
the action of certain ion groups. On the psychic level, biological expansion is perceived as pleasure, contraction as
unpleasure. There is a functional antithesis between vegetative center and periphery. It becomes possible to make a
further correlation between psychic sensation and energy
movement. The movement of energy from the center of
an organism to the periphery is identical functionally with
biological expansion and with the perception of pleasure.
Conversely the movement of energy from the periphery to
the center is functionally identical with biological contraction and the perception of unpleasure or anxiety.

The representation of this mechanism involves the same
diagram used in the preceding chapter to portray the somatic basis of the psychic levels of functioning.

One notes the absence of a muscular system which is
related to the development of the reality principle. The ego
is limited to the surface membrane. Expansion and contraction are basically id phenomena.

Before we proceed it is important to clarify the distinction between unpleasure and anxiety. So far as I know
neither Freud nor Reich has formulated the difference
exactly; Reich equates the two terms. The question may
be posed thus: If biological expansion is experienced as
pleasure, why is the corresponding contraction not ex-

perienced unpleasantly? The word "unpleasure" does not describe a perceptual sensation. In the pulsatile state of expansion and contraction, the tension which builds up prior to release is accepted and submerged in the anticipation of the release which will follow. The anticipation of pleasure permits the tolerance of states of tension which otherwise would be distinctly unpleasant. In the pleasure principle itself there is the rudiment of the reality function which later becomes the dominant principle of mature human behavior.

If tension develops in situations in which the anticipation of the pleasurable release is not possible, anxiety is experienced. Anxiety, however, is not necessarily a pathological condition. Our judgment must always be based on the reality principle. Anxiety is pathological when it is out of proportion to the external situation which provoked it. Even if not pathological, anxiety is always experienced as a threat to the ego which the mature organism seeks to remove. Or we can say that tension becomes pathological when it becomes a chronic state and out of control of the organism. Within these concepts health can be defined as the ability of the organism to maintain its ryhthm of pulsation within the limits of the reality principle. Pleasure has been contrasted variously with unpleasure, anxiety and pain as part of the total principle: tension-relaxation, contraction-expansion. It is now possible to define the third term of the series, pain.

If unpleasure describes the state of energy charge preceding discharge, anxiety implies an energy charge in which the movement forward to discharge is blocked or held back. If the intensity of the charge increases to a point where it threatens the integrity of the structural elements of the body, pain will be experienced. This statement is justified by the theoretical concepts underlying this exposition; it can also be shown to apply to all situations in which pain is experienced. It is not denied that the nervous system plays an important role in the perception of pain as it does in all perceptual functions. By its very structure the entire nervous system can be compared to an inverted tree intimately related in its minutest branchings and ramifications to the upright arborization of the blood system which is the main channel for the free energy movement of the body.

It seems that there could be nothing simpler or more fundamental than the operation of the pleasure principle. Yet in 1920 Freud published a most controversial book, *Beyond the Pleasure Principle*. In it he postulated the existence of two instinctual forces: one, the death instinct (primary masochism) leading back to inanimate nature, and the other, the life instinct (or sexual instinct) which leads life onward in its development and evolution. Freud's exposition of his thesis is concise and masterful. It is not my purpose to debate his formulation here. The question at issue is whether these forces, or any instincts, operate beyond the pleasure principle or within it.

Freud (1950b, p. 71) was led to these concepts by two clinical phenomena. The first was the problem of masochism. It seemed as if there were certain individuals who did not want to get well. In contradiction to the pleasure principle, these individuals appeared to seek painful situations, to be dominated by an inner compulsion to "hold on to the suffering and to experience it again and again." In analytic therapy this manifested itself as a "negative therapeutic reaction." Analytic experience had revealed the operation of a principle which seemed to explain this phenomenon. This is the "repetition compulsion" which, in the opinion of one analyst, is "so imperative that even the pleasure principle is fully disregarded." Freud (1950a, p. 81) himself had said, "my assertion of the regressive character of instincts also rests upon observed material—namely on the facts of the compulsion to repeat."

Let us look more closely at this "repetition compulsion," for, strangely enough, it can be shown to be one aspect of the operation of the pleasure principle. We are aware that all organisms experience the desire to repeat certain activities. One thinks immediately of eating, of sleeping, of sexual activity, etc. By and large the repetition of these activities is based upon certain recurrent needs which set up a state of tension in the organism so long as they are unsatisfied. The resulting drive aims to relieve this tension, and we know that the release of these states of tension is experienced as pleasure whether the activity is eating, sleeping, defecation or sexual discharge. (*See* Fenichel, 1945, p. 542.) Other repetitive activities may be undertaken even if pleasure is not immediately expected—if our sense of reality tells us that it will lead to future pleasure. The patient who comes regularly to the analytic session is functioning on this principle. But the reality principle has been recognized to be a modification of the pleasure principle and not a denial of it.

Is there a repetition compulsion which is beyond the pleasure principle? Freud refers to two sets of observations which support this idea. The first is the condition known as the "traumatic neurosis" which occurs occasionally after an accident involving a risk to life. In this neurosis dreams "have the characteristics of repeatedly bringing the patient back into the situation of his accident, a situation in which he wakes up in another fright." These dreams seem to contradict the "wish-fulfilling tenor of dreams," and as Freud (1950a, p. 11) says, may drive one to "reflect on the mysterious masochistic trends of the ego."

It is known, as Freud points out, that the traumatic neurosis fails to develop if there is a gross physical injury. Freud's psychological explanation, though involved, is correct, for the hypercachexis of the injured organ permits a binding of the excess of excitation. In bioenergetic terms, the mechanical agitation and shock produces an amount of free energy which is bound to or discharged on the injury. This free energy is necessary to the healing process. When no such release is possible, an hysteria-like syndrome develops. Let me illustrate this with a case. A young lady came to therapy because of an inability to develop an attachment to a man, although she was sought after by several personable males. Her history as she related it was significant. Some years earlier she was married to a young man whom she loved deeply. After six months in this happy state she experienced the tragedy of seeing her husband crash to his death in a plane. She did not utter a sound but turned and walked away. At no time did she release the feeling in tears. She separated from their mutual friends and soon after enlisted for service with the armed forces. As she lay on the couch during the second session I could sense from her breathing a catch in her throat. Palpation revealed a powerful spasm of the throat musculature. A quick pressure on these muscles produced a scream of fright which was followed by deep crying. The traumatic incident flashed into her mind. During several succeeding sessions I produced the screams and the crying. Each time she relived the horrifying experience. Then it was over. I continued the therapy for a while longer and shortly afterward she fell in love with a man and they were married.

I do not know if this patient had relived her traumatic experience in dreams. We do know that the dynamics of the problem requires the complete release of all affect involved in the experience and that this release should occur on the conscious level. One can explain her inability to fall in love as a result of the immobilization of this great amount of affect or libido. We should interpret any dream in which the patient re-experiences the traumatic situation as an attempt to effectuate a discharge of the repressed affect. This must fail because of the lack of conscious participation. Repeated dreams are repeated attempts which also fail. This failure gives the whole endeavor its masochistic stamp. The masochistic element derives from an underlying character disturbance which is itself amenable to analytic therapy. The clinical picture, however, in no way contradicts the pleasure principle for the organism is striving to release an inner tension, that is, to avoid unpleasure or pain.

The other clinical observation of the compulsion to re-

peat is based upon the transference phenomenon of neurotics. I, too, experience daily the tendency on the part of
patients to "repeat all of these unwanted situations and
painful emotions in the transference and to revive them
with the greatest ingenuity." (*See* Freud, 1950a, p. 22.)
This is especially true in the analysis of the masochistic
character. If the problem is a difficult one it still is not beyond solution. Reich's elucidation of the psychological
aspects of the problem of masochism is one of the brilliant
chapters in the history of psychoanalysis. My own remarks
on the subject will, I trust, add further insights into the
problem. Other analysts, too, I am sure, have found effective ways of handling this problem. Difficulties in analytic
therapy must not lead us to postulate inherent impossibil-
ities in treatment. If we bear in mind that every analytic
therapy also involves a re-education much will be gained.
The individual who figuratively and literally has not stood
squarely upon his own feet before will find them quite wob-
bly when he makes his first efforts.

I have spent some time on the repetition compulsion
precisely because it is part of the pleasure principle. One
further example will illustrate this. I will use Freud's observation about a girl who was forced to open her mouth
at the dentist. At home she attempted to play at being
the dentist and to repeat on a younger child the same experience. This play demonstrates a "peculiar, fully unconscious tendency of being forced to repeat actively what
one has passively experienced." Children play at these activities constantly and it is to Freud's merit that he pointed
out the underlying nature of these activities. I, too, see it
as a compulsion to abreact the traumatic experiences of
their young lives. But just this is within the meaning of
the pleasure principle as modified by the demands of reality. Let me illustrate with an analogy.

If we indent the surface of a rubber ball or inflated balloon it will recover its original shape as soon as the pressure is released. In recovering its original form the surface
of the ball or balloon repeats in reverse direction the ex-

act movement it made when it was subjected to the initial pressure. I have no hesitation in saying that the repetition compulsion follows the same energy laws as the ball or balloon. The living organism and the inflated balloon obey laws deriving from the fact of surface tension maintained by an internal pressure or energy charge. The traumatic experience is to the child an insult to its ego which is comparable to a pressure upon the surface of the balloon. When the pressure is removed the ego will try to abreact the experience by an active movement which repeats in reverse direction the original reaction. Further, if the child fails to react actively to such a traumatic experience it is because the energy system of the child does not exert sufficient pressure outward. The ego is partially collapsed and the situation is similar to the surface tension in a partially deflated balloon.

On the psychological level we can speak of the drive to master threatening situations. The identification with the active process enables the child to integrate the total experience into his consciousness. It is not masochistic for the individual who falls from a horse to remount immediately so as to overcome his fear. Whatever the psychological interpretations of behavior, basic patterns are determined by underlying energy processes.

Both Freud and Reich agree that the pleasure principle translates basic bioenergetic laws. Freud, as we know, related pleasure and unpleasure to "the quantity of excitation that is present in the mind but is not in any way 'bound'; and to relate them in such manner that unpleasure corresponds to an increase in excitation and pleasure to a diminution." Reich identified pleasure and unpleasure with the movement of energy in the organism. The movement to the periphery decreases internal pressure, raises the surface tension and facilitates the discharge to the outer world. Movement inward has the opposite effect. We are thus led to the problem of energy discharge in the living organism which is a function of its relation to the outer world.

The very existence of a living organism creates the first antithesis in the dynamics of its energy processes—between the individual and the outer world. It matters little that the organism is not aware of its individuality. For, regardless of the fact of its dependence on the external world, each living organism is also an independent entity. Out of this dependent-independent relationship stems the basic inner antithesis: towards the world—towards the self (center). In terms of libido this can be expressed as object libido vs. narcissistic libido. This latter formulation, however, is psychological. We can observe the corresponding somatic process most clearly in the amoeba. Freud, himself, compared the sending out and withdrawal of a psychic interest to the putting forth and retraction of a psuedopodium. If we ask what causes an outward movement in an amoeba, we must answer that it responds to a stimulus in the environment. But this stimulus only determines the direction of the movement, not its motive force. The latter must derive from a build-up of tension in the organism. Tension as a physical concept describes a state of stretch or strain in relation to an applied force. In a unicellular animal we can conceive of this as the result of an inner pressure applied against an elastic limiting membrane. Human beings experience tension in a similar way. In some cases it may become so severe as to produce a sensation of bursting or exploding.

All tension is essentially a surface phenomenon. Surface tension can increase as a result of a contraction of the elastic surface membrane or by an increase of the inner force or charge. Tension could decrease as a result of the reduction of the internal force or by an expansion of the limiting membrane. It is a characteristic of the living organism that it can adapt to an increased internal charge by expansion of the surface membrane. This is implicit in the concept of growth. Expansion as opposed to stretching decreases surface tension. But as we shall see this mechanism is functionally operative only within narrow limits.

One manifestation of the difference between the living

and nonliving elastic membrane is seen in the phenomenon of color. When a colored rubber balloon is inflated, there is a decrease in the surface color due to dispersion of the color particles. The living membrane, such as the skin, shows a heightening of color with expansion. In pleasurable expansion the skin reddens as blood vessels dilate. In anxiety, pallor and contraction of the blood vessels occur. The simple explanation is that the non-living membrane stretches in a passive mechanical way. The expansion of the living membrane is an active process resulting from the movement of charged body fluids to the surface and increased surface charge. We may say then that expansion of the living membrane corresponds to decreased surface tension and increased surface charge, contraction to an increased surface tension and decreased surface charge.

Reich's (1949, p. 285) description of these phenomena is worth quoting. "The pallor in fright, the trembling in an anxiety state correspond to a flight of the cachexes from the body periphery to the center, caused by the contraction of the peripheral vessels and dilatation of the central vessels (stasis anxiety). The turgor, the color and warmth of the peripheral tissues and the skin in sexual excitation are the exact opposite of the anxiety state and correspond psychically as well as physiologically to a movement of the energy in the direction from the center to the body periphery and with that, toward the world."

What happens when the inner tension reaches a degree beyond the expansile limit of the membrane? The tension may then be reduced only by the decrease of substance and the discharge of the inner force or energy. In the single cell organism this is accomplished by the process of cell division. In the metazoa this process is split into the functions of sexuality and reproduction.

We can now distinguish two aspects of the mechanism whereby tension is decreased. In one the movement of energy to the periphery produces an expansion of the surface membrane, in the other, substance and energy are discharged into the outer world. Both processes are pleasurable, the degree of pleasure depending on the quantity and gradient of the reduction in tension. Of the two the second is by far the more important. Let us look at it more closely.

Energy and substance are introduced into the organism in greatest part through the ingestion of food and the respiration of oxygen. This, of course, increases the inner tension which can then be released by expansion of the surface membrane (which includes the expansion of the total organism in growth as part of the same mechanism) or by the discharge of energy and substance into the external world. This may take the form of work, in which energy alone is discharged or sex and reproduction with their discharge of substance and energy.

Freud (1953a, pp. 94–95) had postulated as his first set of antithetical instincts—hunger and love. His later comment is interesting. "In my utter perplexity at the beginning, I took as my starting point the poet-philosopher Schiller's aphorism that hunger and love make the world go round. Hunger would serve to represent those instincts which aim at the preservation of the individual; love seeks for objects, its chief function which is favored in every way by nature, is preservation of the species."[*] The antithesis of hunger and love merits further consideration of its energy dynamics.

The satisfaction of both the hunger need and the sexual need is pleasurable yet the one results in an inflow and the other in an outflow of substance. Both have this in common: the satisfaction of the need in each case requires a movement towards and contact with the outer world. Yet one is determined by a feeling of lack (hunger)

[*] "Thus first arose the contrast between ego instincts and object instincts. For the energy of the latter instincts and exclusively for them I introduced the term *libido;* an antithesis was thus formed between the ego instincts and the libidinal instincts directed towards objects." Sigmund Freud, *Civilization and Its Discontents*. London, Hogarth Press, 1953.

and the other by a feeling of excess (sexuality). The big problem is how a movement outward which must derive its motive force from a central tension can proceed from a feeling of lack. Reich's (1949, p. 283) analysis of this problem is brilliant. Let me quote.

"A protozoa must move plasma from the center to the periphery, that is, increase the tension at the periphery when it wants to take up food, that is, to eliminate a negative pressure in the center. In our language: it must, with the aid of a libidinal mechanism, approach the outer world in order to eliminate its 'negative pressure,' that is hunger. . . . That is, the sexual energy is always in the service of the gratification of the hunger need, while conversely, the taking up of nourishment introduces the substances which finally, by way of a physiochemical process, lead to libidinal tensions. Food intake is the basis of existence and of productive achievement, beginning with the most primitive one, locomotion." To say it simply: one needs food to carry on movement and movement to obtain food. If we interpolate an energy phase it will read: energy is needed to produce the movement to obtain the food which in turn will provide the free energy for further movement. Can the relation between free energy and libido be demonstrated more clearly than in this formulation?

In the protozoa, the distinction between hunger and sexuality is greatly reduced. The fusion of two protista and the engulfment of food particles are very similar processes. One also sees the interlacing of hunger and libidnal need in the function of nursing. Libidinal pleasure and food intake are a unitary experience for the suckling. If one loses sight of the interdependence of these basic functions, one can arrive at the fallacy that the infant is normally passive in the act of nursing. While hunger employs the libidinal mechanism to reach out to the world, Eros has need of the motor system of the hunger drive to achieve satisfaction.

The pleasure principle stands at the threshold of life. Beyond it stretches the vast spaces of inanimate nature which shows in its infinite phenomena the operation of the same laws which prevail in the realm of the living: laws derived from the fields of chemistry and physics. With the emergence of the faculty of consciousness in the evolution of living organisms, life as we are acquainted with it begins. This is a step forward in the organization of behavior for it implies that the organism will exercise some conscious awareness in the choice of activities and responses which have as their fundamental goal the striving for pleasure and the avoidance of unpleasure. But we cannot move ahead without commenting that we leave untouched the central mystery of this discussion—the nature of pleasure itself. We shall find, too, that consciousness itself is no less a mystery although we can elucidate some aspects of its nature.

4

The Reality Principle

If we start first with the concept that the pleasure principle is closely related to the life principle, it follows that it cannot be contravened by the living process. But we also immediately think of the reality principle which is antithetical to the pleasure principle. Strangely, the reality principle, so important in all analytic therapy, is only superficially understood. Reich, who so brilliantly analyzed the bioenergetic basis of the pleasure principle, does little more than refer to the reality functions. In this respect the reality function is in somewhat the same situation as the ego—also poorly comprehended on an energetic basis. We shall see that we are dealing with two aspects of a single function, and the elucidation of one will lead to the comprehension of the other. For just as the pleasure principle is the modus operandi of the id, so is the reality principle the working method of the ego.

Fenichel (1945, p. 35) states this clearly. "The origin of the ego and the origin of the sense of reality are but two aspects of one developmental step. This is inherent in the definition of the ego as that part of the mind which handles reality."

The reality principle, in that aspect in which it is opposed to the pleasure principle, demands the acceptance of a state of tension and the postponement of pleasure in accordance with the demands of an external situation. In return the reality principle promises that such action will lead to greater pleasure or to the avoidance of a greater pain in the future. The essence of this function is the interposition of a time interval between the impulse and its expression in overt action. During this interval a state of tension is created and maintained until the appropriate moment for release occurs. If, now, we ask how this tolerance to tension develops, what is its mechanism, and why does it arise we meet with some confusion. The answer—that reality demands such behavior—tells us nothing. The lower forms of life have no such faculty although they live in the same world as we do.

We all know that the infantile ego is not capable of tolerating much tension. Frustration of a need quickly leads to a motor discharge, mainly in the form of crying. Does tolerance of tension develop with and as a result of motor control? This is Fenichel's (1945, p. 42) view. "Walking and control of the sphincters form the foundation of the child's independence, these abilities help to develop the reality principle and to overcome receptive dependence and the necessity for immediate discharge."

This statement is but partially true. Clinical experience has shown that where sphincter control is acquired at too early an age, neurotic traits develop which consequently impair the reality function. The same can be said of walking. The child who learns to stand and walk too early may end with a lack of security in the organs of support and locomotion. Analysis has often demonstrated the fact that individuals with marked oral traits of dependence and immaturity have a history of early intellectual and emotional growth. The precocious child is typical of this problem. The infant who makes his adjustment to adult reality too soon loses out in the long run. A full and pleasurable babyhood and childhood is the best guaranty of a strong ego and a good reality function.

We constantly risk losing sight of the fact that the reality principle is functionally identical with the pleasure principle even if antithetical to it in its superficial aspect. We must know, therefore, how the reality principle develops out of the pleasure principle on a bioenergetic basis.

We know that the basic bioenergetic function which gave rise to the pleasure principle as a determinant of psychic function was the movement of energy from the center to the periphery and back again. Energy flow in the direction, center to periphery, decreases tension whether it is accompanied by the discharge of substance or not, and it is perceived as pleasure. Energy movement in the opposite direction (periphery to center) increases tension and is equated with unpleasure which is not perceived. This is not the same as anxiety, which only develops where the energy of an impulse fails to be discharged.

This basic pattern of function characterizes the energy dynamics of the simplest unicellular animals such as the amoeba. In the amoeba, the extension of a pseudopodium can occur in any direction and fluid and substance can pass through any part of the surface membrane. Since charge and discharge can take place at all points of the surface membrane which are more or less equidistant from the center, we can describe the amoeba as having one degree of movement. In other words all movements have the same meaning regardless of direction. At this stage, too, sexuality and hunger are closely related; the inner tension is released by the one basic mechanism of cell division. This simple animal shows no surface differentiation and not even elementary specialization for charge or discharge, sexuality or hunger. The amoeba may be said to function purely on the pleasure principle.

The amoeba shows little polarity in body organization or movement.* In some protozoa and in all metazoa a definite polarity is evident. In the course of evolution a head end

---

* In describing the worm, N. R. F. Maier and T. C. Schneirla remark on the fact that it shows a "permanently elaborated anteroposterior gradient in sensitivity, in conduction and in activity." *Principles of Animal Psychology*. New York, McGraw-Hall, 1935, p. 62.

and tail end became differentiated in such a way that the head end develops at the forefront of the direction of movement. This new development is best seen in the worm. Instead of impulses moving from the center to the periphery in any direction, they are now oriented along a longitudinal line from one end to the other passing through the center. This polarity stems out of the basic center to periphery orientation and it develops as a result of the dominance of certain tendencies which were present though latent in the earlier phase. The factor most responsible for polarity can be described as the antigravity tendency of the life force.

The worm offers a good illustration of this phase of evolution. All higher animals show its basic structure; a longitudinal orientation and a metameric arrangement. In the worm movement is essentially in one direction, ahead. The head is differentiated in that it is the region where the taking in of substance occurs while the tail end is limited to the function of discharge. Differentiation of the two ends is not very great as a glance at any worm will tell, yet they can be distinguished. Hunger and sexuality are distinctly different functions, as compared with the situation in the case of the amoeba. We can say that the worm has two possible degrees of movement. In addition to the pulsation, core—periphery, which takes place in the worm as well as in the amoeba, there is the super-imposed pulsation, head end—tail end.

Despite the evolution of the worm as compared with the amoeba, its reality function is most elementary. The worm has some control over the sphincters at both ends, yet it can hardly differentiate the objects it encounters as it moves forward. The worm literally eats its way through the ground as it advances. Nevertheless, in its orientation and structure, the worm possesses the elements out of which the reality function of the higher animals, including man, develops.

Evolution seems to proceed by a process of condensation and differentiation. The head end of the higher organism results from the fusion of several metameric segments. In addition, the energy economy of the more advanced animals functions at a higher level of charge and discharge. Structural differentiation is greatly increased and developed.

The steps in this development can be shown diagrammatically (Fig. 7). The first stage (A) is that of the amoeba, which shows no evidence of any function according to the reality principle. We portray this type of function by a circle.

The second stage (B) is exemplified by the worm. Evolution through growth, development and specialization has produced the following improvements: a marked polarity in body organization, development of a muscular system to facilitate movement and a nervous system to coordinate the activities of the different muscles. The diagrammatic representation of these changes is shown by elongation of the body and its polarity and muscular system.

In the third stage (C), of which man is the highest development, we find a greater condensation plus a higher differentiation. This polarity has greatly increased and this, added to the upright position, has resulted in a specialization and differentiation of the limbs.

When we study the structure and energy dynamics of the human organism we find that these processes have advanced to their highest degree of development. The body plan shows three main segments, head, thorax and pelvis, and two constrictions, the neck and the waist. These constrictions serve as fulcrums around which a certain amount of rotary movement can take place. This adds a third degree of movement—rotation about the longitudinal axis. The constricted segments are zones of passage which speed up the flow of body fluids according to known hemodynamic laws. Pathologically they can become the areas where blocking or reduction of the energy flow can most easily occur. In contrast to these narrowings, the two terminal segments are enlargements which serve as reservoirs or lakes where a slowing down and ac-

A   FIG. 7.

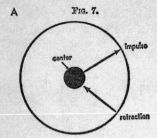

Tension is discharged by the expansion of the surface membrane, as in the extension of a pseudopodium, or through the discharge of substance in cell division. There is no available means for restraining the impulses.

B

Impulses are oriented along the longitudinal axis, although the metameric type of movement also requires segmental impulses of expansion and contraction.

C

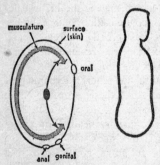

Left: The musculature is now more concentrated along the back. Impulses are strongly oriented longitudinally although some discharge occurs in female mammary organs. Intake is confined to upper, discharge to lower end. *Right:* Condensation has reduced metameric arrangement to three segments: head, thorax and belly. These are separated by two constrictions: neck and waist.

cumulation of energy occurs prior to release through the natural openings in these segments.

Let us study these two segments in more detail. The greater pelvis includes the belly in front, the buttocks and the organs of discharge. The latter include the urinary apparatus with its opening through the urethra, the excretory end of the intestinal tube with its opening at the anus, and the genital system. We can also add the lower appendages, the legs, which, as prime movers of the total organism, are organs of energy discharge.

It is in the function of the genital apparatus that the nature of the reality principle is most clearly demonstrated. The intensity of the genital discharge must depend upon how much energy can be accumulated in the reservoir system prior to release. The genital apparatus itself functions similarly to an electrical condenser which automatically discharges as soon as the charge reaches the capacity level. The reality principle as contrasted with the pleasure principle demands that release of charge or tension be postponed in the interest of greater pleasure. This physiological holding of tension or charge depends upon the size of the reservoir and the capacity of the condenser. A small reservoir function and a reduced capacity lead to impulsiveness and, specifically, prematurity of ejaculation in the male. Prematurity results in decreased pleasure.

Disturbances of the genital function as seen clinically can be best understood in terms of the above concept. Prematurity in the male, which is a common problem, is associated in all cases with tensions and spasms of the tissues and muscles in this area which decrease the reservoir and condenser capacities. Improvement of this condition depends upon the elimination or reduction of these chronic tensions, whether achieved psychologically or through somatic intervention. We can understand why prematurity is frequently absent when a second act of intercourse follows the first. The prior discharge reduces the energy level at the same time that it releases some of the tension. The subsequent build-up is slower thereby overcoming the prematurity, but the decreased charge may lead to a lower level of discharge and less pleasure. In masochism, where there is fear of genital charge, the energy is held in the belly which is already contracted. Thus, while the reservoir is full to the point of bursting with great anxiety, the genital system is weakly charged. Not infrequently erective impotence is also manifest.

The genital apparatus as a condenser system determines the speed of discharge not its intensity. Great pleasure in the sexual act depends upon the amount of charge which is held in the belly or pelvis. From this reservoir, energy is fed into the genital apparatus slowly. At the acme of the orgasm, discharge occurs as a series of pulsations with ejaculatory squirts in the male and rhythmic, involuntary pelvic movements. At this point energy flows freely from the reservoir into the condenser producing a series of charges and discharges. Without the aid of the reservoir function, orgasm would occur as a single nonrhythmic discharge. From another point of view, we can say that the ability to control the sexual impulse depends mostly upon how much energy can be held in the pelvic tissues without overcharging the genital apparatus. The genitals, themselves, provide no natural mechanism for the restraint of the impulse.

What we have been describing so far is the sexual act in the mammalian kingdom. Man, by virtue of his erect posture, is capable of further developments in his sexual potency. The more highly developed thigh muscles in man which serve the function of support to a greater degree than among other mammals can give man a control over the sexual movements which is impossible in the quadrupeds. His ability to move the pelvis under control (gently in the first phase of the act and later with increasing thrust) allows energy to build up to higher peaks than would be possible if the whole act were involuntary. By the same token any chronic spasticity of these muscles decreases the control and favors prematurity. Or the amount of control can be extended neurotically to a point where all spontaneity in the act is lost.

Consider the problem in the case of the excretory functions. The frequency of micturition is not dependent on the urinary sphincter but upon the capacity of the bladder. At most, the sphincters can regulate the moment of discharge. It permits one to control the release until the proper facilities are available. But how much value would this sphincter control have without the enlarged capacity of the bladder which is characteristic of the adult organism? The urinary sphincter is a derivative function of bladder capacity and of lesser importance in the reality function than the role of the bladder itself. The function of defecation in the infant shows the same principles. In his earliest days the infant has frequent and loose bowel movements. Long before any question of sphincter control is raised, the frequency of the movements tends to become decreased and regularized. This ability to hold and organize impulses develops as part of the natural growth of the individual. It is related to the development of those organs and structures localized in the belly and pelvis—namely, the colon and rectum, the bladder, and the organs of reproduction and genital discharge.

Medical pathology shows cases where this reservoir function is severely disturbed. I have in mind the conditions of chronic ulcerative colitis and chronic spastic colitis. These are diseases in which the psychosomatic factor is clearly recognized. I have treated several cases of colitis including one of ulcerative colitis. From a structural point of view they were all characterized by narrowness and rigidity of the lower segment. The belly was small and held in tightly. The muscles inserting into the bony pelvis were all severely contracted. The internist sees mainly the spasticity of the organ. Too frequently he overlooks the rigidity of the organism. In this condition, the lack of a reservoir in the intestinal channel is immediately apparent. The analytic observer sees the consequence in the symptom of diarrhea. My experience with these cases led me to postulate three factors in the production of the symptomatology. One is the lack of a reservoir function in the belly. This is the predisposition. The second is quantitative. Diarrhea develops only when the amount of excitation or energy is greater than the limited ability of these individuals to hold feeling. Consequently the individual with colitis is benefited by rest, a bland diet or any reduction of emotional excitement.

The third factor is characterological. It is the rigidity of the total organism and the inability to respond in appropriate movements to situations of stress or of tension. In the case of the individual with ulcerative colitis, psychological tests (including a Rorschach) showed an emotionally flat and immature personality with the more mature levels of expression blocked. The discharge tended to occur on the most primitive level.

Analytic study of these problems on the bioenergetic level revealed insights into the functions of the two principles. One young lady developed persistent diarrhea in the course of therapy. Her body structure was narrow and very rigid, the belly being held tightly contracted. The predisposition to colitis was given and the second, quantitative factor was also present. The patient was under considerable emotional stress when she began her therapy, yet at this time and for some period afterward, although both factors were operative, there was no diarrhea. The diarrhea developed only when the patient began to improve, specifically in her work function. Sexually there was some improvement but it was inconsistent. It is important to add that previously the patient had used drugs, stayed up late, rose late and led an unrealistic life.

I had assumed that the diarrhea would depend upon whether or not the excitation or energy could be released in appropriate action. Diarrhea would occur if such a release failed to happen, given, of course, the presence of the first two factors. In this case, however, there was no diarrhea in the first stage of therapy when the patient's behavior was most irrational. One must assume that the irrational behavior served to prevent diarrhea, and that the diarrhea developed when such behavior ceased and closed some neurotic outlets of discharge.

So long as the patient functioned on the pleasure principle in opposition to the reality principle, no chronic colitis developed. It was only when the patient attempted to hold her energy in accordance with the demands of reality that the inability of the belly to function as a reservoir manifested itself as a somatic disturbance. Not only was the belly contracted, it was highly overcharged. The rigidity of the total organism, visible in a tight and spastic musculature, makes it impossible for these individuals to support any additional pressure. Outside pressure is immediately transmitted to the soft inner organs with consequent disturbance. It is the flexibility and elasticity of the voluntary musculature which holds the key to the proper functioning of the reality principle. This flexibility permits adaptive reactions which are impossible without it. On the other hand the reality principle itself depends on the unity of all the segments.

We have discussed some aspects of the reality principle as it shows itself in the functions of the lower half of the body. Impulses moving towards the head end have a different quality than those moving downward. The head end is differentiated to take in food, water, air and sensory impressions. It is in the service of those instinctual impulses whose function is to charge the organism, in contrast to those directed downward, which aim at discharge. In man and the anthropoid apes the forelimbs become associated with head end functions while the hind limbs specialize even more in support and locomotion. But even in respect to the impulses whose aim is to charge the organism, a reservoir function is apparent. Where the worm takes in all matter in its path, the higher organisms scrutinize their environment carefully before reaching out to it.

In the upper half of the body the organ which restrains the impulse is the brain. Before the impulse is fed into the motor nerves which control muscular discharge it is subjected to the examination and censorship of the sensory and association areas. If perception or memory counsel holding back, no motor discharge occurs. The main energy of the impulse is frozen on the subcortical level or withdrawn back into the id system. One cannot comprehend the reality principle if one ignores the fact that the brain and, in fact, the whole head, can contain the most powerful impulses. The brain, too, functions like a condenser, equal in capacity to the condenser-like function of the genital apparatus. The actual amount of energy which can be held and focused in the human brain is tremendous. In very healthly organisms it creates a glow about the head.

Theory and clinical observation agree that the reality function is quantitatively equal at both ends. The actions at each end differ qualitatively. The individual will demonstrate an identical attitude towards reality in his thinking as in his sexuality. The aggression which is characteristic of the psychology of the phallic character is "equally" evident in his sexuality. The fantasy life of the oral character is reflected in the lack of contact with the partner in the sexual act. The psychological "holding" of the compulsive character derives from a similar attitude towards the functions of discharge and elimination. These are basic psychoanalytic ideas, what is new is the framework of reference. The reality principle derives from a bioenergetic swing between head end and tail end which is pendular in nature. It can go no further in one direction than the other.

The question to answer is this: To what extent is discharge possible through the head end? We disregard for this purpose such minor forms of discharge as spitting, sneezing, etc. We can phrase the question differently: To what extent can fantasy serve as a means of bioenergetic discharge? Structural considerations alone indicate the answer to the question. The bony envelope of the head, the fact that the major opening into the cranium carries impulses to and from the brain, lead to the conclusion that little real discharge occurs through the head end. The movement of energy upward leads always to increased charge. This is true of all upper end functions: eating, the use of the arms to capture or take food, breathing, sensory impressions and fantasy. Sexual fantasy increases the sexual charge, acting similarly to forepleasure in the sexual act. If it does not lead to discharge via the genital apparatus it becomes a pathological condition of impotence. When the energy moves downward it is fed into the muscular system for discharge.

We can equate the function of charge with the more general function of expansion. The formula would be: tension——→reaching out——→charge. The formula for discharge which is a function of muscular contraction, in the higher animals at least, is: discharge——→contraction ——→relaxation. Fantasy can serve the function of relieving tension temporarily; it leads to a general expansion of the organism, but if the cycle is arrested at this point and not completed a condition of unreality results. Muscular activity both in reaching out and in rhythmic contraction is avoided. Neither the ego nor the reality principle is involved. The result is a dissociation of the perception from the actual state of tension which exists so long as the fantasy is operative.

Fantasy used this way is not the same as intelligent thinking and imagination. The latter derive from the same function but they are not distorted as substitutes for reality. Fantasy and its derivatives, imagination and constructive thinking, have an important role in reality. They lie at the beginning of a cycle which must end in action; they cannot be an end in themselves.

As the ego grows out of the id, so the reality principle develops out of the pleasure principle as the longitudinal, antigravity orientation of the organism becomes established with growth. Despite the evident antithesis, the connections between these related functions must never be severed. The reality principle cut off from its motivation and energy source in the pleasure principle becomes sterile. An ego which denies its id foundation becomes dry and brittle. These relationships can be clearly elucidated through the study of the energy dynamics of the sexual act.

The sexual approach begins as an expression of the ego. Long before any physical contact occurs the two personalities meet through their eyes. Shindler, following

Clapared, places the center of the ego "between the eyes."
I, too, localize the upper point of the energy swing in the
region of the glabella, between the eyes. Certainly, the
ego shows itself in the eyes to such an extent that a
trained observer can evaluate the ego by their expression.
The physical contact which follows is still a reality function—it is exploratory. Activity is still dominated by the
conscious search for more pleasurable sensation with the
ego still in full command. Pleasure now serves the function of deepening the excitation and of arousing the deeper
id sensations. The participation of the id system in the
total experience gradually increases.

With penetration, the id system extends its influence.
Pleasure increases according to a curve which Reich outlined in *The Function of the Organism*—gradually at first,
then rapidly to a climax. The end point is reached when
an involuntary reaction occurs which leads to discharge.
This end point occurs when the ego system is overwhelmed
by the id, or when the reality principle becomes submerged in the deeper pleasure principle. The relative
strength of the two components determines the time of
its happening. Premature ejaculation results from a weak
ego system which cannot hold the strong id sensations.
On the other hand, if the ego is developed at the expense
of the id, the end point can be postponed by diminishing
the id participation with a corresponding decrease in end
pleasure.

Let us assume that ego and id work together, not antag-
onistically. If the ego identifies itself with the deeper id
sensations, the conscious perception of pleasure increases
in the course of the sexual act. The streaming of energy
to both brain and genital intensifies. A point is reached
where the brain, which is in an enclosed container, can
no longer take any increased charge. The reservoirs are
full. The sensations are so strong that consciousness is
overwhelmed. The ego system is drowned in the strong
tide of id impulses, the reality principle fades away, all
barriers disappear. The reservoirs empty in a mighty flood

which surges toward the genitals for discharge. For a few moments the id is supreme; the organism loses its identity in the sexual union. As the storm ends and the flood recedes the ego is reborn to a new day, refreshed and revitalized at the deepest sources of life's energies. Reality intrudes itself as consciousness is reawakened, or this may be postponed if sleep intervenes.

In summary we can say that the ego differentiates itself out of the id only to lose itself in the id in life's supreme moments. The reality principle serves to further the pleasure principle.

It is obvious from the foregoing that I equate the ego system with the reality principle, the id system with the pleasure principle. The justification for this is apparent from everything we have discussed. The ego is a perceptual phenomenon, it describes a subjective awareness. The reality principle describes an attitude viewed objectively. The somatic basis for both is the longitudinal streaming of the energy. The relationship between ego and id, reality principle and pleasure principle, can only be expressed in terms of a formula which derives from the basic unity and antithesis of living processes.

We can say further that if we compare man with the other animals, the following bioenergetic differences are evident. Man is characterized by the most highly developed reality system. This implies a greater energy pulsation and a better developed reservoir function. He has the best brain at one end and the most highly charged genital apparatus at the other. One is the corollary of the other. By definition, his ego is the strongest. All of this, however, would not be possible without a deep and powerful source of impulse formation. The ego can never be bigger than the id from which it arises and of which it always remains a part. It is also due to man's highly charged energy system that he became erect. Bioenergetic energy is by its nature antigravitational in its effect.

5

The Bioenergetic Concept of the Instincts

In the preceding chapters we studied several aspects of the nature of impulsive activity. The impulse itself is an energy movement from the center of the organism to the surface where it affects the relationship of the organism to the external world. This movement of energy from center to periphery has two purposes or ends. One is related to the function of charge, such as the taking in of food, respiration, sexual excitement, etc. The other is related to the function of energy discharge, the foremost expression of which is the sexual discharge and reproduction. All activities can be classified according to this simple criterion; that is, whether they fulfill the function of energy charge or discharge. The goal of these activities is not a constant level of tension or energy charge; rather charge and discharge are part of the living process, the goal of which is beyond our comprehension. Certainly the phenomena of growth and evolution negate any concept of constancy as a dynamic principle of life—which seems to move towards unknown goals in paths which are determined by the pleasure principle.

Individual growth and species evolution follow a line of development in which the simple pleasure principle is modified to provide more effective means of interacting with external reality. This modification of the pleasure principle is known as the reality principle. It has its origin in the separation of the basic functions of charge and discharge. The first specialization of structure is the differentiation of a part of the organism for the function of energy charge. Although absent in the amoeba it is already present in other protozoa. The separation of these basic functions creates an internal polarity which will determine the future organization of all higher life forms. Concomitant with the development of the reality principle and its internal expression in increased differentiation and specialization, we find increasingly higher levels of energy function.

Differentiation, specialization and increasing organization, on the one hand, are the functional manifestations of higher energy levels. Let me show this relationship by a simple analysis. The structural and functional improvements in the airplane would be meaningless without the development of more powerful engines and better fuels. The Wright brothers' jenny had no need of retractable landing gear nor radar devices. Greater power requires greater control, greater control means increased specialization and organization. So it is with living organisms. Power, however, is only the motor expression of an increased energy level. Greater sensitivity, heightened awareness and more control are the other aspects of the same energy process.

In biological thinking we must avoid teleological statements. One describes what one sees and attempts to understand the dynamics of the process. All moving systems are governed by the relationship of free energy to structural mass. No improvement in function results if increased energy production is balanced off by increased structural mass. The story of the disappearance of the great dinosaurs is related somehow to the appearance of the mammals in whom an improved energy function obviated the handicap of great mass which doomed the former. Today we see the same thing in the replacement of the vacuum tube by the transistor as the vacuum tube itself replaced older, more cumbersome methods of power control. This principle forms the basis of Norbert Wiener's (1956) concept of cybernetics as it applies to both living and non-living systems.

As compared with all other forms of life, the mammals as a class show the highest degree of motility. One may take exception to this statement in the case of the birds, but here motility as displacement in space is achieved at the expense of motility in relation to objects. Increased motility results from an increased energy level of functioning which also manifests itself in the ability of the organism to rise from the earth. The mammalian limb is certainly a great improvement over the reptilian limb. All biological concepts, however, are subject to the great law of antithesis. The long-legged giraffe lacks the motility of the cats or the canaries. If motility is evaluated in terms of its antithetical relations—that is, motility as displacement in space versus motility in terms of the ability to manipulate objects—the biped primates show the highest degree of over-all motility.

This increased motility, which is so evident in man, is the direct result of his upright posture, which freed his forelimbs from their subservience to the functions of support and locomotion. Here again is a major development in the reality and principle. The differentiation of the body structure in terms of charge and discharge is extended to the limbs. The whole upper half of the body can now be devoted to the function of energy charge. Energy discharge becomes even more specialized as a function of the lower half of the body since this half will take over the important function of moving the organism in space. This development of the reality principle is itself the product of a new and higher level of energy function. In fact, one dares to make the statement that the ratio of free energy to mass is so great in the human organism that it lifted the whole front end of the organism off the ground and made possible the differentiations, specializations and control which we identify with the human being. Compare the parts of Figure 8.

With this development of the reality principle on the biological level, the problem of the coordination and control of motility transcends for the first time the problem of increased motility.

Psychologists have known for some time that the growth of ego consciousness has been related to the increasing strength of the spiritual feeling in man. Before this happened, however, a long period of development took place. Erich Neumann, in *The Origins and History of Consciousness*, traces this development in the psychic sphere. In the beginning there was the unity of the unconscious—a world without beginning or end, represented symbolically by the circle or round. This is the world of the pleasure principle. This unity is destroyed by the appearance of light which is, psychologically speaking, the light of consciousness. Neumann (1954, p. 104) describes what follows: "Only in the light of consciousness can man know. And this act of cognition, of conscious discrimination, sunders the world into opposites, for experience of the world is only possible through opposites."

Consciousness has a twofold aspect. There is first the consciousness of feelings and actions, and secondarily, the consciousness of knowing. Neumann (1954, p. 126) says, "The important thing is that consciousness as the acting center precedes consciousness as the cognitive center." As this higher ego consciousness develops, it tends to set itself up in opposition to the body, which becomes the representative of the unconscious. The light which is the glow of consciousness is differentiated from and opposed to the current which created and maintained it. Yet we know that a light can never be stronger than the energy source which feeds it. This current is the stream of impulse formation in the body which, moving upward toward the head, excites the cerebral tissues and causes them to glow. But this is only one step away from saying that the strength and glory of man's ego consciousness is a reflection of the strength of his impulses and a product of the heightened energy processes in his organism.

On the unconscious level all activities are instinctual, all

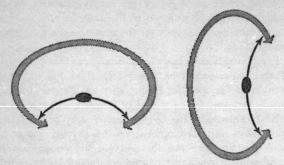

FIG. 8. *Left*. Mammal. The energy of the impulse is still dominated by the mass, or muscular system. *Right*. Man. The strength of the impulse is greater than the mass, or muscular system. Sensitivity, awareness, communication and control become equal to or greater than motility.

impulses are equal and unitary, and all can be reduced to the common principle: the pleasure principle. Charge→ discharge; tension→relaxation. Consciousness is synonomous with the splitting of this unity. The impulse is no longer simply an action; it can now be dissociated into the energy of the impulse and the movement itself. The former is perceived as a feeling, the latter as its expression. This dissociation is part of the reality principle, otherwise one could not restrain actions. What is restrained is not the feeling but its execution. Other animals share with man this consciousness of action for the animal can also voluntarily control his musculature.

In man alone this development goes further. Consciousness of cognition is a consciousness of the control; not only is there the fact of control over the voluntary muscles, there is the experience or knowledge of this fact. This experience can only result from a situation in which the feeling can be appropriately expressed with a minimum of muscular participation. The ego must have an organ of expression other than gross physical movement. Such a function devolves upon the organ of speech. Thus one can say, "I am furious," without having to express it in movement.

The possibility of opposites, the concept of antithetical relationships stemming from a preceding unity, derives biologically from this splitting of the impulse. This is the point from which Freud began his study of the instincts. Let us follow his thinking.

In the preceding chapter we saw that Freud postulated as his first set of antithetical instincts hunger versus love. This would correspond to the directions inward and outward. These he later identified with the instinct for self-preservation as opposed to an instinct for the preservation of the species. Later, this became formulated as an antithesis between ego libido (narcissism) and object libido (sexuality). But these are all merely different aspects of the inward and outward relationship. As such they are secondary manifestations; the problem of splitting the impulse was not touched until 1920.

The reasons which led Freud in 1920 to abandon his previous concepts in favor of a new approach to the nature of the instincts were discussed previously. If we disagree with his arguments, we must nevertheless recognize the daring and scope of the new formulations.

Elaborating on the nature of the ego instincts, Freud (1950, p. 48) concluded that these instinctual drives were essentially conservative and "tended toward the restoration of an earlier state of things." Phrased in other words, Freud (p. 58) said, "For on our hypothesis, the ego instincts arise from the coming to life of inanimate matter and they seek to restore the inanimate state." On the other hand, Freud found in his original concept of the sexual instincts a force which tended to "preserve life itself for a comparatively long period." These, he assumed, "are the life instincts, which lead, by reason of their function, to death; and this fact indicates that there is an opposition between them" (p. 53).

As a consequence of this reasoning, Freud (1950, p. 54) abandoned the concept of the ego instincts and the sexual instincts as primary forces in the phenomena of life. In their place he proposed the idea that these forces are, properly, death instincts and life instincts. "It is as though the life of the organism moved with a vacillating rhythm. One group of instincts rushes forward so as to reach the final goal of life as swiftly as possible; but, when a particular stage of the advance has been reached, the other group jerks back to a certain point to make a fresh start and so prolong the journey." Freud placed the seat of the "death instincts" in the musculature.

Freud (1950a, p. 68) named the life instincts eros, the "Eros of poets and philosophers which binds all living things together." In this eros, Freud recognized the libido of the sexual instincts.

Originally the concept of libido was restricted to the energy of the sexual instincts directed toward an object. Freud declared later that the libido could be withdrawn and turned inward as narcissism. This in no way disproves its original character as an energy or force. One cannot agree with Freud when he equates eros with the sexual instinct. One is a force. The other, as we defined it, is the channel in which the force moves. In this respect Jung is closer to the facts when he uses the word "libido" to mean instinctual force in general. Freud (1950a, p. 71), however, comes close to the bioenergetic concept in the remark, "The difference between the two kinds of instinct, which was in some sort of way *qualitative*, must now be characterized differently—namely, as being *topographical*." Just what this topographical difference is we shall see in a moment.

If one visualizes the gallop of a dog or a horse, the nature of mammalian movement is clearly evident. The alternate coming together and extension of the two pairs of legs represents a process of charge and discharge which can be portrayed (Fig. 9). As the energy sweeps through the muscular system, which is essentially on the back of the animal, the two ends of the animal approach each other and contact the ground. Energy is discharged through the four legs into the ground. This discharge of energy produces a leap in which the legs are extended. Extension

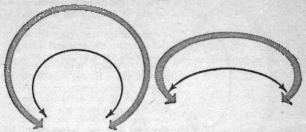

FIG. 9. *Left:* Discharge = muscular action. *Right:* Charge = action of eros, blood-borne.

of the back opens the volar aspect of the animal and leads to the inspiration of air. A new impulse forms which charges the front of the body first and then moves into and charges the main muscle mass of the back. The organism is now in a position for a new discharge and another leap.

Here we have Freud's concept of alternance. One group of instincts moving the animal forward, but in the process discharging its energy; the other group recharging the system for another movement. The failure to recharge the system would result in death.

In man, the upright position permits a dissociation of the two phases. The function of charge does not necessarily lead to discharge; that is, it can be dissociated from the muscular system. The energy of the charge is then localized along the front of the body, increasing its sensitivity but decreasing its motility. The increased sensitivity gives rise to certain feelings which can be expressed either in action or verbally or both. There are fundamental differences in the two modes of expression—most important of which is the fact that only muscular action can discharge the large quantity of energy produced by the alive human being. Speech, as an extension of thinking, works with much smaller quantities of energy. Let us look at these energy processes in the human (Fig. 10).

In my original exposition of these pathways of energy

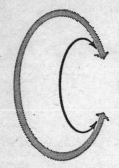

FIG. 10. The shaded line represents the flow of energy along the back. The solid line portrays the flow along the front of the body. The points of confluence are the peripheral structures in the upper and lower halves of the body which react with the environment. The main point above is the region of the glabella between the eyes, below it is the genitals. The upper point of confluence includes the eyes, nose, mouth and hands. The lower point may include the region from the anus to the genitals and the feet.

movement, I derived my concepts from the observation of patients, from personal experiences and from the analysis of animal movement. They had, as their starting point, the concept of the longitudinal energy swing, but I had not as yet worked out its relationship to the ego or to the reality principle. Let me mention some of the experiences which led to these insights.

In the course of my analysis with Reich, I became aware that one can feel a movement downward along the front of the body in the process of a deep and easy aspiration. If one is fully relaxed, the feeling would end as a genital sensation. Reich assumed that this feeling and the accompanying movement reflected a flow of energy downward to the genitals; it had its point of origin in the chest. There was no suggestion by Reich of a movement upward nor any statement that the flow of energy was pendular in nature.

It was while listening to Chopin's music one day that I became conscious of the flow of feeling upward. One can recognize Chopin's music by its emotional quality. The best word to describe that quality seems to be "longing." The feeling of longing is so strong that it almost amounts to a yearning. One senses in his music the failure of the feeling to reach satisfaction; it is as if the feeling got caught in the throat.

I soon realized that all music has this feeling of longing.

In singing, one can experience the movement of the feeling upward from the diaphragmatic region to the head. There are other forms of expression in which an impulse rises upward to vocal utterance. Crying and laughter are such expressions which also include ordinary speech. Vocal utterance, whether in song, speech, crying or laughter, is one of the means of reaching out for contact with others. But there are other ways of expressing this reaching out for contact. The arms raised upwards in prayer, the lips held out for the kiss, the upstretched arms of the infant, have the same fundamental meaning: the reaching out to someone or something outside ourselves. I call this basic feeling "longing." It is a longing for contact.

In the sexual act, the same feeling moving downward toward the genitals has another quality. Given the contact in the upper half of the body, this feeling is experienced as melting and the desire to flow out.

In music the feeling of longing is the basic for the melody. Too, music has a rhythmic component. Whereas the melody soars upward, like the flight of a bird, rhythm is earth bound and finds its natural medium in the movement of the legs and feet. Rhythm is by its nature highly pulsatile and, by virtue of that fact, it is related to all other phenomena of energy discharge. This is seen most clearly in the dance: The upper half of the body carries the melody, the lower half carries the rhythm.

In a study I made of the art of dance, I reached the conclusion that the feeling which underlies the dance is joy. If the expression "one dances for joy" is true, we can also say that whenever one dances there is joy. At that time, however, I did not make the connection between rhythm and joy, although I knew that the greatest experience of joy results from the one activity in which the greatest rhythmic discharge occurs, the sexual orgasm.

As frequently happens in thinking, the various elements fell into place spontaneously to complete the picture. We begin with walking, which is a rhythmic activity—left, right, left, right, in equal measure. If we become more excited, we may jump, hop, skip or run. The increase of excitation leads to more intense discharge. Walking, running, jumping, dancing are interactions of our organism with the ground. Singing and speech are interactions with air and space. We move by the discharge of energy into the ground. In this respect, the ground or earth shows a basic function. All energy finds its way eventually into the earth; this is the principle known as "grounding." It explains the discharge through storm and lightning of an overcharged atmosphere. This principle must also underlie the sexual act. Without elaborating the point, let me say that the sexual embrace of a woman is for the man an embrace of the earth. The woman carries a bit of the earth within herself. Woman in the embrace of a man embraces the spirit.

The polarization which led to the reality principle is derived from these observations. Energy moves from the sun via the atmosphere to the earth. Figuratively speaking, all organisms reach upward to the sun for energy, and this is literally true in the case of the plants. The reaching upward or outward (longing) is part of the function of charge: food, oxygen, exitation. We saw how they involve the upper half of the body. Discharge is downward to the earth. Prior to its discharge, the energy promotes two other living functions: growth and movement. Only the excess, greater in adults, where growth has ceased, than in children, is discharged to the earth as sexuality.

I linked these movements in a common pulsation which had its center in the heart. These are feelings which seem to stem from the heart. Heart feelings are tender feelings which draw the individual into relationships for charge or discharge. But something was lacking. The formulation was incomplete to explain certain clinical experiences. These feelings, while they add strength to the ego, fail to account for the weakness of certain character structures who show a lack of aggression. Too, they did not explain such emotions as anger or rage.

For some time I limited my thinking to the swing of energy which had its center in the heart. One could feel that the pathway of this movement was in the anterior aspect of the body. I had known for some time that anger was experienced in the back of the body, specifically in the area between the shoulder blades. This is the region where the hair of animals erects in anger. Darwin had observed and commented on this phenomenon. In *The Expression of Emotions in Man and Animals,* he describes an ape in anger. "I saw the hair on the baboon, when angered, bristling along the back from the neck to the loins."

I have personally experienced this "bristling" along the back in anger. We also say of a person that he has his "back up" in anger. This reminds one of the cat. In the lion, the expression of this feeling in movement is the leap, paws outstretched to seize or strike, jaws open and set to bite. In man, the energy is directed more strongly into the arms, which take over the aggressive functions of the teeth.

Once my attention was directed to the swing of energy along the back, I became aware that this movement was also pendular. It sweeps upward in anger or rage, moving over the scalp and into the upper teeth. The downward movement along the back occurs in the sexual act. The energy which produces the pelvic thrust can be experienced as an impulse which moves down the back, around the buttocks and perineum to reach the genitals.

I reached the conclusion that the pendular movement along the back has a different quality than the movement in the front. Their relationship became clear as I studied the movements of animals in motion.

The diagrams presented earlier were the immediate result of this thinking. It was only later that I saw the connection with the development of the reality principle and the growth of the ego.

Originally, in figure 10 (p. 78), I portrayed the energy flow along the back by a *red* line (now *black*), and that along the front by a *blue* line (now *light*). While the use of these two colors was fortuitous, they subsequently proved to have a deeper meaning.

The *blue* line which portrays the flow along the front of the body represents feelings whose general quality is tenderness. They comprise such specific sentiments as compassion, pity, charity, faith, etc. Their aim is the identification of the individual with other persons or things. The object, of course, varies and determines the specific quality; tenderness towards a sexual object, religious sentiments in relation to God, pity for one who suffers, etc. Their source seems to be the heart. If these feelings are unassociated with a component from the back of the body, they have a blue tone, or give rise to the blue mood. The red line represents feelings which have the general quality of aggression. These would include anger, rage, sexual aggression, the hunting for food, etc. There is nothing tender about these feelings as there is nothing soft about the back. Since the main muscular development is the region of the back, we would expect that the energy flow in this region provides the motive power for spatial movement of the organism. They are aggressive because their aim is to "move the organism towards" objects, which naturally should be the same objects of the other instinctual force. Again, the objective determines the specific quality. I tend to localize the source of this energy swing in the region about the insertion of the diaphragmatic crura. These feelings when isolated from the tender component produce heat and a sensation of redness. They are the basis of the red flush of anger, of the heat of sexual passion and the blood lust of the hunt.

The use of the two colors has a deeper implication. The tender feelings have a spiritual quality. They are closely related to the respiratory function and the intake of air. Their blue color reflects the dominance of a spiritual or heavenly element. The feelings of the back have a materialistic orientation. They are related to the digestive system by the search for food. Significantly the two functions of respiration-circulation and eating-digestion occupy similar places in the body, the former being more anterior than the latter. Food as opposed to oxygen is derived from the earth; the aggressive feelings are basically earthy and this, too, justifies their red coloration.

Every action has a component from each aspect of the individual. In the action of reaching out one's arms to another person, for example, impulses from both front and back are represented. The quality of the movement is determined by the ratio of these two elements. In the previous example, if the tender component dominates, the gesture is one of an embrace. On the other hand, if the aggressive element is the stronger, the action shows a threat of force which would be out of place in a love relationship but appropriate in a wrestling match. In the neuroses, as we shall see later, the ratio of the two instinctual drives tends to be fixed within narrow limits regardless of the situation. The oral character tends to approach all situations with an attitude of sympathy; the phallic character's basic attitude is one of aggressive determination. The ratio is characteristic for each type of character disturbance.

It must be evident to the analytic reader that there is a very close similarity between the bioenergetic concept of the instincts outlined above and Freud's views as expressed in *Beyond the Pleasure Principle*. This similarity only became apparent to me after I had constructed my present formulations. If analysis on the somatic level yields the same result as analysis of the psychic tendencies, the fact proves the unity of the two functions.

The problem of the instincts is confused for Freud since he does not draw a distinction between primary pathways which determine the nature of an instinct and its aim, which determines its specific quality. Freud (1950a, p. 73) admits that the ego instincts have a libidinal component attached to them. He also "recognizes the presence of a sadistic component in the sexual instinct." We shall see later that the ego instincts can be analyzed into an aggressive component, motor in nature, and a tender component, sensory in nature, both of which move upward. It is the upward direction which determines their ego identity since both components bring an energy charge to the head. Similarly, the sexual instinct is composed of two components, both moving downward toward the genitals.

One must also draw a distinction between the pathway of movement and the energy force itself. There is only one energy or force in the organism. This force or energy is identical with the psychoanalytic concept of the libido and also with Freud's eros. This single energy acts in both instinctual pathways. In the case of the aggressive instincts, it activates a motor system, becomes a source of power for muscular contraction. It is used as a motor force to create movement. When the energy is dissociated from the muscular system, either because action is restrained or the need for conscious awareness and control dominates the need for movement, the free energy tends to move along the front of the body. The feelings it gives rise to are tender feelings because the tissues are fluid and soft. The absence of a strong musculature makes this a sensitive region. The energy dominates the structural elements which are mainly vehicles for its movement. Expression of these feelings is mainly by vocal utterance.

The ego is the creator of opposites as it is the synthesizer of antitheses. It is a catalyst which can separate and combine. Actually, it does both. By restraining the muscular expression of a feeling, we can dissociate it into a motor action and a sensory feeling component. One cannot become aware of the tender feelings if one immediately acts out every impulse, for the ego is then dominated by the physical action and its consequences. In the same way, one stops movement to increase sensory perception. The splitting of the unity of the impulse is the basis of ego consciousness, for it permits a later recombination of the components for a more effective response. However, the split must not be too great for re-fusion of the two components to occur.

If we looked for an antithesis to eros to satisfy a dualistic concept of the nature of the living process we would find it in the concept of unorganized matter, the clay of the biblical expression. Eros, then, is the breath of life which God breathed into the clay to make it come alive. Here, however, we are far from the instincts themselves and close to the physical domain of matter and energy. Life is not a mixture of matter and energy but energy in matter, bound in such a way that dissociation is impossible so long as the living process continues. Eros thus is related to the concept of the spirit; the structural elements of the body are derivatives of the matter out of which they are constructed. Death is the condition in which the dissociation of the spirit or soul from the material body occurs. We say the soul leaves the body.

Every cell, as every organization of cells in tissues, organs or organism, is a mixture both of clay and spirit, of body and soul, of matter and eros. The living process results from this mixture, it is not the mixture itself. This relationship can be understood if we compare life to a flame. A fire requires both a combustible substance and oxygen. Yet the fire is not one nor the other nor the combination. Under given conditions, a fire could start. Once in existence it is a new element, neither matter nor energy but a process. It has its own tendencies to grow and to start new fires. Life has been compared to the flame which while it can be extinguished in one spot can start new flames that will carry on the same process.

Life itself has no tendency to die, anymore than a fire has an innate tendency to extinguish itself. Life is a self-perpetuating fire and this is its great mystery, not the inevitable eclipse of any individual flame. The fire will continue so long as it is assured of a combustible substance, oxygen and the elimination of waste products. Life, too, has these needs: food, oxygen and the elimination of waste matter. But here the analogy ends. Life follows certain laws of growth, organization and reproduction which we do not as yet understand. Now it may be that when the potential for growth, organization and reproduction which is bequeathed to the living organism at conception is exhausted the individual organism dies, but this does not prove the existence of an instinct toward death.

The concept of a death instinct is illogical. Since the word "instinct" implies life, it is as if one said, "life equals life plus death," or A equals A plus B. Death can be contrasted with life, it is not a part of it. The animate develops as part of its structure, a framework of inanimate matter which may cause a drag or inertia on motility. It cannot be designated as a tendency or instinct.

Freud assumed the "presence of a sadistic component in the sexual instinct," which he felt was a representative of the death instinct. I do not, however, accept the connotation of sadism as appropriate to this component. We must distinguish between sadism and aggression. The lion who kills for food is aggressive but not sadistic. The action of a lynch mob is sadistic. In sadism, the pleasure is derived from the act of destruction per se. In the case of the lion, the destruction only makes possible the pleasure which is derived from the satisfaction of the hunger need. We can apply the same distinction to the sexual act. If the pleasure is derived from the feeling of domination over or injury to the woman's ego, the act has a sadistic element. Where the pleasure is derived from the experience of communication, both physical and spiritual, which is the essence of the sexual act, no sadistic quality can be ascribed to the action.

The sexual act is bioenergetically a phenomenon of energy discharge. This necessarily involves two components: an aggressive factor which provides the motive power and the tender feelings which give the action its meaning. Feelings of love in themselves are powerless to achieve discharge without the aid of the aggressive drive. This is not an uncommon problem. Female patients who have a dominant oral character structure experience strong sexual excitement but frequently are unable to bring it to a climax. Bioenergetic analysis of their structure shows marked weakness of the aggressive drive associated with a lack of motility in the back and legs. The opposite situation also exists. The rigid structure of the phallic narcissistic male permits discharge to occur at the expense of the tender feelings. The result is a feeling of release and minor satisfaction with little meaning. When the aggressive component is not tempered with love or tenderness, sadism is manifest. But this is a pathological condition.

As part of his death instinct theory, Freud introduced the concept of primary masochism, that is, the death instinct is a destructive tendency, which is originally directed inward. Eros turns it outward in the form of sadism. The clinical evidence for the existence of a primary masochism does not exist. All analytic therapists have to deal daily with the problem of masochism or masochistic tendencies and if they are unable to solve the problem the therapy ends in failure. When we examine these cases analytically it does appear that the aggression is turned inward. Therapeutic success, however, disproves the idea of a primary biological tendency to failure. How can we explain, then, the observed self-destructive tendency?

The bioenergetic structure of the masochistic character shows an overdeveloped musculature that is at the same time severely contracted. Freud associated the muscular apparatus with the death instinct. At the same time, the tender feelings are greatly suppressed, not repressed. The supression of the tender feelings produces a markedly contracted and tense abdominal musculature. If one charts the energy flow in terms of movement along the front and back of the body, the following picture emerges (Fig. 11).

In the natural un-neurotic state every impulse is the result of the fusion of the two components: one aggressive and motor, the other tender and sensory. It may be weighted more on one side than on the other depending on the external situation but there is little conflict between the two tendencies. In the masochistic structure, these two tendencies cross each other and create a condition of ambivalence. This is one type of instinctual defusion to which Freud called attention in his discussion of the instincts.

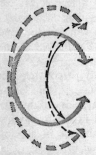

FIG. 11. Masochism. The heavy broken line shows the overdeveloped pathologically contracted musculature. The tender feelings are bottled up and create internal pressure and anxiety. Aggression is turned inward. There is a crossing of the two instinctual tendencies. The light solid and broken lines show the normal instinctual relationship.

To anticipate briefly the detailed study of the masochistic character structure, we can mention the two basic causes of this condition. The overdeveloped musculature is a result of an exaggerated emphasis in childhood of the material side of life. Generally this is done by an over-protective mother who places the main importance on food or toilet training or both. Such a muscular development is designed to "hold in" impulses as contrasted with the elongated and relaxed muscles needed for movement. Since body movement and bowel movement are closely related, any marked interference with the natural intestinal functions leads to a generalized decreased motility in the organism. In these cases, too, one finds that the tender side of the mother-child relationship is suppressed. The mother shows her love through her attention to food and defecation; the child is expected to respond by being a good eater and having regular, controlled bowel movements. It is obvious that there is little tolerance for the expression of the personal wishes and interests of the child; his other emotional needs are ignored and his resistance is crushed. These mothers smother their children with an attention they do not want. We shall see the exact interplay of these forces in the detailed case histories to be presented later. At this point, my purpose is to show that the concept of an aggression turned inward is bioenergetically true but it must be considered a secondary, neurotic condition.

But we should also ask ourselves: Is it not true that it is eros which directs the aggression outward and that without eros the musculature would contract to a condition of rigor mortis? The answer must be "yes." Even our own diagram says the same thing. But eros is not the sexual instinct, it is the force which motivates all instinctual activity. Living activity, as such, would be impossible without it. Eros is the life force and there is only one such force or energy. In this respect, our ideas are monistic. But this force or energy operates through matter. The front of the body is therefore the sensory side, the back is the motor side. The dominance of the solid elements in the back accounts for the material quality of the aggressive drive. Conversely the preponderance of energy over matter in the front of the body determines its spiritual quality.

Compare this concept with one Freud (1950b, p. 56) advanced in *The Ego and the Id*. "Both instincts would be active in every particle of living substance, although in unique proportions, so that some one substance ought to be the principle representative of Eros." Freud does not say what that substance might be but he does name a special organ by means of which "the death instinct of the single cell can successfully be neutralized and the destructive impulses be diverted towards the external world . . . This special organ would seem to be the musculature." I would venture the suggestion that the special substance "which is the principle representative of Eros" is the blood. This may explain why the identification of members of a family are referred to as "blood relationships." We also set up in this way an antithesis between the fluid elements of the body and the structural elements.

We need go no further into this question now. We are interested in knowing how the two "classes of instincts" function in any specific action. Here, too, Freud has pointed to a theoretical answer. According to his conception, the "two classes of instincts are fused, blended, and mingled with each other." Reich has suggested a mechanism which would explain this phenomenon. It is his concept of superimposition which is, simply stated, the observation that when two moving waves going in the same direction meet, they fuse into a common wave with greater amplitude and force.

Instinctual "defusion" does occur. Freud (1950b, p. 57) suspected "that the epileptic fit is a product and sign of instinctual defusion," a motor discharge completely divorced from any component from the tender feelings which would relate the action to the external world. Sadism is another example of instinctual defusion. Here a destructive action is directed against an object which would normally be the recipient of a tender feeling. We can find an example of a tender feeling which lacks a motor component. The individual who yearns or pines for an object has an identification with it, but the aggression necessary to achieve satisfaction through union is lacking.

Complete defusion of the instincts characterizes the psychotic condition. Incomplete defusion is responsible for the ambivalence which is a common symptom of the neuroses. In analyzing the ambivalence expressed in the love-hate polarity, Freud (1950b, p. 61) arrives at a construction which is essentially bioenergetic. First, he recognizes that "in many circumstances hate changes into love and love into hate." The mechanism whereby this change is effected is conceived as follows: "An ambivalent attitude (incomplete fusion) is present from the outset and the transformation is effected by means of a reactive shifting of cachexis, by which energy is withdrawn from the erotic impulses and used to supplement the hostile energy." The assumption upon which this statement is based is the psychic equivalent of bioenergy. "We have reckoned as though there existed in the mind—whether in the ego or the id—a displaceable energy, which is itself neutral, but is able to join forces with an erotic or with a destructive impulse."

Let us summarize the ideas so far presented. One basic energy motivates all actions. When it charges and flows through the musculature, especially the voluntary muscles, it produces spatial movement which we equate with *aggression* (to move to). When it charged the soft structures such as the blood and skin, it produces sensations which are erotic, tender or loving. Each of these aspects of the emotional life of the individual tends to be localized topographically: the motor component in the back and legs, the sensory component in the front of the body and in the hands. While this tendency to topographical localization is not absolute, for the practical purpose of bioenergetic therapy, this distinction between front and back is valid.

In un-neurotic behavior, this one energy is distributed into the two pathways to produce an action which is rational and appropriate to the situation. Impulses from the two pathways merge or super-impose into an action which, seen at the surface, is a unitary expression. Fusion is a surface function, that is, it is a function of expression and under the control of the ego. Where complete fusion has occurred it is impossible for the observer to delineate the two components. Incomplete fusion creates ambivalence and produces irrational behavior. It is easily seen by the observer, as in the case of the patient who cries when moved to anger or becomes angry when moved to tears. Complete defusion must be synonymous with the psychotic split.

We are now in a position to advance our thinking. We recognized the antithesis of matter and energy and we postulated an antithesis between a motor, aggressive pathway and a sensory, tender pathway. Now, on a higher level of organization, we can speak of ego and sexual instincts. The sexual instinct includes both fundamental components—sensory and motor, tenderness and aggression. The erotic component moves down the front of the body and joins with an aggressive component which swings down the back around the perineum and into the genitals. The sexual nature of these impulses is determined by their aim, a sexual act with a sexual object, and by their point of confluence in the genitals. On the other hand when the direction of movement of both impulses is upward towards the head, with a major point of confluence in the eyes, we can designate the common pathway as an ego instinct.*

Due to its opposite direction, the ego instinct becomes antithetical to the sexual instinct. It explains the observation that at the height of the sexual orgasm the ego becomes extinct. It permits us to determine the quality of the ego from the expression in the eyes, the bearing of the head and neck, the expressive quality of the face, etc. It ties in with our discussion of the reality principle in which we postulated a basic longitudinal swing between the head and genitals, between the organs of charge and of discharge. If, now, that longitudinal energy pulsation can be divided into two more basic components, the division has meaning only in terms of a disturbed function, that is, instinctual defusion. At the level of the ego and sexual discharge only a single current is discernible. The movement in the living organism is pulsatile. The energy movement upward and downward is pendular in nature. The ego instinct can be no stronger that the sexual instinct, the ego itself no greater than the sexual feeling. If there is an ambivalence on the ego level a similar ambivalence will be found in the sexual function. This swing as the basis of the reality principle is the cornerstone of all bioenergetic principles and therapy.

We have now concluded our discussion of the theoretical principles which underlie bioenergetic therapy. In

* Compare this with Paul Schilder's ideas on the ego. "In the tendencies of the body there is therefore not only aggressiveness. The tendencies of the ego provide food and self-defense." *The Image and Appearance of the Human Body*. New York, International Universities Press, 1950, pp. 121–122.

the next three chapters theory is united to technique in such a way that the presentation of character structures which follows will have both a practical and a theoretical value.

6

Bioenergetic Principles in Analytic Therapy

Psychoanalysis had its origin in Freud's attempt to comprehend a somatic disturbance (hysterical symptom) in terms of a psychic conflict. The next big problem to command Freud's attention was the distinction between the anxiety neurosis and neurasthenia. Throughout its development psychoanalysis has never been able to dissociate itself from the physical manifestations of emotional conflicts. Yet with respect to the physical function of the organism the psychoanalytic attitude has been to approach it from its psychic reflection. One can proceed in the reverse direction with greater effectiveness, that is, from the physical problem to its psychic representation.

We saw in Chapter 1 that Ferenczi supplemented the traditional method with techniques which sought to involve the body more directly in the analytic procedure. Reich placed even more emphasis upon the somatic functions, especially upon the relation of respiration to the problem of emotional control. In addition, Reich introduced the concept of a physical energy as a counterpart to Freud's concept of a mental energy. But neither in Reich nor in any other analytic writer is there a systematic presentation of the relationship between somatic function and psychic problems. Such a presentation will occupy the second half of this book. At this point I should like to set forth some basic bioenergetic principles and show their validity for analytic practice.

Some time ago I treated a colleague who suffered from an inability to work following several episodes of depression, one of which had necessitated his hospitalization. He had undergone a traditional psychoanalysis and also a form of group therapy. No doubt he was helped by these treatments but this work function had not improved. Finally he was referred to me for bioenergetic therapy in the hope that I could reach him with our more active techniques where others had failed.

After about eight months of bioenergetic therapy with one hour sessions once a week he was able to resume the practice of analysis. Some time later a mutual friend complimented me on the result and remarked, "I don't know what you did to get him on his feet, but no one was able to do it before." I answered that I literally put him on his feet. Very little of the bioenergetic therapy was done with the patient lying on a couch in a relaxed position. Most of the time he was on his feet either moving or talking.

I wonder how much it is possible to achieve with a patient lying supine on a couch or sitting comfortably in a chair. Since all of my patients suffer from some degree of lack of aggression, the physical passivity enjoined by the prone position or the sitting position must constitute some handicap in the therapy. If we think of "aggression" in terms of its dictionary meaning, to move to, the standard analytic position imposes a limit upon aggression and movement.

I do not mean to imply in the foregoing case that simply putting a patient on his feet could overcome such serious problems as depression and the inability to work. Much more is involved than this. I use the case to illustrate the literal significance of such expressions as "to stand on your own two feet," to be "on your toes," to "hold your ground," etc. Sometimes, very rarely, the patient is spontaneously aware of the immediate connection between his emotional problem and the somatic disturbance. When this happens the therapeutic endeavor is greatly facilitated.

A young man came to therapy following his discharge from military service. His complaint was that he didn't know where he was going nor what he wanted to do. He was very tall, six feet five inches, thin and walked with a slight stoop as tall people are wont to do. In the initial interview he described certain sensations which I believe accounted for his inability to "know where he was going." I quote his exact words.

"Just before I went overseas was when it dawned on me. When I moved my leg (while walking) in the mechanical sense, there was an instant, almost immeasurable, when my leg was swinging free and out of control, like the pendulum swing of a weight. As I initiated the movement of walking, my leg was originally under control. In the reaching out, I had a feeling that it was out of control as if I wasn't sure it would come back. The cumulative effect of these experiences, instantaneous but continuous in all walking, had an effect on me. There is a vague feeling in the body that at some vital point in movement, one is out of control. It seems to me that this is akin to schizophrenia. There are two different situations, one while sitting and one while walking. It seems to me that my personality has two aspects, one when sitting and one when walking. When walking, I feel as if I am on stilts." Then he added, "I feel that I am still learning to walk and this gives me a very infantile feeling. As you said, the lower half of my body is infantile looking. Ultimately, you feel split off from your legs; above your legs is you, below are the legs, something alien to the self."

It makes sense to me that an individual who feels that he has no control over his legs should also feel that he doesn't know where he is going. Of course his height doesn't help him. Tall persons frequently have some loss of contact with their legs or with the ground. Sometimes one gets the impression of a patient that they are "up in the clouds." One is tempted to say to such an individual, "Come down to earth." But the technical problem in such a case is how to bring the patient down to earth and how to anchor him there. The sense of belonging, of having roots, must be directly related to the feeling of intimate contact between the feet and the ground. Another patient expressed this relationship very clearly, she said, "I had the feeling that I wasn't in life, that I wasn't in things. I was walking a foot above the ground."

The problem of lack of contact with the feet and the ground may be manifested in other ways. In interpreting drawings of the human figure as a method of personality investigation, it is observed that "legs and especially feet are sources of conflict and difficulty in many drawings." Machover (1949, p. 65) states that "we may understand why insecurity of footing, literally interpreted, is shown in most problem drawings." The functional importance of the lower extremities cannot be overestimated. Machover's observation repeats common knowledge. "In addition to the potentiality for contact, which the legs and feet share with the arms and hands, they bear the added responsibility of supporting and balancing the body proper and of making possible locomotion of the body."

The problem of emotional security cannot be divorced from the question of the physical security of one's footing. While the problem can be tackled on the verbal level, it yields more quickly and more completely to a therapy which combines analysis "from above" with direct work on the physical disturbance below. In these cases bioenergetic therapy aims to bring the patient into contact with his feet and with the ground and at the same time to make the patient aware of the relationship between his emotional problem and its physical counterpart. The therapy proceeds on two fronts simultaneously, although at one time the analytic work may predominate while at another time the emphasis shifts to the physical side.

When Ferenczi spoke of "analysis from below," he had in mind the function of the sphincters which govern the processes of discharge. It took me many years of analytic work with the body to realize that for such a technique to fulfill the promise it holds out it must literally start from the ground up. It is an everyday truism that a house is no stronger than its foundation. Not until one examines the legs from a dynamic point of view does one become aware how weak are the foundations which support some seemingly strong ego structures.

I treated a patient some years ago who suffered from severe hypertension. He had been a press agent for several Hollywood stars and movie producers. He was a good eater, a fairly heavy drinker and a smooth talker. He had a round florid face and a full body. When he took his clothes off, I was shocked at the pair of thin spindly legs and narrow hips that were revealed. The conclusion was inevitable that the seeming security and strength of the upper half of the body was a compensation for the weakness below. His main activities were confined to the upper half of the body and were essentially oral in nature. The functions of energy discharge were severely restricted and the discharge of energy in movement and sex was greatly reduced. Bioenergetically one could interpret the hypertension as the result of a preponderance of energy charge over energy discharge. I understood, too, why this patient had a strong interest in boats. With his weak legs he was bound to feel insecure on land.

Recently I saw a young man who was a jet pilot in the navy. He had a history of reading difficulty which he managed to overcome through special exercises. He also complained of a feeling of insecurity. His body showed very little disturbance of form. He was fairly well proportioned, trim and lean. The jaw was clean cut and determined, the legs seemed a little too heavy. His problem was revealed when I asked him to strike the couch. Everytime he struck a blow his feet left the ground. When I pointed this out to him, remarking how difficult it was for him to hold the ground, he said, "Now I know why I feel so much more secure up in the air." Experiences such as these confirm the importance of studying the human being physically as well as psychologically.

Reich maintained that there could be no neurosis without a disturbed sexual function. This observation met with strong objections from many analysts at the time it was made. But one can go much further than Reich. There is no neurotic problem which does not manifest itself in every aspect of the individual's function. This follows logically from the gestalt concept of the organism as a unity. Because we express our personalities or character in every action and in every attitude it becomes possible to determine character traits from such diverse expressions as handwriting, the walk of the person, etc. The bioenergetic analyst does not depend on any one manifestation. The history, the appearance, the manner of speech and even psychological tests are used to arrive at a correct diagnosis of the character structure. Most important, however, is the physical appearance at rest and in movement. No words are so clear as the language of body expression once one has learned to read it.

We begin with the legs and the feet because they are the foundation and support of the ego structure. But they have other functions. It is through our legs and our feet that we keep contact with the one invariable reality in our lives, the earth or the ground. We speak of a people as being "earthy" to mean that they have a good sense of reality. The contrary, "to be up in the air," denotes a lack of contact with reality. The bioenergetic treatment of the psychotic or schizoid character consists in part of establishing in the patient an awareness of his legs and feet and of the ground on which he stands. To be successful in these cases one must know the mechanism of the bioenergetic disturbance. Once good rapport has been established with the patient, consistent work on the physical level to develop body awareness and motility produces results that are astounding.

The lack of contact with the feet and the ground is related to another common symptom, falling anxiety.

This symptom is manifested in dreams of falling, in fear of heights, and in the fear of falling in love. Where there is a basic insecurity in the lower half of the body, the individual compensates by holding on with arms and eyes to objective reality. One may question why I include the fear of falling in love with symptoms of basic insecurity. Of course the very expression "to fall in love" relates this phenomena to the others, but we also know that to fall in love is a form of ego surrender. All forms of falling anxiety translate the fear of loss of ego control.

In addition to the functions of support, balance and rooting, the legs are the most important structures in the function of body movement. Where the function of support is weak, we may also expect a disturbance in motility. We measure the motility in the legs by the ability of the individual to freely swing the pelvis without using any part of the trunk in the movement. This is very close to the motion demanded by such dances as the samba, the mambo and the rhumba. This requires a relaxed, flexible knee joint, a looseness of the pelvis on the trunk and relaxation of all the leg muscles. We find that there are three conditions which impair this basic motility: weakness, massiveness and rigidity.

Individuals with underdeveloped leg muscles, weak ankles and a collapsed arch will have great difficulty in executing and maintaining such movement. First, they suffer from a lack of control over the necessary muscles, and secondly, they tire too quickly. The thick, fat and massive thigh presents another problem. In these cases the lack of motility is so pronounced that we say that such persons have "lead in their legs." The accumulation of fat around the buttocks and thighs must be interpreted bioenergetically as the result of a stagnation of energy in this region due to inhibited motility. In the rigid leg the muscles are so spastic and contracted that balance is frequently impaired. One patient told me that he understood why it was so difficult for him to get out of bed in the morning. He said that his legs were so stiff that he was afraid to put his weight on them. Rigidity must be regarded as a compensation for underlying feelings of weakness. The walk of individuals with spastic leg muscles is mechanical and fast since with relaxation feelings of weakness and insecurity manifest themselves.

The legs may be weak, they may be abnormally heavy or they may be rigid. Frequently the legs will show a mixture of these elements. In the analysis of structure, attention is paid to each component as well as to the total aspect. The feet may be narrow or broad, the toes pinched together or spread apart, the arch collapsed, relaxed or tightly contracted. The calf muscles may be shapeless or knotted. The position of the feet in the person's natural stance may be straight and parallel, turned outward as a result of spastic gluteal muscles, or pigeon-toed. Each disturbance is interpreted in terms of its effect on the functions of support and movement.

I have discussed the bioenergetic analysis of the legs and feet in some detail to illustrate the principles of this therapeutic approach. Where even the traditional Freudian analyst will observe the facial expression, few analytic therapists study the form and movement of the lower half of the body. Actually, we direct our attention first to the posture of the individual. Is he straight, sway-back or hunched over forward? Does the weight of the body rest upon the legs or on the sacrum? Is the patient standing on his heels or on the balls of his feet? When the weight of the body is directly over the heels, the standing position can be upset easily by a slight push backwards. Here again the common expression describes the situation well. We say of such a person that he is a "pushover." When used with respect to girls it has only one meaning. I had a patient whose main complaint was that she couldn't resist the sexual aggression of men. In a standing position she tended to rock on her heels. I have heard two expressions which describe this trait. These girls are said to have "round heels" or to be "ball girls." Aggression or movement is not possible except by pressure exerted through the front of the foot.

The relation of the pelvis to the legs and trunk is very

important because of the genital function. The pelvis may
be free swinging, which gives the individual grace in
movement, or it may be immobilized in either a backward
or forward position. A break in the natural line of the
body is evident in both of these latter positions. With the
pelvis held forward and pulled up there is tension in the
abdominal muscles, spasticity in the rectus abdominis
and contraction of the buttocks. The impression is that
the individual is closing off the natural outlets of discharge.
Holding and retentive tendencies are strongly marked in
the character structure. An immobile pelvis is associated
with a decrease in sexual potency. The pelvis well backward, fixed in a retracted position represents a severe
sexual repression.

One reads little about the backbone in analytic therapy.
As an important structural element in the body, a weakness in the backbone must be reflected in a serious personality disturbance. The individual with a sway back cannot have the ego strength of a person whose back is
straight. On the other hand backbone rigidity while adding
strength to support decreases flexibility. In addition, such
individuals frequently develop lower back pain. I have
treated many patients with this complaint. In each case
reduction of the tension in the lumbosacral muscles, mobilization of the pelvis, analysis of the repressed conflict and
a resolution of the problem of the inhibited drive results
in the complete disappearance of the pain and disability.
The rigidity of the backbone is not only evident in the loss
of flexibility in movement, it can be palpated in the tension
of the lumbar muscles.

Ever since Reich called attention to the importance of
respiration in the flow of feeling, the study of the respiratory movements occupies an important position in bioenergetic analysis. We look to see if the chest is expanded
and held rigid or soft and relaxed. A blown up chest is
the invariable concomitant of a blown up ego. It reminds
one of the fable of the frog who attempted to blow himself
up to the size of a bull. On the other hand, a soft chest,

although related to more feeling, is not necessarily a sign of health. It is found in certain impulsive character types who have a pregenital structure. What we look for is a relaxed structure in which the respiratory movements show the unity of chest, diaphragm and abdomen in inspiration and expiration. Respiration is not analyzed independently of the total structure but as one aspect of the organismic function.

The position and motility of the shoulders are as significant to the ego functions as the legs and pelvis are to the sexual functions. Several attitudes are easily discerned. Retracted shoulders represent repressed anger, a holding back of the impulse to strike; raised shoulders are related to fear; square shoulders express the manly attitude of shouldering one's responsibilities; bowed shoulders convey the sense of burden, the weight of a heavy hand. The shoulders play an important role in the motility of the chest since the shoulder girdle extends from the spine in back via the rhomboids to the sternum in front via the pectoral muscles. Disturbance in the shoulder girdle will therefore affect the respiratory function. Since the basic function of the arms in the primates is to reach out to take or give, to seize or strike, the extent and quality of the reaching out is a measure of the ego. Clinical experience has enabled us to make certain characterizations and to relate them to specific physical disturbances. The schizophrenic character does not reach out to the world, the oral character reaches out only under favorable conditions, the masochist reaches out then withdraws and so fails; the rigid types, phallic-narcissistic males, tend to be grasping.

The specific functional disturbance in the schizophrenic body structure is the dissociation of the arms from the body. In movements, the body and the arms do not function as a unity. This gives the movement of the arms a mechanical quality which can be observed in such actions as reaching out with both arms or striking out. Very deep tensions in the shoulder joint are responsible for this dissociation. In addition, one notes that the shoulder girdle itself is "frozen" and partakes to a very limited degree in the arm movements. Because the body does not take part in the movement of reaching out, we say that the schizophrenic does not reach out to the world.

In neurotic structures the arms and body form a unity. This unity, however, is subject to the limitations of the character structure. The oral character complains of feelings of weakness and impotence in his arms. In his body structure we observe that the muscles which hold the scapula to the body and control its movements are overdeveloped and chronically contracted. The most visible ones are the pectoral muscles in front and the trapezius behind. Par contra, the muscles which hold the arms in the sockets are weak and underdeveloped. This accounts for the difficulty the oral character has in reaching out to take or give. The masochist shows a muscle bound condition in his arms as in the rest of the body. His movements are atactic, ungraceful, and difficult. Reaching out is an effort which the masochist finds difficult to maintain. In the rigid structures, for example, the phallic-narcissistic male, movements are co-ordinated and highly charged; the tensions are peripheral. In the upper extremities they are located mostly in the hands and forearms. The high charge acting against a strong peripheral tension gives the hands a grasping, claw like quality.

We saw that there is an antithesis between the upper and lower halves of the body. It is not uncommon to see a broad-shouldered man with narrow hips and thin, weak-looking legs. It is as if all the energy were concentrated in the upper half leaving the bottom half impotent. We find in practice that as the legs strengthen and as sexual potency increases the shoulders drop, the chest becomes smaller and the center of gravity drops appreciably. The distribution of the musculature in the human body is such that the greater part is concentrated in hips and legs. This gives man support for his ability to maintain the upright position. The muscles of the upper half of the body have been spared, the function of supporting or moving the body. They should be soft, relaxed and available for quick, sensitive movements.

The bearing of the head is in direct relation to the quality and strength of the ego. Our theoretical principles support this concept, which is ultimately derived from clinical observations. We are acquainted with the long proud neck and the short bull-like neck which represent familiar attitudes. Certain schizophrenics carry the head at an angle in such a way as to give one the strong impression that it is disjointed. When I observe this in a patient it is sufficient to put me on guard against psychotic tendencies. There is another expression when the head is carried at an angle. Here the impression is that the head is too great a burden for the body and so is allowed to droop. This represents the patient's attitude towards reality. Sometimes one is reminded of pictures of Christ descending from the cross and this impression is reinforced by an attitude expressive of martyrdom in the rest of the body.*

When we study the expression of the face as a measure of the character and of the personality we are on more familiar ground. Since this is a procedure we carry on unconsciously all our lives, I shall add only a few words to show the bioenergetic basis for our practice. We are aware of the dominant feature but our attention should be directed first to the eyes. We saw that other writers such as Schilder (1950, pp. 96–98) place the ego near or in the eyes. It must be with some reason that the eyes are regarded as the mirrors of the soul. Our own research indicates that the two instinctual pathways converge above in the eyes as they do below in the genitals.

---

* Compare with Paul Schilder's comment, "We meet here for the first time the important principle that the individual character expresses himself in the body-image model." *The Image and Appearance of the Human Body*. New York, International Universities Press, 1950, p. 89. We make a further premise that the functional motility of the body will correspond to the body-image.

We can determine the intensity of the expression as well as its quality. Some eyes are bright and sparkle, some shine like stars, others are dull and many are vacant. Of course, the expression changes. We seek, therefore, for the typical look. Some eyes are sad, others are angry; some are cold and hard, others are soft and appealing. These are not qualities one can measure with an instrument anymore than one can measure the beauty of a lovely female figure or the sense of masculinity in a lithe and agile male. But if one is unaware of these things psychiatry becomes a lifeless profession. Many an experienced psychiatrist can spot schizophrenia by the vacant, far-away look in the eyes.

Not infrequently two conflicting expressions are shown by one face. The eyes may appear weak and withdrawn while the jaw is strong and protruding. Or it may be that the jaw is weak while the eyes are strong. If the jaw muscles are overdeveloped there is a block in the flow of energy to the eyes. The jaw is a mobile structure which resembles the pelvis in its movements. It can be immobilized in both a retracted or protruded position either of which represents a decrease of motility. A jaw that cannot move forward with aggression or soften with tenderness is considered pathological in terms of function. Many expressions are related to the position of the jaw. As it moves forward it first expresses determination, a further advance gives it a fighting expression while extreme protrusion, as in the case of Mussolini, clearly means defiance.

The number and variety of expressions which may appear on the countenance of an individual is great. As we watch our patients we are, of course, aware of this play of feeling. A sneer appears on a patient's face and we inquire why they sneer. To our surprise the patient answers that he did not sneer. Absorbed as persons are in the reactions of others, they are frequently unaware of their own expression. These expressions are like slips of the tongue, the importance of which Freud pointed out many years ago.

Of greater significance to analytic therapy are those unconscious expressions which are frozen into the countenance, so much so that we take them for granted as part of the personality. I recall a professor whose brow was so raised that lines of surprise and astonishment were engraved on his forehead. No one paid the slightest attention to it, least of all the professor. Yet when one raises one's brow strongly, the feeling of surprise and astonishment is so immediate and so strong as to be disturbing. Why was the professor unaware of his expression? We must conclude that when an expression becomes ingrained into the features, one looses consciousness of it. Like our old clothes, these expressions become so much a part of us that we become aware of them only by their absence. A very common expression which we take for granted is the look of disgust caused by the retraction upward of the alae of the nostrils. Have you not seen people who show a perpetual expression of pain on their face? Are these people in pain? Certainly! Depth analysis of the unconscious would reveal that these expressions portray repressed feelings—surprise, disgust or pain.

Enough, you might say. How far can this go? Are not weak, myopic eyes due to heredity, which has nothing to do with the ego? Or a patient remarks, "My father has a weak jaw, his father had a weak jaw, does not that disprove your ideas about my own jaw?" Or it might be that everyone in a family has the same legs and this is adduced to show that their structure has nothing to do with environmental influences.

These arguments are valid and have to be considered seriously. There are two questions here, each of which requires a separate answer. Whatever may be the cause of myopic eyes they represent a weakness which affects the ego. Clinical experience has repeatedly confirmed the fact that the ego is determined by dynamic and structural factors regardless of their etiology. Certainly, infants are very different at birth and this difference will have a profound influence upon their future development, physically and mentally. How much of this difference is due to heredity one cannot say. At the time of birth, the infant has already been subjected to a vital experience of nine months' duration. The quality of this experience cannot easily be assessed but its importance cannot be overestimated. There is today in medicine a growing awareness that many congenital malformations and disturbances are due to illnesses and deficiences to which the mother was subject during the pregnancy.

Theoretical considerations alone should force us to re-examine our attitude towards the intrauterine life of the individual. Two seeds from the same flower or fruit are almost indistinguishable if both are equally mature. Yet the trees or bushes into which they grow may show marked differences. Of course the seeds are not identical but neither are the two pieces of earth where they root and develop. Not only may the soil show differences in its composition but drainage and exposure are rarely the same at two different locations. The womb is a bit of earth into which the mammalian seed is implanted for nine months. No two wombs are alike in terms of fertility. Some are rocky and stony with imbedded fibroid tumors. Some are hard and contracted with a diminished blood supply. Some are small and immature while others have been through several pregnancies.

The infants born from these wombs will differ. Every obstetrician has seen these differences. They range from the lusty energetic vital infant to wizened and shrunk infants who look like old people. It would follow, too, that the early extrauterine life of the infant will repeat the quality of his intrauterine existence. Without special preparation, the attitude of the mother to the child will repeat the unconscious pattern given in the relationship of the womb to the embryo. People do not change easily. The experience of the child with its mother is a continuous one which begins at conception. The developmental potentialities of the child take form and shape only as reality permits, and reality for the child is its mother.

This is a concept which is gaining wider acceptance in analytic circles. The attitude of the mother as it interacts with the child's needs for support and affection on the one hand and independence on the other will determine and set the emerging pattern of the child's personality. Set modes of response become hardened and frozen in time into the dynamic character structure which confronts the analytic therapist. The role of the father and other persons in the environment must be taken into account but these are, obviously, of later and secondary importance.

There can be no substitute for the love of the mother as it manifests itself on both the physical and mental levels. The development which takes place under optimum conditions produces a body structure and personality which evokes our admiration. However, analytic therapists are confronted daily with individuals whose structure and personality are defective even to the point of being inadequate to handle the pressures of reality. In their struggle to survive such individuals develop compensating mechanisms to overcome their weaknesses. Adler's theories about organ inferiority and the striving for power and superiority derive from such clinical observations. Unfortunately, compensating mechanisms never correct the fault or weakness. Bioenergetic analytic therapy attacks the basic disturbance as it manifests itself in the adult pattern of behavior thereby eliminating the need for compensations and adjustments.

A patient came to bioenergetic therapy after many years of analysis. She said that she had gone about as far as she could with verbal analysis and that our approach seemed to offer more. She had a heavy, fat body, a short but well formed neck and an expression of grim determination on her face. Her arms and legs were thin, she tended to be knock-kneed and the feet were small and weak. Despite her determination she could not restrain her appetite. Her work function was good but she had little in the way of social relationships. It was her ability to work which kept her going amidst depression, anxieties and discouragement.

This patient began her bioenergetic therapy with characteristic determination. For several weeks there was a marked improvement in her mood and she ate less. Then she became anxious and depressed again. This was as far as her determination and enthusiasm could carry her. Now she had to face the hard work of strengthening her legs, acquiring body motility and relinquishing the attitude of grim determination. This determination must be considered bioenergetically as a compensation for the weakness in legs and genitals. No amount of determination can replace the natural security and motility one derives from well-balanced legs. Further, the characterological set determination in the ego structure prevents the charge and release of genital excitation. The natural pendular swing of the energy is blocked by the immobility of the jaw. Still, while we point out and analyze this characterological attitude of determination, our main effort is directed towards eliminating the weakness.

Determination as a fixed attitude is not a real source of ego strength. It implies a lack of ego flexibility. It freezes energy into a pattern of behavior at the expense of other possible reactions. It is an ego defense against depression and failure but like all defenses it impoverishes the emotional life and may lead to the very calamity it is organized to prevent. It is a limitation of motility at the same time that it attempts to overcome the limitation. If one increases the natural motility of the organism, the characterological determination vanishes and is replaced by an ability to be determined when the appropriate situation arises.

Another patient began bioenergetic analytic therapy after five years of traditional analysis. Many of his compulsive patterns of behavior had been worked through and he had gained some insight into his motivations. He used to run after women compulsively until he understood that this was an attempt on his part to live up to an ego ideal of himself as a young and handsome male sought after by women. His actual behavior changed in that while he still sought after women he no longer started affairs with them. Following his former analysis he had developed a compulsive tic in his eyes. As is usual in these cases his sexual potency was not strong. His own orgasm was weak, his sexual interest lay in large part in his desire to satisfy the woman. The psychoanalytic interpretation of his actions was correct, but it offered no choice other than the surrender of his ego ideal and its associated behavior. Unfortunately this did not stop his interest in other women nor his compulsiveness.

He showed a body structure which while well-developed was disproportionate. His big chest and hunched shoulders gave the upper half of his body a massive appearance. The hips were narrow, the belly pulled in and contracted and the pelvis held back. His leg muscles were spastic. Pelvic motility and genital charge were both reduced. Another interpretation of his behavior is possibly based on the bioenergetic dynamics of his structure. His running after women was an attempt to increase the charge and excitation in the lower half of his body. This action was compensatory in that he sought to remedy a weakness by the response of the female. His lack of manhood then revealed itself by the identification with the female in the sexual act at the expense of his own orgastic pleasure. He ended each experience with the same dependent need as before. In one respect his ego ideal was valid in that it reflected his real dissatisfaction with himself as a male and his desire to improve.

Bioenergetic therapy was directed at the lower half of the body to increase its motility and charge. By strengthening the structure where it is weak, the need for an irrational compensatory behavior is eliminated. As the patient developed a stronger genital charge his sense of his own manhood increased. This brought about a change in his ego ideal. He could conceive himself as more aggressive in business and more responsible in his family life. The compulsive tic in the eyes developed out of the feeling of weakness in the eyes as an attempt to gain more strength. A compensatory mechanism was at work here as on the genital level. The weakness in the eyes was conditioned by overdeveloped jaw muscles which expressed an exaggerated determination. It was interesting to see how his eyes brightened and relaxed as the tension was released from the upper half of the body at the end of each treatment.

Psychoanalysis aims primarily at uncovering the ego defenses and compensating mechanisms. We analyze a pattern of behavior to show the ego drives which motivate it. But this is the easiest part of any therapy. More difficult and more important is the endeavor to strengthen the natural ego functions to a point where the patient has no need of defenses and compensations. For this purpose psychoanalysis has available only two technical procedures: one is the working through of the transference, the other is the analysis of the everyday behavior of the patient in outside life. Both involve an analytic and a didactic element. Implicit in the latter is the personality of the analyst as a force guiding the patient to more rational behavior. A patient cannot develop the needed positive attitudes except through identification with the analyst and will do so only to the extent that they form part of the personality of the analyst.

When the neurotic symptom serves an ego defense it may be possible to eliminate it by exposing its defensive function. This is especially true for the conversion symptoms produced by a displaced genitality in the hysterical character. The phobias and obsessional symptoms are not so easily resolved. Despite analysis of its mechanism, the phobia is not eliminated until the individual faces the feared situation. In the case of obsession or compulsion, exposure to the imagined danger is equally necessary. The problem is even more difficult in the character neuroses, for here we deal with immature ego structures. Many of these patients know and understand the nature of their problems almost as well as the analyst. If, then, they have not remedied their situation, we say that insight is lacking. But this can only mean that they do not have the courage or strength to adopt a more mature attitude. Under such conditions the analysis continues until, out of desperation, the patient quits or asserts himself. Difficulties such as these led Ferenczi to adopt his "activity techniques."

Bioenergetic therapy works directly with those forces in the organism which can give strength and courage. The strength is not easily acquired nor the courage quickly gained. The feared situation must be faced repeatedly. This we saw was part of the technique used to overcome the phobia. In bioenergetic therapy the fear is related to difficulty in the expression of feelings of anger, of love, etc. Basically, every emotional disturbance is a reduction of motility. The word emotion itself means a movement outward. "Outward" in the higher organisms is synonymous with discharge. Every emotional disturbance involves a block in the flow of energy to the organs of discharge among which the genitals are primary. The more peripheral the block is, the less severe is the disturbance. When the blocks are more centrally located they tend to be more severe. Strength and courage depend upon the availability of the energy at the zones of discharge. Let me illustrate:

I once treated a young man who told me that he was very much disturbed because he had turned and run away from a situation in which someone pulled a knife on him. That action itself does not indicate a lack of courage. The problem lay in his feeling of disturbance over his behavior for he sensed in himself a lack of courage. During the subsequent therapy we both realized that he did not face the problems of his life. One day he became upset and nauseous and had to throw up. As he did this we were both shocked to see a yellow streak appear on the midline of his abdomen. The expression "yellow bellied" flashed into our minds simultaneously. One tends not to take such phrases literally, but here was a visual demonstration one could not ignore. The yellow coloration disappeared when his stomach was empty.

We have another common expression for people who act as if they lack courage. We say they "lack guts." Since, however, everyone has guts the expression must mean that the individual lacks the feeling of his guts or has no belly sensation. When a patient complains that his guts are tied up in a knot or that he feels empty in the belly, we cannot expect him to be brave.

This patient suffered from hyperacidity of the stomach and frequent heart burns. I could smell the acidity in his breath. When he threw up the vomitus was lemon-yellow colored. On occasion his skin showed a lemon-yellow tint. How the "yellow streak" appeared and disappeared I do not know. Years of observation has convinced me that skin manifestations frequently represent underlying dynamic processes which reach the surface. The patient himself was aware of a block which he felt was responsible for most of his difficulties. This block was a deep seated tension at the pit of the stomach which he called his "Gordian knot." So much energy was tied up in this deep seated tension that the belly was relatively undercharged.

There were other manifestations in this patient of his basic insecurity. Under tension his legs would shake so severely that he literally left the ground. We remarked earlier in this chapter about the expression, "to hold your ground," as an expression of courage. Consistent attention to the dynamics of the structure in this case produced excellent results. The marked hyperacidity noticeably decreased. His legs and thighs relaxed and his ability to hold the ground improved. At the same time he was able to tackle problems in his life from which he had previously run. And he began to experience pleasure in the belly which was a new experience for him.

The feeling of strength depends upon the surge of the life force or energy. I have no hesitation in making such a broad statement. We are not dealing here with such mechanical properties as weight lifting, etc. The child who is fully alive feels his strength as well as the man in the prime of life. The feeling of strength is basically ego strength. We have all seen men with broad shoulders and well developed muscles whose strength lay in their ability to take punishment. A pattern of behavior which we call passive-feminine and which manifests itself in the lack of aggression towards women belies the strong man physique. The overdevelopment of the musculature is a compensation for this underlying weakness. Muscles can be used for holding back impulses as well as movement. *A therapy which encourages expressive movement increases the motility of the organism, improves its aggression and creates a feeling of strength on both the physical and psychic levels.*

How much can one change structure? If the shoulders are too high can they be lowered? If the neck is too short can it be lengthened? If the thighs are too heavy can they be trimmed down? These things have been accomplished but the patient who presents a problem which is structurally related does not expect to be made into a new person. To the degree that structural pathology is reduced, function is increased; to the degree that function improves, pathology decreases. Structure is frozen function.

We mentioned earlier the problem of the broad shouldered male. I am not speaking of those men whose broad shoulders are in harmony with a broad body. The harmony of the body configuration is itself an indication of relative health. The broad shouldered male with narrow hips, the dream type of American male, invariably shows passive-feminine tendencies. Such men quite frequently suffer from premature ejaculation and depth analysis reveals an identification with the female. The relationship to the woman is ambivalent; at times he acts in a father role to the girl child, at others he is the "little boy" to his mother. The broad shoulders give the impression that he is a pillar of strength, that he can shoulder his burdens. Analytic investigation into the background reveals that the patient had a mother whose basic attitude was one of suffering and self-sacrifice for her children. This boy may have been her favorite. She shared her sorrows with him and he felt her unhappiness. As a child he had determined to bring some joy into his mother's life and he made himself responsible for her well-being. Of course, the whole Oedipus conflict is involved; there is rivalry between the boy and his father. But what is important for our discussion is the fact that in his broad shoulders this man shows his exaggerated sense of responsibility for the welfare of the woman. This feeling of responsibility is frozen into the structure of the shoulders.

Such an attitude carries its own antithesis. There is an equally strong feeling of resentment and a fear of women. One can find this resentment in the tension at the back of the neck and the fear in the immobilization of the pelvis. This latter accounts for the narrowness of the hips. In this hypothetical case, to drop the shoulders means to drop the load, to express the feeling, "I don't care," to free one's self of the exaggerated responsibility.

What are the energy dynamics of this structural attitude? The shoulders do not broaden simply because the child feels responsible for the welfare of its mother. The structure crystallized out of a relationship that began at birth. Shoulders rise as part of the reaction of fear. These shoulders show fear but not to the extent of fright. They are held midway between a forward position and a backward one. This position is a dynamic equilibrium between the forward reaching and the backward holding, between anger and defiance. The position is a compromise between two opposing attitudes and as such it produces an immobility. The block limits the energy to the muscles of the shoulder girdle at the expense of the hands.

The rigidity of the shoulders decreases the mobility of the chest. Respiration is reduced and there is a decrease in the level of the energy economy. The feeling tone is quieted down and the genital function is weakened.

This problem is attacked bioenergetically on several

fronts simultaneously. Psychologically, the attitude of responsibility for and identification with the female is analyzed. Movement to free the shoulders is encouraged. The motility of the pelvis is increased and genital charge is strengthened. The heightened feeling of manhood acts to sever the feminine identification. There is an increased flow of energy downward from the shoulder region, and as the shoulders regain their natural motility the chest relaxes. The squareness and exaggerated width disappear as the natural slope of the shoulders is restored. The elimination of the neurotic function coincides with the change in the structure. The restoration of the natural function produces the natural structure.

Every bioenergetic change acts on two levels simultaneously. On the somatic level there is an increase in motility, coordination and control; on the psychic level there is a reorganization of thinking and attitudes. No permanent change is possible unless this double effect is achieved. A new function must be integrated into the conscious ego before the patient can claim it as his own. It is not possible to do bioenergetic therapy without a thorough working through of the present day attitudes and behavior and of the genetic and dynamic forces which brought them into being.

Bioenergetic interpretations are never made of isolated structural features although a problem is quickly recognized. The clinical diagnosis is made only after an intensive study of the history and presenting problems and their integration with the structural aspect. Every aspect of the individual is viewed as the expression of a unitary personality. Where all facets of the personality are known and their interrelationship established, we are in a position to describe the specific character of the patient. Analysis and therapy then proceed with this character as the framework of reference. It is important, therefore, to understand the technique of character analysis and to know something about the dynamic forces which form the character structure.

7

Character Analysis

In 1933 Wilhelm Reich first published the results of his psychoanalytic work during the previous nine years in a book which he called *Character Analysis*. The theoretical principles and technical concepts subsumed under that title marked a major advance in the psychoanalytic comprehension and treatment of the neuroses. The first edition of this work was eagerly received by the analysts. Today, many years later, the book is still regarded by analysts and psychotherapists as one of the basic texts in analytic theory and practice. In my opinion it represents the highest achievement of psychoanalytic technique and forms the bridge which leads from psychoanalysis to the analytic comprehension of muscular tension and energy blocks. Psychology and biology meet in the study of character. It is for this reason that the bioenergetic principles set forth in this volume are expressed clinically in terms of character structure.

Since the publication of the first edition of Reich's *Character Analysis* no further work extending or deepening the knowledge of character structure has been published. Reich himself moved ahead to the investigation of muscular armoring, energy blocks, the somatic illnesses and the nature of the biological energy itself. Other analysts found the principles and techniques of character analysis valuable in their analytic work but they did not follow up this direction. The present author was trained by Reich in character analysis and vegetotherapy and has followed him in the further development of his work on the muscle tensions and energy blocks. This study grew out of the necessity to integrate into a unitary scheme basic psychoanalytic concepts and the newer bioenergetic principles which form the basis of our therapy. This unity is achieved clinically by the application of character analytic principles. The character is the unitary expression of the individual's function on both the psychic and the somatic realm: its comprehension requires a thorough knowledge of ego psychology and of energy concepts.

In the preface to the first edition Reich (1949, p. xix) remarked that his study of character was incomplete. "Today as nine years ago we are still far from a comprehensive and systematic characterology. This book will serve, however, to decrease that distance a considerable stretch." Since the later editions have added no new material, we still face the problems Reich posed in 1933 and which he only partially answered. These are: "a genetic-dynamic theory of character; a strict differentiation of the contents and form of the resistances; and, finally, a clinically well founded differentiation of character types."

The concept of character did not begin with Reich. In 1908, Freud published a paper entitled "Character and Anal Erotism" in which he pointed out the relationship between the regular combination of three traits: orderliness, obstinacy and parsimony, and anal erotism. In his conclusion Freud, postulated the idea of a character structure. "At any rate, one can give a formula for the formation of the ultimate character from the constituent character traits; the permanent character traits are either unchanged perpetuations of the original impulses, sublimations of them, or reaction formations against them" (1908, p. 50). The formula proved inadequate for it was not possible to derive the character from any combination of traits. Rather the traits are aspects of the unitary structure.

During the following years Freud developed the concepts of ego psychology. The character traits were observed, studied and interpreted but no attempt was made to formulate basic character types. In 1921 Abraham published a paper on the anal character in which he discussed many of the traits found associated with anal problems and, by induction, related them to certain childhood experiences. Then in 1924 and 1925 Abraham extended this study of character types by two additional papers on the oral character and on the genital character. The attempt to relate character types to the libidinal development of the child has obvious merits. Unfortunately, these character types of Abraham are described in terms of specific traits and no synthesis is attempted by means of case histories. The problem is further complicated by the fact that the literature contains references to other character types such as the compulsive character, the hysterical character, the masochist, etc. which were not integrated into a general framework.

Reich approached the study of character not from theoretical considerations but as a practical problem in analytic technique. He did not isolate the traits but he attempted to understand the character first in its role as a resistance to analytic interpretation and second to comprehend its function in the libido economy of the organism. The first led to the principles of character analysis with which we are concerned in this chapter. It is in this sense that Wolfe (1949, p. xiii) defined character as the "characteristic behavior of the patient in defending himself against analytic insight and unconscious material."

The relation of character to the libido economy requires an understanding of the formation and structure of character which will be the subject of the next chapter. Abraham's (1925, p. 407) definition relates character to libidinal organization. "According to the traditional view, a character is defined as the direction habitually taken by a person's voluntary impulses." It is important to recognize that however we define the character it is the basic attitude with which the individual confronts life whether in the analytic session or in the external world. Once the character is understood the nature and meaning of the resistance which the patient sets up is readily appreciated.

It is not generally appreciated that the character describes an objective reality. It can be fairly easily observed by others but only with great difficulty does the individual himself become aware of his own character. We look at others critically, at ourselves favorably. The main thing about the character is the fact that it represents a typical pattern of behavior or an habitual direction. It is a mode of response which is set, congealed or structured. It has a "characteristic" quality which always stamps it as the mark of the person. In this sense every character structure is pathological. The individual whose libidinal energies have never been structured in a typical mode or habitual direction cannot be said to have a character structure. Such individuals, who are quite rare incidentally, are difficult to define, to portray or to nickname; they have a lively expression and spontaneity which defies the attempt to seize it.

It would be well to differentiate the concept of personality from that of character. Both are experienced by the observer; the former, however, is generally more subjective. We speak of an individual's personality as pleasing, magnetic, strong, depressing, etc. It describes our feeling response to another being. Character, on the other hand, must be determined by the observation and study of a person's behavior. The personality is an expression of the life force in a person and is probably the extension of that force into the environment. There is a relation between personality and character but the terms should not be used interchangeably.

The relation between the ego and the character is involved. The ego is fundamentally a subjective perception of the self whereas the character and personality are objective appreciations. But the patient's description of his own ego is noteworthy for its unreliability. The patient thinks of his ego in terms of his ego ideal which expresses some inherent capacity rather than an actual function. Thus the analyst has to construct the true ego from a determination of the character structure and an appraisal of the personality.*

A young man whose case will be discussed more fully later came to his sessions with a grandiose air and a patronizing smile. He told me what a great guy he was with the girls and how well he functioned at work. At other times, however, he was quite depressed and dejected. The reality of his situation was that he had failed at everything he tried previously and became grandiose at the slightest possibility of success. He acted as if he had a strong, highly developed ego structure but it was blown up out of all proportion to reality. Deflated, it was rather small and undeveloped. His blown up ego picture of himself was a defense against the perception of his true ego structure. Yet there was something in him that made me feel that he had latent possibilities far greater than those manifested in his function. If the difficulties in the realization of his latent possibilities were immense, one cannot say that his ego ideal did not express a valid aspect of his ego. To free the ego from its character involvement and make it available for the legitimate aspirations of the ego ideal seems a worthwhile goal for an analytic therapy.

Unfortunately the neurotic individual identifies with his character of which the ego ideal is also a part. This is so because the character structure represents the only modality in which the instinctual life has been able to function. The determined individual may regard his determination as his greatest asset. In one way it is, in another way it is

---

* Compare this with Otto Fenichel: "The mode of reconciling various tasks to one another is characteristic for a given personality. Thus the ego's habitual modes of adjustment to the external world, the id and the superego, and the characteristic types of combining these modes with one another, constitute character." *The Psychoanalytic Theory of Neurosis.* New York, Norton, 1945, p. 467.

the enemy which will prevent the realization of a fuller, more successful life. But one cannot insist upon its surrender without offering a better modus vivendi. This can be a seemingly difficult situation. In the case of a patient who pushed himself and whose pushing created frustration and anxiety, I suggested that he stop it. His reply was, "If I don't push myself to get up in the morning, I would lie in bed all day and not go to work." I had to concede that it was better to go to work than to lie in bed all day. However other analysts may handle this problem, we have a solution in bioenergetic therapy. During the session he spends with me he does not have to push. He would make more progress if he let the movements develop spontaneously with feeling than by pushing out a lot of noise. At the same time, the tension that makes pushing necessary is worked on.

The character is a resultant of opposing forces, the ego drive and the ego defense which also employs ego energies. If we can separate the ego from the character structure in which it is embedded, the way is open to change the structure. But to achieve this identification of the patient with his ego as opposed to his character, the ego defenses must be overcome and eliminated. However done, this is the task of every analytic therapy. When Reich (1949, p. 3) wrote, "Every neurosis is due to a conflict between repressed instinctual demands—which always include infantile sexual demands—and the repressing forces of the ego," he stated the basic problem of all analytic therapy. The problem, however, must be viewed in its entirety. The character itself is the basic disturbance and no real progress can be achieved in analytic therapy until this is recognized by the patient.

Character analysis has, therefore, one basic objective—to make the patient feel his character as a neurotic formation which limits and interfers with vital ego functions. The task is a big one. Both Ferenczi and Reich have pointed out that whereas the patient feels the neurotic symptom as alien to the ego, the character is accepted as the ego itself. The analytic problem requires persistent and consistent analysis of the behavior pattern showing how each action fits into the total picture. Through bioenergetic analysis we can also show how the dynamics of the body structure reveal the same character structure. As Ferenczi had remarked, nothing is so convincing as experience on the physical level.

The principle of character analysis requires that no interpretation should be made on the infantile level until the character has been dissociated from the ego. Otherwise the interpretation will be used to justify the character structure making it all the more difficult to change. Failure to observe rigidly the rule that the character is the main object of attack leads to confusion and eventual collapse of the therapy. This was the situation when Reich (1949, p. 5) first introduced character analysis as a technical procedure:

"If, for example, a certain resistance situation is presented in the seminar, one analyst will say it calls for this measure, a second another, and a third, still another. If the analyst, then, provided with all this advice, again approaches his case, there appear innumerable other possibilities, and the confusion is worse than before. And, yet, one must assume that one definite analytic situation— given certain conditions and situations—admits of only one optimal technical procedure which in this situation is better than any other. This applies not only to an individual situation but to the analytic therapy as a whole."

That this confusion exists today among analysts cannot be denied. I have treated a number of analysts who had previously undergone psychoanalysis, some for extended periods. Each one of them stated that he felt that the analysis had not gone deep enough, that his fundamental problem was not understood. This can happen only through failure to conduct the analysis from the standpoint of the character structure. Analysis of the symptoms and problems as they arise leads to superficial understanding which does not touch the inner dissatisfaction. I recall the case of an analyst whose training had been completed by a well-known psychoanalyst. He came to me because he had become aware of the rigidity in his chest. His father had had several heart attacks and my patient was afraid. But he was afraid of many things: He was afraid of the water and he couldn't swim. It was very difficult for him to say "No" to a woman. He was afraid to commit himself to a course of action, a program or a person. His pattern of behavior was marked by superficial friendliness and good will which covered an underlying distrust and rebellion. Since the character of the patient was not in question during the psychoanalytic treatment, these basic problems were not worked through. The analyst took his patient's friendliness and ready acceptance of analytic interpretation at face value. This is just what Reich warned against in character analysis. The result in this case was the failure of the treatment. It is to the credit of the patient that he recognized that the analysis had not gone far enough.

I know this problem well for I, too, had made many such mistakes. It was only as I deepened my understanding of the nature of the character structure that I learned to avoid these failures. This is a point which Reich takes up so well in his own book that I need do no more than refer the interested reader to it. I should like, simply, to illustrate the problem by some remarks and a case from my own experience.

We are all aware of the patient who smiles at the analyst. Sometimes the smile occurs in response to an interpretation, at others it may be the typical expression which the patient shows the analyst. Most frequently the patient is unaware of the smile since it is an habitual form of response. One notes it especially in those situations in which the patient find himself in an awkward or embarrassing position. It is rare that such smiles are simply friendly gestures to the analyst and I never accept such an interpretation under these conditions. Masquerading under the smile is a negative attitude. But what attitude? It differs for each patient and it shows through in some slight distortion of the total facial expression. In one the smile is patronizing, in another it is derisive, in a third it may be the silly grin of the fool who thus avoids the responsibility for his own actions. The correct interpretation of the expression may be guessed intuitively, this is the art of analysis. The proper evaluation depends upon a knowledge of the total neurotic mechanism of the individual; that is, upon the character structure.

One patient had such a smile which was out of all keeping with the seriousness of the problem he posed. When I pointed it out to him, he became immediately aware of its defensive function, but try as he would he could not wipe that smile off his face. He disliked it intensely but even as he uttered the words, there was the smile. He observed it in all his interpersonal relations outside of the therapeutic session but to no avail. It was the smile of a good little boy who was trying to please. He was a good little boy trying to win the approval of everyone he met. And the harder he tried, even to remove the smile, the more he was that good little boy. Bioenergetic analysis revealed that he had a masochistic character structure with erective impotence.

He told me, spontaneously, that he had always been the good boy. His popularity at school was due to the fact that he antagonized no one. Yet he recalled that as a boy of seven or eight he was regarded as a terror by his family. He had very violent temper tantrums. It is my belief that his masochism set in following the subsidence of the tantrums. Masochism is a pregenital character structure. The analysis proceeded on two fronts; the goodness as a defense against aggression, and the boy as a defense against the man. Bioenergetic analysis took precedence over the psychoanalysis. The main emphasis was given to freeing the aggression and developing genitality. Then, without attention, the patient remarked one day that his smile was gone. So it was in the treatment and outside.

If the analyst does not comprehend the basic problem of masochism, he can easily fall into the same pitfall that the masochist himself is in. The smile covers a very deep layer of negativeness and resentment. This layer is like quicksand. I shall describe the dynamics of this character structure more fully in Chapter 10. At this point I would like to say that therapeutic success in this problem depends on the ability of the therapist to introduce a positive element into the patient's attitude. Neither the good boy nor the bad boy can succeed in adult life, what is needed is the man. The patient, however, will not develop this more positive attitude until the character structure is thoroughly worked out. Every symptom, every expression, every dream is analyzed backward to the character and then forward in terms of the character. Only when the latter begins to yield is the analysis permitted to proceed to the infantile layers. This is well illustrated by the following case.

I treated this patient for several months prior to my departure from this country for study abroad. She continued her analysis with another therapist for about five years. During this extended treatment she had very many strong emotional breakthroughs, that is, affective discharges, following each of which she said that she felt better. When I resumed her therapy I found that she was in no better condition than when I left. The strong affective discharges had led nowhere. They had begun during her previous therapy with me. At that time they took the form of crying with choking sensations which were mixed with anger. As I observed these outbursts, I realized that they were ineffectual to promote the therapy. She did not cry or become angry because of the awareness of a past trauma. Her reaction was one of frustration without any direction. I interpreted it as a resistance in the sense that the patient was "blowing off steam." This "blowing off steam" made her feel better temporarily, but at the same time it had the effect of preventing the build-up of sufficient inner tension to bring her into better contact with her character armor. I had only to point this out several times to bring an end to these reactions, and it was only when they ceased that I could proceed with the analytic work.

Such breakthroughs have to be distinguished from the

spontaneous affective release which is triggered by sudden conscious awareness of a repressed conflict or experience. The experienced analyst can frequently sense the difference. In general I distrust these emotional breakthroughs. First, the discharge breaks through the character structure at its weakest point. This follows a law that is valid for all explosive discharges. The strong and pivotal points of the character armor are spared and they may even be strengthened. Secondly, this kind of emotional release has the function in many impulsive individuals of preventing too great a strain upon the character and muscular tensions. In reality, then, these releases are part of the neurotic mechanism. This is the problem of acting out in the therapy. The analyst who permits the patient to function neurotically in the analysis blocks himself from an effective attack upon the neurosis. The acting out of the neurotic character is the fundamental resistance.

The therapy with this patient now proceeded by the analysis and treatment of the resistances. But soon I met with another and more severe block. Each successful attack made the patient cry but she could not give in to her crying. She choked, began to cough again, sputtered and gasped. Even the attempts to relieve the spasm of the throat musculature were unsuccessful. She repeated to me what she had told the other analyst. When she choked while crying, she said that she had the sensation that her mother's milk was sour. As soon as the feeling swelled up in her throat, the experience of this sour taste made her choke. As she told me this, I recalled what I had read in *Character Analysis* about the interpretation of early infantile material. This was certainly early! I was suspicious. Her memory of her mother's milk was probably a true one, at least I could not deny it, but why did it come at this time when I was analyzing her present situation? Further, she was a definite hysterical character type and the problem of her relation to men had not been solved.

I refused to accept her interpretation but the choking continued. I should have asked myself what role did the choking have in her present day function, but I doubt if I would have known the answer then. The analysis continued on her present day problems. Some months later I saw the true picture in a flash. I had the correct interpretation and it was just what I needed. Not sour but bitter was the sensation this girl felt although she never used that word. She was bitter though it was so well covered up that I had not suspected its presence. She was bitter because of her continued feeling of frustration. In retrospect I saw that her earlier outbreak of mixed rage and crying were reactions to this feeling of bitterness. As reactions to it and not against it they changed nothing.

Now I could go further. One had simply to ask and find the answers to two questions. Under what circumstances does bitterness arise? And what was she bitter about—in the present and in the past? The other obvious trait which this patient showed was pride. It was not expressed but like the bitterness it, too, was repressed. However, one could not miss the meaning of the long stiff neck. I had not been able to get at the pride either analytically or by work on the tense muscles of the neck so long as the bitterness lay concealed. The exposure of this bitterness opened the way to therapeutic success just as the failure on the part of the preceding therapist to interpret properly this symptom had condemned his efforts.

Let me answer the above questions to bring this case to its conclusion. The bitterness in the present related to the patient's inability to develop a successful relationship with a man. And as long as the bitterness would persist a sweet affair would be impossible. As a child she had experienced the same frustration. Her mother was the queen bee type. Her father was over solicitous about his wife and indifferent to the femininity of his growing daughter. He treated her as a boy with a good feeling of companionship and she accepted the role. She wore boy's clothes and played boy's games, competing with them on their ground. As she took on the feminine role in late adolescence she already had marked ambivalence towards the male. She was bitter about the earlier insult to her femininity, exceedingly proud to cover the sense of hurt and determined not to be dependent on a man and to so prevent a repetition of the earlier experience. And yet she needed a man desperately to confirm her sexuality.

Once this picture was fully clarified the patient began to change. Pride, bitterness and determination slowly loosened their grip on her behavior. She lost some of her restlessness, her figure took on more feminine lines and she began a new relationship that was more mature than any previous one. As she developed more positive attitudes, the bioenergetic work on the physical level became more important. Progress from then on was rapid.

To master the concepts implied in the technique of character analysis the theoretical basis of the character structure must be understood. One must know the nature and function of the character structure and one must be thoroughly familiar with the basic character types. In the following chapter I will present a genetic-dynamic theory of character formation which will be followed in the succeeding chapters by a detailed discussion of the basic types with case histories. Here, let us examine more closely the nature and function of the character and relate it to the technical problems of transference analysis.

We mentioned earlier that both Reich and Ferenczi made a distinction between the neurotic symptom and the character itself. Reich (1949, p. 42, 43) pointed out that the neurotic symptom is experienced as a "foreign body and creates a feeling of being ill." It is "never as thoroughly rationalized as the character." The neurotic symptom is experienced as something alien to the ego. The character is not really rationalized, it is only the way a neurotic individual experiences his ego. It is rationalized only after it is brought under attack. When the character structure begins to crack up in the therapy and a more spontaneous way of being makes its appearance, this new way, even though it is a healthier way than the old one, is felt as strange by the patient.

Of course the patient would like to be different than he is. That is why he is in therapy. That is also the meaning of his ego ideal. But it is like gazing at the opposite shore of a river without knowing how to get there. It is like asking a person to swim who is afraid of the water. The patient feels that he is being asked to leave familiar territory for unknown regions. As he starts out he finds that he is frightened, weak and insecure; the resistance is strong. The motivation must be equally strong. To achieve this the therapist must make the patient aware of his character as a disturbance and at the same time make the patient feel the possibility of a better way of functioning. If he can experience this better way the task is greatly eased. In this difficult situation, the transference plays a very important role as we shall soon see.

A person identifies with his character and will not question it so long as it enables him to function without too much conflict in his social situation. If it fails to insure his function he will first question the demands of his environment. It is only repeated failure and deep dissatisfaction which will bring an individual to doubt his very way of being and acting. But he can do no more than question it. To embark upon a new way without guidance is like taking a step into the void. A character structure, however, is the result of a compromise; it is the expression of a dynamic equilibrium of opposing forces and as such it is only relatively stable. In the changing circumstances of life it will frequently prove inadequate. If the repressed forces break out either as a hysterical symptom, a violent rage or a compulsive reaction, a threat to the ego is experienced. By contrast, a character trait which is integrated into and forms part of the character structure is regarded as an eccentricity or peculiarity at most by the individual. If the repressing forces are too strong, which may happen when a person moves into a more liberal environment, the individual feels himself as alien to the social situation. This, again, proves the extent of the identification with the character. Destroy the character structure even temporarily and the individual will become confused. He will ask, "Who am I?", "What is the real me?"

From the foregoing statements it can readily be appreciated that when the analysis touches the character, resistance will develop. Since everyone would like to be free of his neurotic symptoms resistance will be encountered only when the character is challenged. Therefore we equate resistance with the character and thus agree with Wolfe's definition. The passivity of the passive-feminine character, the distrust of the masochist and the dependency of the oral character are not only resistances, they are fundamental modalities of behavior. They cannot act otherwise whether in the analytic sessions or elsewhere. I, therefore, do not interpret such attitudes only as resistances. I prefer to point out that the resistance is merely one more manifestation of the character structure which is also responsible for the problems which brought the patient to therapy. Although this pattern of behavior was the best solution in the given conditions of the patient's childhood, it constitutes a severe impediment in the more fluid environment of the adult.

The emphasis in bioenergetic therapy is upon flexibility of response and positive attitudes. If a child develops a distrustful attitude as a result of repeated negative experiences in his childhood, we must regard this attitude as a defense against further disappointments. The child is bound to his environment. Can he change his parents? Can he leave the parental home? But the adult is not so limited. His continued distrust prevents him from seeing those who are his friends. Even if he is hurt again in a relationship, can he not change it? Choose another friend, a new partner? These possibilities are implicit in every analytic therapy, it is well to make them explicit.

Now let us see how the character structure operates in the transference situation. Most patients start therapy with a positive attitude, their very coming is an indication of it. This positive attitude is, however, very superficial. It is based upon hopes for a quick cure, the promise of happiness and fulfillment implied in analytic therapy and a real desire to be different. Underneath lies the resistance of the character—fear, distrust, doubts, resentments, etc. If the analysis could be conducted without touching the character everything would be well. Since this is not the case, we must expect that the negative attitudes will come out. We must expect that every patient will react to the analyst in accordance with his own character structure. If both aspects of the transference are kept clearly in mind, much confusion over the question of transference can be avoided. It is a good policy to point out to the patient that while one does not question the sincerity of his expression of good will, there are elements in his character structure which suggest that a negative attitude is also present. The further the character analysis advances, the less hidden are these negative feelings. The sooner the character analysis is begun, the less will be the difficulty presented by these negative attitudes.

Few patients show the cooperation one meets with in the passive-feminine character. It covers his antagonism to the therapy as it covered his hatred of his father. His cooperation is not just an effort to further the therapy, it expresses his fear of the therapist and his desire not to provoke him. This fear of provocation rests upon a deeper layer of hatred and antagonism. Despite his cooperation or just because of it, the therapy will fail. Then, with good cause, he will attack the therapist, prove him inadequate and so justify his attitude of passivity. The analyst is placed in a difficult situation. He needs the cooperation of the patient but he must unmask its motivation.

One word about the situation which produces the kind of transference in which the patient gets "hung up" on the analyst. It means that the patient has developed a very positive transference which prevents the further progress of the therapy. The more positive the transference becomes, the more deeply repressed are the negative attitudes. Finally the character becomes inaccessible. This happens when the therapist assumes the role of the parent who is most responsible for the character structure. When the break comes, the sudden release of the repressed negative attitudes smashes the therapy. I treated a patient who in her previous analysis had developed a very strong transference to her analyst. She told me later that he was like her mother to her. He knew her as well as her mother did but he could not help her. Instead of working on her need for support and lack of independence, he relieved her symptoms. This created further dependence and the situation became hopeless.

The analytic situation is based upon a real relationship of two people united in a common effort. The reactions of either party will be strictly in accordance with their character structures. This is true of the analyst or therapist as well as of the patient. It is just as true of the analyst who assumes a formal, stand-off attitude, for here the patient reacts to the unconscious in the analyst, to those subtle expressions which reveal character. In fact, the formality of the analyst prevents the analyst from attacking the character of the patient since the latter also will respond in a similar fashion. If the analytic therapist is open and free in his manner and has worked through his own character problems, the transference provides the best material for use in the delineation of the patient's character.

The character structure can be worked out from the many details of the patient's daily behavior. It can be ascertained from the dynamics of the body structure and expression. It can be determined from the patient's attitude toward the therapy and the analyst. Then once the character is fully determined and set forth, a separation of its composite nature must be made. The positive ego forces must be separated from the negative ego defense functions. The latter are analyzed, but they are not eliminated until the former are strengthened. One of my patients made a very appropriate remark to this effect. He said that he felt his ego to be crystallizing out of the mixture which was his character.

The concepts of character structure and character armor are not synonymous. The character is the medieval knight, his armor is his defense. Like all armor, the character armor creates a limitation of motility and a decrease in sensitivity. The hindrance to motility hampers the aggressive functions of the individual. To some extent, the decrease in sensitivity increases aggression. In contrast to Reich, I reserve the use of the word "armor" only for those character structures which include as part of the neurotic mechanism an ability to decrease sensitivity to hurt. This excludes all pregenital character structures.

Reich moved from the concept of a character armor to the concept of muscular armoring as manifested in muscle tension and rigidities. Actually it is more correct to say that character and body structure are merely two aspects of an individual's way of being. But regardless of definition, the link was forged between psychology and biology. It is now possible to determine the character type of a person either by a study of his behavior or by an analysis of the body attitude as it reveals itself in form and movement. This was a big step forward for it not only opened the physical aspect of the individual to analysis and interpretation, it made possible the direct attack upon muscle tensions and rigidities as a means of changing character. Let me illustrate with a trait which formed part of a character structure.

At the first session with an attractive young lady, I was struck by her strong jaw and the set of her head. The impression this jaw gave was one of grimness. It is only a matter of degree from a determined jaw to a grim one but I did not doubt my impression. She was aware of a lack of joy both in her personal life and in her family background. She understood immediately what I said about the quality of grimness in her. With her head drooped slightly to one side and the shoulders raised a bit her body had a resigned expression, as a martyr grimly bearing her fate. While I worked on the total body attitude I spent time each session softening the jaw and releasing tensions at the back of her neck. Each time I worked on this region she would cry softly following which she brightened perceptibly. I persisted in this work and I was agreeably surprised a few months later when I could detect no trace of the grimness in her expression. The character structure was beginning to yield a little, but this one trait had disappeared at least for the time being.

I would not like to give the impression that character analysis and the resolution of the character structure is an easy task. The ability to diagnose character from the body structure requires knowledge of the bioenergetic processes and considerable experience in the observation of patients. Reich used to describe a good analysis as "going through the mill." The best description of what is involved in a bioenergetic analysis is given in the story of the *Divine Comedy* by Dante. You may recall that the poet Dante finds himself lost in a woods. There is no way back and ahead he sees a fierce tiger. Helpless and frightened, he calls on heaven for aid. His appeal is heard by his protector, Beatrice, who sends the poet, Virgil, to guide him home. Virgil tells Dante that the way home passes through hell, purgatory and heaven. Hell is full of dangers and frightful scenes. No one can traverse it without a competent guide. Virgil says that he has been through it himself and knows the way. In hell, Dante sees the suffering of those who were sinful and are being punished according to the nature of their transgressions. Dante is spared the punishment but not the realization of sin and its consequences. With Virgil's help he comes through hell.

Virgil can represent the analyst who had previously faced the problems of his own character and resolved them. Dante is the patient. Hell is the suffering caused by the individual's secondary, neurotic drives. In purgatory one is freed of these neurotic tendencies so that he may taste and partake of the joys of heaven.

It is well to close this chapter with a quotation from Dostoevski. In *The Brothers Karamazov*, Father Zosima tells his monks, "Hell is the suffering of those unable to love." Each of us must face and go through his own hell to find the way to heaven and home.

8

Character Formation and Structure

There is no aspect of psychoanalytic literature which is more confused than the one dealing with character formation and structure. Fenichel (1945, p. 525) has remarked, "The description of pathological character types is rather confusing. The different criteria that have been used for classification overlap one another and this necessitates frequent repetitions. It would be advantageous if psychoanalytic characterology were to give us a dynamic classification."

As early as 1908 Freud mentioned the desirability of formulating a general theory of character formation. He did not return to this suggestion until 1931 when, after having explored and subdivided the mind into the categories of id, ego and superego, he suggested that it might be possible to distinguish human character types according to the dominant subdivision. Thus, there could be an "erotic" type in which the personality is dominated by the instinctual demands of the id, a "narcissistic" type which is ego centered, and a "compulsive" type whose life is regulated by a superego which controls their personality. This classification has much to recommend it in addition to the authority of Freud. If it has not been more widely used, it is because the classification is based on symptomatology and lacks a genetic-dynamic foundation.

Underlying Freud's failure to comprehend character is his tendency to equate the neurosis with the neurotic symptom. However, as Fenichel (1945, p. 463) states: "There has been a fundamental change in the clinical picture of the neuroses during the last decades. In the classic neuroses an integrated personality was suddenly disturbed by inadequate actions or impulses. In modern neuroses, however, it is not a question of dealing with a hitherto uniform personality that is merely disturbed by some immediate event but, rather, with one that is patently torn or malformed, or at any rate so involved in the illness that there is no borderline between 'personality' and 'symptom.'"

Many cases come to therapy today which do not present any outstanding neurotic symptoms. Yet the neurosis is clearly established and can easily be recognized. I have in mind a typical example. A young lady of 26 came to therapy with the complaint that she was not aggressive enough. She was petite in her body build, rather good-looking, and well proportioned in her body structure. She was well dressed, her manner was reserved and quiet and her voice was small. She posed no sexual problem in the present. Her work function was not as satisfactory as she wished it to be. She said she was afraid of strong-willed persons.

On the couch she lay still, her breathing very subdued. These facts made me think that her neurosis was severe. The skin of her cheekbones and across the bridge of her nose had a waxy quality which gave her face a lifeless look. The absence of any spontaneous remarks or movement was striking. On occasion she crossed her hands on her chest, and all one needed was a lily to make you think she was lying in a casket. Just this lifelessness was the neurosis. I did not realize at first how difficult it would be to reach the life in that organism and to bring it to the surface. For reasons to be discussed in a subsequent chapter I diagnosed her as an hysterical character structure. Within that broad group she had a specific quality which could be described as mannequin-like. She worked with women's clothes and she said she wanted to be a designer. Could not this be interpreted as a desire of the mannequin to become alive?

Such cases are ordinarily very resistant to symptom and resistance analysis. To the many questions I posed about her past, she had one answer, "I don't know." Could you expect other from a mannequin! That the character was finally broken through was due to the use of a technique which could circumvent the rigid exterior to reach the biological core.

I mentioned this case to show that symptom formation is not a necessary sign of the neurosis. It demonstrates, too, the problem of affect-block. There was a tendency in early psychoanalytic days to draw a distinction between so-called impulsive types and affect-block types of personality. The distinction is a valid one although it lacks a genetic base.

Interest in character structure and character formation was stimulated by the work of Abraham and Reich. Abraham's characterology was based upon a conglomeration of traits. His character types were not dynamic concepts even if genetically determined. The basis for an analytic characterology was set forth by Reich with the first publication of *Character Analysis* in 1933. In that book, for the first time, the question of analytic characterology is studied in all its aspects. First, the economic function of the character is clearly set forth. "Economically, the character in ordinary life and the character resistance in the analysis serve the same function, that of avoiding unpleasure, of establishing and maintaining a psychic equilibrium—neurotic though it may be—and finally that of absorbing repressed energies" (1949, p. 48). Second, character formation proceeds from the same infantile experiences which produce resistance in analysis or symptom formation. In fact, the character is the strongest resistance in analytic therapy. "The situations which make the character resistance appear in the analysis are exact duplicates of those situations in infancy which set character formation into motion. For this reason, we find in the character resistance both a defensive function and a transference of infantile relationships with the outer world." Third, the book contains a clear exposition of the technique of character analysis. And fourth, Reich presents detailed case histories to illustrate some of the more important character types.

Is it possible to arrange the different character types schematically so that we have a broad picture of the essential neurotic disturbances? Such an arrangement presupposes a relationship between the character types and some developmental pattern. Is it possible then to formulate a genetic-dynamic theory of character formation which would serve as such a pattern?

The close relationship between character structure and ego development found expression in Abraham's concept of the oral, the anal and the genital character. Most analysts are agreed that character types, if they are to have any meaning, must be related to ego structure. Obviously, this basis for establishing a dynamic and analytic characterology is sound but we face the problem of clarifying our concepts of ego structure.

The genital character as described by Abraham is essentially unneurotic. Reich also uses the concept of the genital character as a symbol of health in opposition to the neurotic character. But many individuals have a libidinal structure which has reached the genital phase of ego organization and who, nevertheless, are neurotic. Actually, if we follow Freud in his later theories, expressed in *Beyond the Pleasure Principle* and *Civilization and Its Discontents*, we must assume that absolute emotional health is impossible under the conditions of civilized living.

I would suggest that we limit the concept of character in analytic therapy to pathological states. Health must be distinguished by the absence of a typical mode of behavior. Its qualities are spontaneity and adaptability to the rational demands of a situation. Health is a fluid state in contrast to the neurosis which is a structured condition. We face the choice, therefore, of using the concept of the genital character as a type of neurotic structure or of choosing another name for the neurosis in which the ego structure is developed to the genital level. I have chosen the latter course.

There can be no question about the oral phase or the genital phase of ego development. There is a serious doubt about the existence of an anal stage in the natural growth and development of the ego structure. Reich in his later publications denied that it was a natural phase of libidinal organization. Yet it is just this so-called anal stage which formed the starting point of character analytic studies and about which so much has been published in the psychoanalytic literature.

The fact that an anal character type exists is based upon descriptions by Freud, Abraham, Jones and others. But we are not justified in assuming that what is a recognized pathological condition corresponds to a natural phase in the ego development of the child. Several considerations impel me to regard this stage as an artificially induced one and not a natural step towards genitality.

The true compulsive character or the anal character are not types which are commonly met with in analytic practice in this country. I have noticed some of the traits which go to make up this structure in many patients, but a grouping of traits of such completeness as to resemble what the European authors have described has been very rare in my personal practice. The few cases I have seen have been individuals who had been raised abroad. There is a big difference between American and northern European attitudes in regard to cleanliness and toilet training. An acquaintance told me that in Switzerland mothers were proud if their children were toilet trained at eight months of age. I was convinced by my own extended stay abroad that the exaggerated cleanliness one finds in some countries, while a treat for the visitor, is obtained at the expense of spontaneity and joy in life.

Personal observation of children who have been toilet trained spontaneously further convinced me that the child has no special interest in this region nor in his feces. Civilized living requires that all children be toilet trained. This means, of course, that some attention will be given to the excremental functions by adults. If left to themselves, children will void and move their bowels anywhere, but away from the place of their usual activities. Everything, then, depends on the attitude of the adults. Can we keep the child in diapers until such time as he can understand the nature of these functions, express his need in clear language and even make some moves to help himself or must we act as quickly as possible to free ourselves of this burden? Can we look upon the excremental functions as natural or must we show horror and shame towards them? Is the regular bowel movement regarded as a measure of health? In these questions American tradition leans one way, European another. One can understand the European attitude towards cleanliness in view of their background of plague and disease. European civilization had been an urban civilization long before proper sanitary facilities were available. Children from more primitive cultures and from warmer climates tend to avoid this problem.

Theoretical considerations indicate that the anal phase is not a natural phase in the normal growth of the ego. Freud (1953b, p. 138) reminds us of Abraham's remark that embryologically, "the anus corresponds to the primitive mouth, which has moved down to the end of the bowel." The anus begins to function as soon as the mouth does, not some time later. If the infant has no voluntary sphincter control in the early days of his life (he does have some sphincter control) neither does he have control over all movements of his mouth. The two ends of the tube develop simultaneously. As a rule both ends are equally disturbed. The mother who is rigorous in her education to excremental cleanliness is forceful and strict with feeding. The disturbance when it is severe upsets the whole alimentary tract with nausea and vomiting above, constipation and diarrhea below.

Most children growing up in civilized surroundings will have some degree of disturbance in the anal function. The attempt on the part of the child to develop sphincter control at too early an age results in spasm and tension in the gluteal and hamstring muscles. An energy block ensues which subsequently overcharges the area and creates an anal erotism which is purely pathological. While we are justified therefore in speaking of anal traits, we are wrong when we assign to the anal function a position of independence in the natural organization of the ego.

Of course, if we admit innate destructive tendencies in the child, then the development of teeth can be regarded as an ominous sign. Soiling the diaper may also be interpreted as anal-sadistic behavior. However, Freud's death instinct is not a true evaluation of the natural aggressive tendencies in the living organism. This is not to say that destructive tendencies do not develop in the child. They can be traced analytically to interference with the child's natural needs and rhythms, and this is what we wish to avoid. So, too, an anal-sadistic character structure can result but it does not correspond to any natural phase of ego growth and it cannot, therefore, be used as a generic character type. It will appear as a variation of one of these types.

Freud (1953b, p. 136) goes further. He agrees with Abraham in the division of the anal stage into two parts: the first contains "destructive tendencies to annihilate and get rid of things," while later, "those tendencies predominate which are friendly to the object, and seek to possess things and hold them fast." There is no justification for regarding these tendencies as biological or other than the derivatives of a special cultural process. Everyone would admit that civilized living is impossible without some form of sanitation. It would be equally impossible to run a home if the children were not trained to excremental cleanliness. But the observations which gave rise to Abraham's concept, with which Freud concurred, relate to the cultural conditions existing in a special part of Europe in the early part of this century. At that time and place toilet training was unusually severe. It was instituted too early and enforced too strictly. Families were large, laundry facilities were woefully inadequate and the fear of germs was widespread. I have observed many children in our time and place who do not show any of the tendencies Freud describes. If the training is begun when the child is mature enough to understand the demand made upon him, the experience becomes one more step in the acquisition of those skills and abilities which constitute the cultured man. It differs in no way from learning to use silverware, take care of one's clothes, etc. The time at which this maturity first comes into being coincides with the beginning of the genital phase.

Even in the present time, there are too many parents who insist upon sphincter control at too early an age. The consequences are disastrous for the children. The motor nerve to the external anal sphincter muscle is myelinized at a late date so no control over this muscle is possible too soon. Bioenergetic analysis shows that children squeeze the buttocks, pull up the pelvic floor and contract the back of the thighs to hold back the movement. Since this is a very painful condition, a serious conflict develops. If the child fights against the pressure from the parent, it will express destructive tendencies. This is a first stage. The parent being stronger will win the fight and the child is forced to submit. It now shows retentive tendencies as a second stage. All that has happened is that fear of the movement is stronger than the natural urge to evacuate. The child frequently becomes constipated and the parent steps in again with laxatives, enemas or other means to resolve a neurotic conflict. The whole problem can be avoided through understanding and patience.

This splitting of behavior patterns into two opposing tendencies is characteristic of Freud (1953b, p. 136). The oral stage is also divided into two periods by the appearance of the teeth. "In the earlier period we have only oral incorporation and there is no ambivalence in relation to the object, i.e., the mother's breast. The second stage, which is distinguished by the onset of biting activities, may be called the 'oral-sadistic' stage. It is here that we get the first manifestations of ambivalence." I have seen some children show an ambivalence towards the breast in the first months when the mother was anxious while others who never felt this splitting throughout an extended nursing experience. For a child to become ambivalent about an object which is at once the source of its nourishment and pleasure requires the introduction of a strong disturbing factor from the outside. In this case, it is the mother's conscious or unconscious reluctance which creates the mixed feelings in the child. It is wrong to regard our aggressive organs as sadistic elements. The teeth can bite in love as well as hate, the arms can embrace as well as crush, the penis can caress as well as pierce.

In our consideration of the growth of the ego, we can dispense with the whole anal phase and with the idea of two stages in the oral phase. We can say simply that the development of the child proceeds from a condition of emotional dependence to emotional independence, from the nebulous pleasure-pain ego of the infant to the crystallized reality ego of the adult, from the oral phase to the genital phase. The growth of the organism both physically and psychically is a continuous process. Those who live intimately with the growing child know that it is impossible to distinguish the changing although we recognize the change. His first aided step may occur at seven months, he may take several steps alone at eleven months, he doesn't walk until much later. The first word doesn't constitute speaking. Growth is also slow and consists of innumerable daily experiences each of which extends the organism's awareness of reality, both the internal reality of its feelings and needs and the external reality of its environment. When we look analytically at the history of an individual we see a spectrum which goes from immaturity to maturity like the color changes in a maturing tomato. Highlights stand out in this spectrum only when we compare distant points, adjacent areas grade into each other imperceptibly.

Let us look at this process of growth and maturation bioenergetically. We can arrive at concepts which are basic and valid for different times and other cultures. The newborn human infant is biologically completely helpless and dependent on his mother for life sustenance. He cannot move from place to place as other newborn mammalian young can and he cannot even hold on to his mother. He must be carried and supported while being carried. Slowly he gains strength and coordination. He can sit up, then he can stand erect, next he begins to walk. But even at the age of three, when he can run and play, his need to be held continues. He tries and has to be carried. If he falls, he wants to be picked up and assured. Biologically, the dependence of the human young is long. He does not reach biological maturity until puberty. By the end of the period of puberty, physical growth is almost completed; the sexual function is well established on the genital level. Emotional growth is not in a linear progression. It is most rapid in the earliest period, leveling off gradually to adulthood.

If we distinguish several periods in this broad spectrum, it is only for purposes of discussion. Life has only two fixed points, birth and death. When we speak of the "oral phase" we refer to a period in the organism's life when it is most dependent, when its need to take in sustenance dominates its activities. As it grows and develops it gradually reaches a period of energy balance with its environment. Once physical growth has ceased, the organism is under the necessity to discharge the net excess of energy resulting from the activities connected with sustenance. It is a quality of the living process that it produces more energy than it needs for its individual growth. When the protozoan reaches this level, it maintains its energy balance by cell division. In the metazoan, sexuality and reproduction serve this function. We can describe this phase of the individual's life as the genital phase.

Living processes are continuous. Genitality does not emerge in full function as Minerva did from the brow of Jupiter. I do not know at what age the child first becomes aware of its genitals, certainly it is early in the oral phase of its life. At one year of age and earlier, a boy baby may have quite an erection. From two, three or four years of age on, children show a considerable interest in their genital activity. It is obvious that this is a function which matures slowly. Yet there is an age, varying for each child, when it enters the genital phase. Soon thereafter genitality becomes established even though the function is not mature. From then on the primacy of the genitals is furthered as the organism gains strength, control and coordination of its movements. As orality decreases, genitality increases. We equate orality with dependence, genitality with independence.

Within the period from birth to adolescence, we can highlight the changes by several events: the emergence of teeth at six to seven months, the beginning of the functions of walking and talking, the acquisition of sphincter control, interest in and play with other children, starting school, the eruption of the permanent teeth, etc. If we could adjust our cultural demands on the child to his natural rhythm of growth and development, much of mental illness would be avoided. Any serious interference with the growth process will produce a pathological character problem which may persist through life. Let us see what form these interferences may take.

We said that the human child at birth is dependent on his mother for sustenance. Sustenance for the infant and child is more than alimentary nourishment. The child needs love, security, narcissistic supplies—however one may describe it. Compare Renee Spitz's studies on the effects of this deprivation which may cost the child his life. The child's relation to its mother is a libidinal one; an energy process is involved. The contact of the infant with the energy system of its mother excites the energy of its own system and causes it to stream towards the point of contact. If this is at the breast, the energy charge at the infant's mouth becomes very strong. The longitudinal pulsation from center to ends is started. The reality principle has begun to operate even if the infant is unaware for the moment of the external reality of breast and nipple. Growth, maturation and the establishment of the bioenergetic basis for the reality principle follow a well-known biological law, development proceeds from the head end to the tail end.

The infant needs the physical contact with its mother as much as it needs food and air. The necessary intimacy is best achieved through the function of nursing, substitution of the bottle for the breast weakens the contact greatly. But when the child is hardly held at all, the loss of contact with the mother is a severe deprivation. Nursing has many other advantages over bottle feeding from a bioenergetic point of view. The nursing child has more control over his food intake than the bottle baby. He can take as much or as little as he wishes. More important, however, is the fact that the teat is sucked deep in the mouth by the action of the tongue against the posterior part of the hard palate. The rubber nipple is sucked mostly with the lips. The former is a more active procedure than the latter.

Here, now, are the important questions. How much contact with the mother does the baby need to avoid any feeling of deprivation? As a corollary, one should know—how long the mother should continue to support, nourish and hold the child? My answers will shock some readers but will also account for the great number of problems we face in mental health. Exact answers depend upon the individual child. We can, however, give some approximate ideas.

Only the child really knows or feels how much contact it needs. Some need more than others. The baby expresses his need by crying. A child may express himself vocally or by gesture. Any child that cries needs some attention. To let a child cry without responding creates a feeling of despair and hopelessness. If this becomes a regular practice, the baby or child stops crying. *What is the use!* But this feeling of "what is the use" persists until it manifests itself as a reason for resistance in the analytic therapy. I have no hesitation in saying that one cannot spoil a child with love. But it must be genuine; that is, it must be a tender feeling which responds to the needs of the child and not what the mother "thinks" the child needs. Although the demands of the infant are our only guide to his needs, we do have objective means of determining whether those needs are satisfied. A happy child is a healthy child; a satisfied child is a beautiful child with bright eyes, a glowing complexion, a lively manner, and a fighting spirit.

How long is the mother to continue to satisfy the needs of the child? Let me answer this question by saying that here, too, the needs of the child determine the response. One must recognize that conditions of civilized living makes such demands upon a woman that she cannot devote herself to her child as a primitive mother can. On the other hand, babies and children are not civilized yet and their demands differ little from those of children born into simpler cultures. The result is that modern woman is in frequent conflict with her children.

Despite the fact that no important biological event occurs at three years of age, it is a significant age in the history of the individual. Primitive mothers generally nurse and carry their children until that age. At about three years, the child gains control of the sphincter muscles, good locomotor coordination and adequate comprehension of the spoken word. At this age, too, the child begins to show a sense of independence and a feeling of responsibility for his own needs. Analytic research has shown that the Oedipus conflict begins around this period. These considerations lead to the conclusion that the genital function becomes established at about this age or that genital primacy is achieved. Bioenergetically, this means that the longitudinal energy swing is now anchored in the head and genital. The issue created by the child's growing independence is biologically linked with its developing genitality.

Knowledge about character structure and character types is derived from clinical observation. For example, where the behavior pattern of the individual is characterized by feelings of deprivation, strong fear of loss of the love object, inner emptiness and despair, we describe the character structure as an oral type. These individuals are dependent in their relationships. They are subject to marked fluctuations of mood, to elation and depression. We shall study a detailed case history of this character type in the following chapter. For the moment we can say that to produce such a character structure the deprivation must be severe and must occur in the first six months of life. If the deprivation is less severe or occurs later the ego structure will be stronger and more developed, but it will show some degree of orality in the form of oral traits. The bioenergetic basis of this character structure is a weakness in the strength of the longitudinal energy swing. Neither head nor genital is strongly charged. The reality function is conditional upon the attitude of the environment. The oral character accepts reality only if it is favorable. An unfavorable environment is rejected, but there is no denial of reality such as one finds in schizophrenia.

Contrast the above picture with the child who does not meet with severe frustration until after three years of age. This is the time when, as we have seen, the child has passed out of the stage of babyhood and shows some independence. Since he can speak and understand the spoken word, parents expect that he should begin to obey their commands. He is to be taught the ways of civilized living. Masturbation and sex play are interdicted. Politeness and manners are stressed. Unfortunately the child has other ideas. His new found independence and his conscious interest in the genitals force him into conflict with his parents. Where one would never spank an infant and only rarely spank a baby, the three to four year old may "get his" regularly. If the genital function has become firmly established, there is no retreat from reality. The child meets frustration, deprivation and pressure by stiffening up. The energy does not withdraw from head or genitals. The child may hide his genital interest, reduce its charge or be openly defiant. He never gives it up. This is what we mean when we say that at about this age the bioenergetic swing anchors at both ends.

The stiffening produces rigidity, both physically and emotionally, and the various character types of this group are marked by the inflexibility of their ego structures. Because rigidity is the outstanding characteristic of this group, we name this type the rigid character structures. This broad group includes various clinical types: the phallic-narcissistic male, the hysterical female, the compulsive character, the obsessive neurotic, the anal character, etc. All of these clinical subgroups have as their common denominator structural rigidity, characterologically and somatically.

The rigid type of character differs greatly from the oral type. Where the oral character withdraws from reality in unfavorable conditions, the rigid character tenses further but maintains the contact. For this reason, their work function is generally good and they are less subject to mood fluctuation. They constitute the group which formerly were described as affect-block types as opposed to the impulsivity which characterizes the oral character. Because of the rigidity, motility is decreased and the individual complains of feelings of lifelessness but not of inner emptiness. Of course, the degree of rigidity varies from one individual to another, and varies in the same individual under different conditions. Fenichel (1945, p. 465) noted this difference in reaction. "In extreme cases," he wrote, "the rigidity is a total one; in less extreme cases a relative elasticity may be preserved so that the rigid pattern becomes pronounced whenever anxiety is felt, and is somewhat relaxed whenever an experience of reassurance or pleasure permits the individual to ease the barrier."

It was the recognition of this characterological rigidity which led Reich to formulate the concept of muscular armoring and to equate it with the psychological attitude. But it is only to this type of structure that the concept or armoring applies, for the oral character has no such defense. Individuals so armored experience little anxiety for it is precisely the economic function of the armor to bind anxiety. By the same token their contact with the external world is also limited, and in the presence of more spontaneous persons these individuals will experience themselves as lifeless, dull, inferior, etc. It is this experience which brings them to therapy. If the armor is broken through in therapy, anxiety is immediately produced. In the case of one such patient, merely opening the mouth and eyes very wide produced a strong reaction. She let out a scream of fright. Her body tingled all over. She begged me not to repeat the experience, it frightened her too much.

When the armoring is incomplete its anxiety binding power is less. Emotional reactions and symptom formation are more frequent and may dominate the picture. If the pressure increases on the armored individual, a dangerous situation may result. A woman in her late thirties came for help because of heart palpitations, insomnia and the feeling that she would crack-up at any moment. It was not difficult under these conditions to open the door and release a flood of tears which then brought out feelings of shame and guilt for letting go. All her life she had carried a heavy load of responsibility with an attitude of grim determination. Her husband had been seriously ill during the past six months and she had managed his business, looked after the home and children and nursed him with a fortitude that was remarkable. Small wonder, then, that she was near the breaking point! Admirable as such fortitude is, it poses a serious threat to the individual. Rigidity cannot be maintained indefinitely without the danger of a breakdown, emotionally or physically.

There is an intermediate type of character structure which lacks rigidity yet does not show the mood fluctuation nor withdrawal from reality which marks the oral character. There is no complaint of inner emptiness and no strong feelings of deprivation. The lack of any rigidity is manifested by a tendency to collapse when inner tension or outer pressure increases: the male may lose his erection just before penetration. Bioenergetically, there is a failure of the energy pulsation to anchor securely in head and genitals. The genital function is not overdetermined as in the case of the rigid character nor conditional as in the oral type. It is hesitant as is the whole personality. There is advance and retreat, effort and collapse, which over a long period reveals a pattern of repeated failures. This is the type of structure which we call "masochistic." It introduces a new factor in the determinants of character structure.

Deprivation produces orality, frustration on the genital level results in rigidity. The former is a factor which operates most strongly in the first year of life; frustration is an oedipal phenomenon. In our culture a third factor may be introduced between the first and third years of life. This comes from the mother who is overprotective, oversolicitous and overwatchful. A material interest in the child's welfare is substituted for the tenderness and affection which has regard for the growing independence of the new individual. It has been called "smothering" instead of mothering. It takes the form of forced feeding, anxiety and interest in the bowel function, and overzealous regard that the child should not be hurt in physical activity. This is done in the name of love, but the effect is to suppress the growing ego of the child. Resistance and rebellion are soon stamped out, self-assertion and self-regulation are not permitted. Under the dictum that "mother knows best," the spirit of the child is literally crushed.

Masochism has its origin in experiences which overwhelm the ego of the child before it can firmly establish itself in genitality. Suppression differs from deprivation in that physical force is used to effect the mother's ends.

While there is no lack of attention to the child, it is focussed upon his material needs to the complete exclusion of his tender spiritual needs. Suppression differs from frustration, where the objective is to adjust the child's instinctual activities to adult forms. Suppression aims to render the child submissive to the mother's superior knowledge and wisdom. While there is no actual deprivation, disapproval and the threat of deprivation are used to force obedience. The fight is not easily won. Before submission is achieved, there are severe temper tantrums, rage reactions, etc. We shall study this problem in more detail in a subsequent chapter. It is important to recognize that the process which leads to masochism begins in the second year of life. It is a pregenital problem and creates a pregenital structure.

We designate as a masochistic character structure a pattern of behavior which is compounded of effort and collapse, attempt and failure. Its underlying quality is the fear of self-assertion in any form. The oral character will assert himself under favorable conditions, the rigid character asserts in a hard, driving, compulsive way. Compulsion is not a characteristic trait of the masochist, it is a reaction formation to it. In masochism there is intense anxiety in all situations where aggression is required. Compulsion is a form of rigidity which binds the anxiety. Masochism as a character structure is not rare, however; it is more common to find masochistic traits in most neurotics.

In the growth and development of the ego structure the child is subject to three major kinds of disturbance, each of which will leave its characteristic mark on his personality. Deprivation leads to orality, suppression to masochism, and frustration to rigidity. There is some correspondence with Abraham's three types of character, but Freud (1931b, p. 248) comes even closer with his libidinal types: the erotic, the narcissistic and the obsessional. Freud's description of the erotic type shows that it is identical with the oral character. "They are governed by the dread of loss of love, and this makes them peculiarly dependent on those who may withhold their love from them." The obsessional character is not a masochist although there are strong masochistic elements in it. However, it is really in the masochistic structure that the superego dominates the personality with "great accompanying tension." The narcissistic type was later described as the phallic-narcissistic character. It is a prime example of the rigid structure.

It seems hardly likely that an individual could grow up in our culture subject to only one of the common disturbances. Most individuals show a varying combination of orality, masochism and rigidity. Character analysis does not depend upon the purity of the type but upon the dominant pattern of behavior. When we make the diagnosis of oral character, this does not mean that the individual has no masochistic traits or lacks rigidity. The diagnosis is the analyst's judgment of the dominant trends in the patient's structure. The character analytic technique demands that analytic interpretation and therapeutic work be directed consistently at this major problem. The secondary neurotic tendencies are analyzed in terms of their influence in shaping the final structure. We certainly cannot agree with Freud's idea that a combination of erotic-obsessional narcissistic trends would be the "absolute norm, the perfect harmony." Mental health is not due to the adjustment of conflicting tendencies but to the elimination of the conflict.

Every adult who comes to analytic therapy does so because of some disturbance in his ability to function on the level of reality. Adult reality requires of an individual satisfactory functioning in his work, social relationships and sexuality. The neurotic does not deny this reality. He may question its standards but he would like to be able to live up to them. The oral character does not function on the oral level but on the genital level. However, this function is weakened by oral tendencies: the need for security, the fear of loss of the loved object, etc. The need of the masochist for constant reassurance and approval limits his aggression in work and sex. Rigidity creates an immobility which impedes function. Psychoanalysis and bio-energetic analysis will reveal the nature of these disturbances and some of the early experiences which led to them. Freud pointed this out in 1933. "Nowadays, we direct our attention more to the facts which indicate how much of each earlier phase persists side by side with, and behind, later organizations, and obtains permanent representation in the economy of the libido and in the character of the individual" (1953b, p. 137).

It is not always easy to make a diagnosis of the character type. Since most individuals present a character structure which contains two or more elements, it is a matter of judgment as to which is the dominant factor in the personality. Considerable clinical experience is needed in addition to a thorough knowledge of the dynamics of each type. Borderline cases are quite common. Most oral characters will show some degree of masochism and, similarly, the masochist will have oral traits. They have this in common: they are both pregenital structures. The combination of a pregenital tendency, orality or masochism, with rigidity can create a character structure which is neither one nor the other. There is a recognized clinical character type among men called the passive-feminine character. Reich described two bases for this character formation, one in which the mother is the frustrating person and another in which the "exaggerated severity of the father" drives the boy from his masculine-phallic position. Freud considered passive-femininity as a type of masochism. My own experience has led me to include this type as a variety of the rigid structures. We shall study the problem more in detail later. What is important here is the fact that it is a borderline character type which sometimes poses difficulty in diagnosis.

This combination of tendencies is responsible for the many clinical classifications. The concept of the compulsive character is widely used in analytic writing. Actually, this is a classification based upon a symptom and not upon the dynamic structure which underlies it. Compulsive tendencies are found in both masochistic characters and in rigid characters. The compulsion itself is a defense against the masochistic collapse, failure or defeat. In the masochist it is a weak defense, in the rigid structure it is a powerful defense. Just because the defense is good and collapse and failure are prevented, we are justified in regarding the compulsive as a rigid character. In his body structure the true compulsive is one of the most rigid structures seen.

The so-called "anal character" is another delineation based upon certain symptoms or traits. The very nature of these traits—orderliness, parsimony and miserliness —requires considerable rigidity to maintain them. The oral character has none of them. Masochists may show them only to the degree that they can or have developed the necessary holding power. If these traits are at all outstanding, one can be sure that the structure is dominated by rigidity. Actually, the masochist rarely suffers from constipation which is a common complaint of rigid structures.

Rigidity is always a genital problem but it can be determined by other factors than genital frustration. The individual with strong oral or masochistic traits will develop rigidity as a means of supporting a genital organization which is weakened by the deprivation and suppression suffered earlier. But what we have here is a weakly charged genital function, which stiffens at the slightest frustration. In the rigid character, genitality is over-determined.

Within each broad group of character types, the development of any special form depends on many factors. No two oral characters, no two masochists nor any two rigid characters are exactly alike. There are variations in the degree of orality, masochism and rigidity which are quantitative as well as qualitative factors. The character which is specific for each individual is the resultant of all the experiences which the individual has from conception to adulthood. Certainly the earliest experiences are most determining. Later experiences give the structure its formal stamp.

Among the masochists I treated, the following individual portraits were seen. One young man had as his typical expression that of the good boy, another was the innocent child, a third had a stupid look, a fourth was angelic. These are typical masochistic attitudes. Each, of course, covered the opposite tendencies. Oral characters in their more elated moods tend to put on regal airs. The rigid characters show much more variety. They all are characteristically determined; some grimly, others bravely, some obviously bitter, others resentful. Some are openly defiant while others are wily and foxy. To ascertain this specific quality is the art not the science of analysis.

It would be valuable in summary to explain the difference between deprivation, suppression and frustration. The infant and baby have a need to take in sustenance which includes affection. Bioenergetically, we say simply that the infant has a need to take in energy. If this energy (food, love, etc.) is not forthcoming, there is deprivation. At about the age of three, the child is less dependent on the adults for his energy intake. He can still suffer deprivation but it is less serious. He has a growing need now to give, to express his affection, to discharge energy. He enters the genital phase when the need to discharge arises, whether in play with other children or affectionately towards the adults in his immediate environment. His libido, formerly turned inward, is now directed out into the world and it needs an object. The lack of an object, or what is the same, of response by the object, causes a frustration. Bioenergetically, frustration describes the inability to discharge, deprivation, the failure or lack of charge. Suppression involves a denial of right. The child is forced into a passive position. His will is subverted. The ego of the oral character is more or less empty, that of the masochist is crushed. The rigid character has a rigid ego, hard and inflexible.

Part Two

9

The Oral Character

In the preceding chapter we learned that the neurotic character structures are determined by traumatic experiences in the early life of the individual. The knowledge of these relationships was derived from the psychoanalytic investigation of neurotic behavior. But while we are in possession of much knowledge about the genetic origin of many traits, the specific dynamic factors which determine the different character types have not yet been fully elucidated. It is our purpose in the following chapters to study these factors in detail by means of case histories and clinical presentations.

The problem of the oral character structure is presented first because it shows more clearly than any other type the great dependence of psychic function upon the underlying bioenergetic processes. The psychoanalytic literature contains many references to oral traits. The relation of morality to depression has been frequently observed and psychoanalytically interpreted. Abraham introduced the concept of the oral character but his paper was speculative and it merely related certain traits to the persistence of tendencies observed in the early infantile period of development. Reich's book on *Character Analysis* does not contain a case history of this type of structure. While the oral character is not the most common type of neurotic character structure, oral traits and oral tendencies can be found in almost all individuals who present themselves for analytic therapy.

The patient whose problem will serve as the basis for our preliminary discussion came to therapy because of the persistence of periods of marked depression. He was a young man in his late twenties. In addition to the fact of repeated depressions, he had considerable difficulty in holding a job. When he first consulted me he was out of work and so the start of the therapy was conditioned upon his obtaining employment. His work record showed a succession of jobs, none of which he held for longer than six months. He had no profession, nor was he skilled or trained in a particular vocation.

When I questioned him in the first interview about his attitude towards work, he expressed strong reluctance to accept the necessity for work. This attitude, I have found, is characteristic of the oral character. I challenged him by asking if he felt that the world owed him a living. Unhesitatingly he said "yes." One cannot argue with such a belief for it translates an inner feeling of deprivation. The individual with this attitude acts like one who believes that he has been cheated of his birthright and will spend his life trying to recover his inheritance. At most, one can only prove its impracticality. I agreed with him that he had been cheated and I offered him my support. This took the form of a statement on a prescription blank that the bearer was entitled to a living which he could claim at any bank or trust company in the United States. I signed my name to it and handed it to him. Then he laughed. He realized that however justified he might feel his demand to be, he could never realize it. He agreed to find a job.

The therapy began two months later. My patient had found employment as production manager in a small factory. This position was the first he had in which responsibility and authority over others devolved upon him. For the first time, too, he was on the side of management in the labor struggle. But the job was not an easy one. He was due in the factory at eight in the morning and frequently he had to stay until the work schedule was finished. It wasn't long before he began to complain about the grueling nature of his work. He was tired at night. It was a big effort to get up each morning to get to work on time. But he admitted that he felt better than he had in years and he had no attacks of depression. In this early phase of his therapy, I concentrated on the problem of his specific muscular tensions at the same time that the issue of work as a necessity in the life of a man was fought out in terms of his daily experiences.

Before we proceed further with a discussion of the therapy in this case, I would like to present the background of this patient. We should have before us, too, a picture of the body structure and some knowledge of its specific tensions and blocks.

The patient was the oldest child of three in a family in which there was constant friction. Although his father was an independent artisan with his own business, the family income was hardly more than enough to cover necessities. He had two younger brothers, one of whom suffered from rheumatic heart disease.

The patient described his home situation as follows: His parents hated each other. His mother was a weak woman who, he felt, tried to lean on him. He was disgusted with her helplessness. His father had frequent flare-ups of violent rage but otherwise showed little interest in the family. The patient recalled that as a child he was frightened of his father. He had no feeling of having received any love from either parent. He characterized his mother's attitude as "mothering in a sticky way." Neither parent, he felt, had any personality.

He had the usual childhood illnesses. Sports and athletic activity interested him little but he read a good deal. In school he suffered from a lack of ability to concentrate on his subjects but he received good grades nonetheless. He completed high school and attended college for one year. At eighteen years of age, he left home and quit college to live with the girl who became his future wife. He remarked that he didn't know what he wanted to do or rather that he didn't have the impetus to get anywhere.

His career was limited to a succession of odd jobs with intervening periods of unemployment. Married life was not too successful. His wife was subject to periods of depression too. They separated for about one year but had resumed their married life before the therapy began.

Two periods of his life stand out with vividness in his memory. At eleven years of age the patient recalled that he was very aggressive with girls. This was met with rebuffs and thereafter the patient said he became aloof. At fifteen years of age he joined a young socialist group and then later an anarchist group. One can surmise that in these groups he made the first social identifications of his life.

In answer to my question, the patient remarked that the outstanding feelings in early childhood, as he recalls them, were feelings of disappointment and loneliness. From adolescence on he suffered from severe headaches and nausea (probably migraine) which he connected with feelings of helplessness.

Prior to the present therapy, the patient had been under treatment with several different analysts for periods not exceeding six months each. One of them, he said, "shattered me." This happened when the analyst painted for the patient a true picture of his ego at the same time that he laughed at him in a good natured way. In his elated moods the patient carried himself as if he was a person of some importance. He had no hesitation in telling one about his talents and abilities which had no relation whatever to his accomplishments. As a result of the deflation of his ego, the patient said that he developed symptoms of diarrhea, indigestion, insomnia and headaches. He felt that he had derived little help from the other analysts.

The early sessions of therapy were marked analytically by the necessity to bring about some balance between the claims the patient made for his rights based upon his evaluation of his abilities and the recompense, which was based upon his productivity. The therapeutic sessions occurred once a week for one hour. Each hour was begun with a statement of how good he was and how poorly he was appreciated. He stated his case well. His speech was fluent and his words were well chosen. His criticism of employer and employee relationships, his analysis of his boss, were well made. He had no feeling, however, for the struggle which is involved in the attempt to develop a small business. He showed an exaggerated narcissism and a lack of feeling for other people's problems.

It is interesting at this point to analyze the physical structure of the patient. He had a well developed figure, slightly taller than average height with a proportionate body build. The biggest disturbance in his physical appearance was a depressed sternum with an outward flare in the lower ribs which gave them a chicken-breasted look. The pectoral muscles were prominent and seemed overdeveloped. The shoulders were elevated. The neck was thinner than what one would expect for this body build. The head and face were regularly shaped with no obvious distortion. The diaphragm was held high and contracted and this probably accounted for the flare outward of the lower ribs. Below, the belly was flat and seemed to lack fullness; the legs did not strike one as being weak.

Respiratory movements were limited to the chest, which seemed mobile. However, the shoulders did not participate in these movements. Neither inspiration nor expiration involved the abdomen to any visible extent, the diaphragm retained its contracted position. Strong extension of the arms produced marked tremors in the shoulders, head and neck. In the action of striking the couch, a clearly defined expression of anger was visible in his face, the teeth were bared, the nostrils flared and the eyes dilated. However, the blows lacked resonance and the patient jumped up each time he landed a blow. Arms, shoulders and body moved as one piece, as if they were frozen together. It was clearly evident to me that an extremely strong ring of tension surrounded the body at the shoulder girdle. This was most manifest in the tense pectoral muscles.

While it was easy to arouse the patient to anger through hitting, the emotion did not persist long. After a few movements he would be out of breath, panting and tired. Not infrequently, the hitting aroused feelings of helplessness and ended in crying.

One would be justified in diagnosing the presence of orality from the history of repeated depressions. One could go further and describe the total character structure as oral. This would mean that the dominant pattern of behavior is determined by oral tendencies. On the one hand, we have the patient's remarks about deep-seated feelings of loneliness, disappointment and helplessness. On the other hand, there is the narcissism, the obvious need for attention and praise (the search for narcissistic supplies) and the desire to be fed. "The world owes me a living." The patient admitted that at one period of his life he had been a gluttonous eater and had been quite fat.

As I describe the therapy of this patient, it would be well to discuss and elaborate on the known psychological aspects of this problem and to compare them with the bioenergetic dynamics of this character structure.

There is first the history of lack of success in work. Generally one finds in these characters an inability to hold a job for any length of time. Another patient told me that as soon as she was sure of a job she had to do something to be fired or else she had to quit. Not uncommonly this may go so far as a rebellion against the necessity of work or, more commonly, against the demands of the work situation.

My patient showed this attitude clearly. Yet the alternative to work, as I could point out to him in his own experience, was depression. Difficult as it was for him, and I would agree that given his problems the demands of reality were difficult for him, there was no other way. As I mentioned earlier this issue dominated the early phases of his therapy. He had to admit week after week that, despite his resentments and complaints, he felt better while working than before. The physical therapy which decreased his tensions, improved his breathing and increased his energy potential aided immeasurably. In this respect he was a most cooperative patient and he would pound the couch regularly until he was out of breath. Gradually his vital capacity increased and he could sustain a continued activity for longer periods.

One of the early problems which arose was a falling off in the patient's genital potency. Following his return from work he was generally very tired and he had little feeling for sexual activity. This disturbed him considerably. I pointed out to him that he had only enough energy at this time to meet the demands of his work situation. Since this was the more important reality function, it took precedence. As he became stronger he could expect an improvement in this realm too. The patient was satisfied with my explanation and we proceeded.

The love relationship of the oral character shows the same disturbances which we find in his work function. His interest is narcissistic, his demands are great and his response is limited. He expects understanding, sympathy and love and he is overly sensitive of any coldness in his partner or in the environment. Since the other person in the relationship cannot fulfill these narcissistic demands, the oral character develops feelings of rejection, resentment and hostility. Given the fact that the partner has his own needs which the oral character cannot easily satisfy, the situation is one of almost constant conflict. The dependence is great but it is frequently masked by the hostility.

The problem of maintaining this patient in a continuous work function was complicated by his dissatisfaction with his wife. This, of course, gave me ample opportunity to analyze his neurotic tendencies and point out their narcissistic character. But as one went into the background,

one found nothing positive to replace it with. He hated
his father and he despised his mother. She was always
dirty and unkempt. One of his earliest memories was of
himself lying in a crib and crying bitterly. His father
loomed above him with stern face and admonishing gesture. His forefinger wagged at the child and he said "shsh
shsh." He was not to make any noise.

Analysis is one thing, satisfaction is another. My patient
felt that he must find another partner. His wife did not
give him enough. This was easy for him, since the marriage was rather loose and there were no children. Each
new liaison was approached with excitement and enthusiasm. Once or twice there was greater pleasure but not
one of his several affairs held up. More and more the patient was forced to the realization that his problem was in
himself.

I need not detail that in the course of a year's work the
patient had many impulses to quit his job. He was not
being paid enough, he was not appreciated enough. His
boss was an ulcerous type who exploited his employees.
Yet in his position as production manager he could see that
if one didn't put any pressure upon factory workers they
would produce little. He held the job because he knew it
was the best job he ever had. Further, he now accepted
the fact that he had to work and he wanted to prove that
he could hold a job for at least a year.

The vicissitudes of a small business made him realize
the problems his boss faced. During a slow period, he
saw that he was earning a salary while his boss had to
sweat it out to keep his business going. This was an important step for the patient, for he lost his resentment at
some of the inequalities of the social system. He declared
that he did not want to change places with his boss.

As we shall see later, the gradual acceptance of reality
is one of the major goals in the therapy of the oral character. It turns him outward. Another major problem remains, however. The fear of rejection, which in the case
of the oral character is a fear of loss of the loved object,
lurks in the unconscious as a great danger and threat.

Analytic thinking relates the depression to this fear. Fate decreed that this threat should materialize for this patient in the course of the therapy.

One can appreciate that it is difficult to live with an oral character. This marriage was not a successful one. My patient discovered one day that his wife was in love with another man. I don't believe that it came unexpectedly to the patient yet it aroused him to a fury that was out of all proportion to the feelings he had for his wife. She called me one night to say that her husband was furious and that he was out looking for her lover to kill him. Some friends of his got him to speak to me on the phone several hours later and I calmed him down somewhat.

When I saw him the next day he was still very angry and determined to "beat the man up." It wasn't too difficult to point out that his anger was misplaced. He had talked of leaving his wife several times. Why did it matter to him so much that she wanted to leave him? Was this not the repressed anger which he had for his father who had prevented him from crying for his mother? When I pointed this out to him, he began to cry deeply.

His hatred had made him strong but he didn't know what to do with it. The analysis now could uncover the whole infantile tendency in his personality. Like an infant, he was interested only in his own needs and in his own feelings; he was narcissistic. His wife left him, in part at least, because he was unaware of her needs. Just as he had not been happy with her, she had not been happy with him. Recently, he had remarked that he felt that he had outgrown his wife as a result of his therapy. Should he not have realized that she had to find some meaning in her own life? His inability to feel for others or to be aware of the needs and desires of those in relationship with him was a weakness in his personality. He had faced the same problem in his job. In that situation, through identification with his boss, he had made a significant advance in his capacity to work. Could he not now achieve a similar improvement in his capacity to love?

In the therapy of the oral character one must bring

home to the patient the fact that what he holds out as love is experienced by others as a demand for love. The statement, "I love you," should be interpreted as "I want you to love me." His attitude in the love relationship is not based on the adult pattern of give and take. Rather it resembles the infantile pattern of need and demand in which the other person is regarded as the provider of needed narcissistic supplies.

Although I pointed this out to the patient, I did not deflate his ego by driving the point home. Instead I aroused his compassion for his wife and her lover. It was not difficult to do since my patient, like all oral characters, was a sensitive person. We spent several sessions on this subject and it proved to be the turning point of the therapy. He realized that a separation was in the best interest of each one and that they would be happier apart. He had gained a new found respect for the problems of others.

As his resentment and hatred disappeared the problem remained of what to do with his anger. I suggested to him that this aggressive force was too valuable to waste on destructive ends. It could be directed to reduce the patient's physical tensions and to strengthen his structure. The patient agreed. The turning point in every analytic therapy occurs when the aggression which has been freed through analysis is consciously directed at the task of improving the present day function.

The physical therapy continued now with more power. The patient felt stronger and more charged each week. He found a new girl and they established a relationship which is still going on as of this writing. Then he lost his job, but this did not upset him much, although at this point we stopped the therapy. Some months later he was in business for himself and when last I heard from him, he was in an executive position with an established firm.

Rather than summarize this case, let us study several aspects of the problem posed by this character structure. I can illustrate the main points with salient facts from this and other cases.

The oral character is marked by the desire to talk and the pleasure in speech. This is typical. One finds it in all such individuals. He loves to talk about himself, generally in a favorable light. He can take the center of the stage easily and he suffers no uneasiness from his exhibitionism. It differs from the exhibitionism of the hysterical female or phallic male which always has a genital significance. In the oral character it is a means to gain attention, interest and love.

This need for verbal expression goes with a high degree of verbal intelligence. His intellectual ability is nowhere reflected in accomplishment but, despite this, the oral character has an exaggerated ego picture of himself. True, this ego inflation is a concomitant of periods of well being and excitement. In moments of despair and hopelessness, feelings of helplessness and inadequacy dominate the picture.

The tendency to depression cannot be overlooked. Wherever it exists it is pathognomic of oral tendencies. Where it dominates the personality, it determines the oral character structure. Depression generally follows a period of increased activity and seeming well-being. The pattern of elation and depression tends to be cyclic, although this may not always be evident.

The masochistic character does not suffer from true depression, although he is subject to periods of reduced activity. The masochist gets stuck in what should be called the masochistic morass. This appears to be a nonreacting state; however, the masochist can be easily aroused by any suggestion which promises pleasure and when so aroused he is as energetic as before. Not so the oral character in depression. This latter is a very resistant state.

On a deeper level one finds a difficulty in the perception of desire. The oral character will frequently say, "I do not know what I want." The truthfulness of this remark struck me many times. Material wants are rarely important. I was impressed by a similar remark from two such patients who said, "above all, I want peace." They have a reluctance to accept the reality and the necessity of struggle in life.

Aggression and aggressive feelings are weak in the oral character structure. The oral character does not make a strong effort to reach out for what he wants. In part this is due to a lack of strong desire, in part to the fear of reaching. The fear of reaching can easily be made manifest. The justification given is the experience of constant disappointment. He hopes to get what he wants somehow without reaching for it; in this way he can circumvent the feared disappointment.

Anger is not an easy emotion to arouse. In its place one sees a hyper-irritability. There may be much sound and fury but the strong feeling is absent. One must not be misled by fantasies or dreams of hostility. A forceful expression of hostility in action or gesture is difficult to elicit.

The oral character is the "clinging" type. In an extreme case this may show itself as a sucking of another person's strength and energy. In all cases the inability to stand upon their own feet is truly characteristic of this type of ego structure.

Another characteristic of the oral character are feelings of inner emptiness. These feelings are present in every true case regardless of the superficial behavior. Loneliness, despite a love relationship, is also frequently present. In the therapeutic situation the demand for assurance and support cannot be overlooked or ignored.

The above symptomatology is more or less common to all cases of oral character structure, although, of course, there is an individuality to each patient. The specific details are determined by quantitative factors as well as later experiences. An oral character structure may sometimes be covered over by behavior which belongs to a more highly developed type of ego organization. Whether the character is determined by the higher organization with the persistence of oral traits or is fundamentally oral in type can be ascertained only after careful evaluation of the behavior.

On the whole, psychoanalytic observations of oral traits show close agreement, with those outlined above. Abraham (1924) mentions the following traits as orally determined: abnormally over-developed envy, neurotic parsimony, melancholic seriousness or marked pessimism, clinging and leeching, an obstinate urge to talk, intense craving and effort, hostility, impatience, restlessness, and, finally, a morbid intense appetite for food and an inclination to various oral perversions. Unfortunately many of these traits are not typical of the pure oral character but are due to the admixture of suppression and frustration to an earlier severe deprivation. Hostility is found in all neurotic characters. The hostility of the oral character is generally impotent as are so many of his actions.

A real comprehension of the dynamics of this character structure requires the reduction of all oral traits and symptoms to one basic disturbance in terms of which each can be explained. Once the pattern of this disturbance is established, the problem of diagnosis and therapy is greatly eased. That pattern can be most easily established by a study of the bioenergetic processes.

The following observations of the structure of the body, the quality of its movements, the location of its tensions, point to an answer.

The oral character tires rapidly when engaged in a continuous physical activity such as striking the couch. Many of these individuals feel that they lack energy. The abandonment of the effort is only partly due to muscular fatigue. When they resume it is not for long. This assumption of a lack of energy finds support in the fact that this structure is frequently associated with low blood pressure and a low normal basal metabolism. While tiredness and lack of energy are not pathognomic for this structure, their presence always indicates a strong oral element in the personality.

The chest is generally deflated, the belly is without turgor and feels soft and empty to palpation. The deflation in the chest may produce the depressed sternum which is found in some oral structures.

Movements of reaching out with the arms are generally experienced unpleasurably. When exaggerated and maintained, the action frequently leads to crying and to the feeling of inner emptiness. Stronger actions such as hitting the couch seem to lack power. The patient may feel the weakness and impotence in his arms and hands. The movements are not supported by an adequate flow of energy.

The legs are never experienced as stable supports for the body. The feeling of weakness in the legs can be shown to be based upon a true perception of their function. The legs tire rapidly in positions of tension. Control of their movements is poor and coordination is inadequate. The oral character tends to compensate the weakness of the legs by locking the knees while standing. This gives the leg a feeling of rigidity which is achieved at the expense of flexibility. The feet are weak and not infrequently the arches are collapsed. The specific quality which characterizes the structure of the oral character may be described as "disjointed." This differs from the schizophrenic dissociation which we described earlier. One such patient remarked that her arms and legs went in all directions and that she had no real control over them. Another product of the weakness of the lower extremities is the loss of contact with the ground. Falling anxiety is common in oral characters. Nightmares and falling dreams are common experiences of these individuals in childhood and later life. The fear of falling can be demonstrated in the therapeutic session.

Headaches are a rather common complaint of the oral character. One can explain their frequency by the tensions in the neck and head. Any effort which produces a strong flow of energy into the head may result in a pressure headache or in dizziness to which these individuals are very prone.

The muscular tensions are particularly disposed in the

oral character. One always finds a very strong ring of tension about the shoulder girdle and at the root of the neck. The scapula is tightly bound to the thorax. The pectoral muscles are overdeveloped in the man. In the woman, the breasts tend to be large, pendulous and to lack tone. The longitudinal muscles of the back are very tense, especially between the shoulder blades, at the level of the diaphragmatic crusa and at the insertion into the sacrum. The muscles of the pelvic girdle are as tightly contracted as those of the shoulder girdle. Marked muscular tension seems absent from the front of the body but this is only because of the deflated condition of the chest and abdomen. Deep palpation will reveal spasticity of the rectus abdominis muscle.

Above all, the muscular system of the oral character structure is underdeveloped as compared with the frame of the body. This failure of muscular development is typically oral wherever it is found. In contrast, the schizoid character frequently shows a muscular hypertrophy, the masochist a condition best described as "muscle bound."

The gag reflex is fairly easy to elicit. This may be due to early feeding disturbances with persistent tendencies to vomit.

It goes without saying that the genital function of the oral character is weak. Orality and genitality are antithetical tendencies. One is related to the function of charge, the other to discharge. The sexual drive of the oral character is for contact with the partner. Discharge is subsidiary. It represents the need to take in, to feed from the partner; that is, the genital organ serves the oral need. Genital discharge in both male and female is weak. In the woman, a definitive climax or orgasm is frequently absent. There is never any frigidity however. What is lacking is the strength of the motor drive to discharge the feelings.

One of my patients whose perception of himself and of his physical condition was acute gave me a diagram of

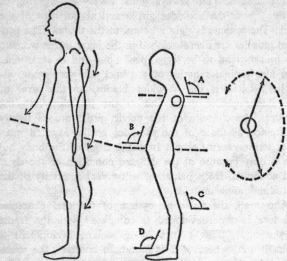

Fig. 12. Oral stance. Analysis of posture diagram shows obtuse angles (A, B, C, D) at points of compression. Legs, from knees down, are contracted and undercharged.

the stance of the oral character (Fig. 12). It is a self perception of course. I am reproducing it here together with his observations since they are particularly revealing. For comparison, he also submitted his concept of the natural stance (Fig. 13). (See also Schilder's [1950] account of the postural model of the body.)

DYNAMIC ANALYSIS OF ORAL AND NATURAL STANCE

1. In the oral character structure the weight of the body rests upon the heels. In the natural stance the weight of the body rests upon the metatarsal arch between the ball of the foot and the heel.

2. The oral character tends to have a sway back. The shoulders are pulled back and this is compensated by a forward thrust of the head. Below, the buttocks and pelvis are held forward. The back, in the natural stance of the body, is straight with the pelvis "cocked" backward. It reminds one of a tail being held high or of a trigger which is cocked for action.

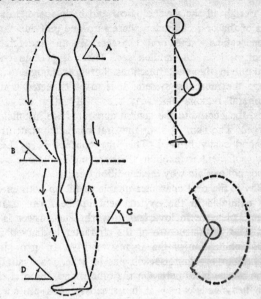

FIG. 13. Natural stance. There are acute angles (A, B, C, D) at points of tension. Analysis of the posture diagram shows a ready-to-spring attitude of movement.

3. Forward movement is initiated by the head in the oral structure whereas in the natural stance it starts from the ground.

4. Since the legs are not strong enough, the body is supported by the spine in the oral character. The back is not available, therefore, for aggressive action. In the healthy individual, the body is supported by the legs which retain the flexibility of the knee joint. This type of structure is marked by its free aggression and its ability to "back up" its actions.

5. In the oral character structure the angles of compression between the body segments as shown on the diagram are obtuse and open. In contrast, these angles in the healthy structure are acute. The body is held like a compressed spring, charged and ready for action.

6. The ends of the organism face forward in the natural stance. This can be interpreted as a reaching out to the world. In the oral character the ends of the organism are pulled backward thereby expressing his rejection of the world.

Through all the psychological and biological manifestations of the oral character, there runs one unifying thread. Bioenergetically the oral character is an undercharged organism; it is an unfilled sac. There is enough energy to maintain the vital functions, but not enough to fully charge the muscular system. It is to be expected that the peripheral regions and structures will suffer most. The limbs, the head and the genital apparatus are insufficiently charged. The skin, too, in the oral character structure, is thin and easily bruised. This one concept is, as I shall show, sufficient to explain all the symptomatology noted. It does not explain why the condition persists.

Why is the oral character unable to fill up with energy? It is available in the environment in the form of food, oxygen, pleasure in love and in work. The answer is evident. The very structure of the character is derived from an immobilization of the aggressive drive. If an organism is afraid to or cannot reach out to take, the availability of the means is no help. On the other hand, the oral character has needs which it must satisfy. His attitude towards these needs is infantile. He expects the adult world to recognize these needs and to satisfy them without the necessity for any effort on his part.

Whether one thinks psychologically in terms of fear, or biologically in terms of muscle tension and the energy of drives, the oral character is marked by an inability to be aggressive. The weakness of the aggressive drive is reflected in a weakness of the back. The tiredness of which they complain can be traced frequently to this weakness in the back, which is localized in the lumbar region. By virtue of this fact, the oral character as a personality lacks backbone feeling. We characterize this character as "spineless" in contrast to the masochist who although his muscles are markedly over-developed also has no backbone feeling. The oral character has great difficulty in taking a strong opposing stand and the tendency is to run rather than face an attack.

Now let us look at the picture again to see how the var-

ious traits in this character structures relate to this concept of lack of aggression and inner emptiness. The envy
can be explained by the feeling of deprivation. Clinging
and leeching are the adult equivalent of the infant's sucking and being carried. The weakness in the arms and legs
also suggest an infantile structure. The abnormal appetite
must be interpreted as an attempt to fill up. Impatience
and restlessness result from the unsatisfied longing. One
should not be surprised if the oral character shows malice
and hostility at times. However, the expression of hostility
is vocal and only rarely physical. The inability to reach
out to the world leads to a terrible loneliness; and disappointment must be the inevitable lot of the adult who
hopes that his wants will be recognized and satisfied without his own effort. We can understand, too, the failures
which haunt such characters in adolescence and adult
life. The more basic manifestations of this disturbance,
however, require some elaboration.

What is the bioenergetic reason for the cyclic phenomenon of elation and depression? In my therapeutic work
with these patients, whenever I observe them going into a
phase of elation with inflated ego thoughts, I caution
them against the ensuing depression which will follow.
A patient whom I treated told me that she felt there was
genius in her and that I had never appreciated that fact.
She was in high spirits but not otherwise overexcited. I
did not deny her statement. Who am I to say that she
did not possess that quality. Besides she was a girl of some
talent. On the other hand, she had never produced anything exceptional. If one asks, why does she tell me this,
the obvious answer is that she seeks my admiration and
affection. This is psychologically true, but one should also
ask, what is the basis for the thought. Her remark stemmed
from a feeling of being a genius and was not consciously
uttered to win my admiration and affection. It was related to her high spirits but it was also a portent of the low
spirits which will follow.

We can also say, psychologically, that this behavior is

an attempt to establish and maintain self-esteem. I will agree with Fenichel's (1945, p. 407) statement that, "descriptively, an immense increase in self-esteem forms the center of all manic phenomena." But this only substitutes another term in the equation. We shall have to understand the origin of this increase in self-esteem which, we must recognize, is not in accord with reality. I always have the impression that this kind of ego picture is like an inflated balloon. It rises easily but it can burst easily and depression will follow. Depression, seen in this light, is always a secondary phenomenon. If the elation can be avoided, depression will not occur. Fenichel (1945, pp. 408, 410) looks upon the depression as primary. Historically, it is. He says, "The triumphant character of mania arises from the release of energy hitherto bound in the depressive struggle and now seeking discharge." I can only add that depression is not a struggle but a diminution of energy processes and impulse formation. The energy does not seek discharge; that is a genital function. Rather it rises to the head seeking contact with the world. Given the severe block in the path of the energy flow to the arms, it follows the infantile path to the head and mouth. It is this that produces the volubility of the oral character in the elated stage. Fenichel is also aware of the illusory nature of the reaction. "The mania is not a genuine freedom from depression but a cramped denial of dependencies."

The lack of independence can be discerned despite the exaggerated self-esteem. The energy flows up, not down. The legs are undercharged and contact with the ground is not maintained. There is no increase in genital excitation. Because of this lack of contact with the ground, which is the counterpart of the psychological lack of contact with reality, one feels that these individuals are "in the clouds," "floating somewhere up there," "out of touch."

When one looks at the phenomenon bioenergetically, the picture becomes clearer. In elation the oral character reverts to an early infantile stage. It is reaching with the mouth for the breast. At this stage there is no need to be independent. At this stage, the infant can rely upon the mother's strong arms to hold it and support it. Its strength is the strength of its parent's body. The feeling of oneness with the parent is very strong. Is it not astounding that a child can be held in any position, if held with love, and not be afraid. Think of a baby monkey as it is carried through the tree tops, secure in its closeness to its mother's body.

The excessive talking can be regarded as symbolic sucking movements. We recognize that in his speech, the oral character seeks admiration and affection, "narcissistic supplies." In speech the mouth can also express the aggressive function of biting, in what we would describe as "biting sarcasm." However, the speech of the oral character is well thought out and rational, excepting the exaggerated ego picture it paints. These individuals possess, too, the clear and straightforward intelligence of the child. We can surmise, therefore, the origin of the exaggeration. For this ego picture is like the ego of the infant: diffuse, uncrystallized and omnipotent. A true ego comes into being with an awareness of the external world and with the anchoring of the longitudinal energy swing in the genital function. The infant has neither the ability nor the perception of give and take. Where the adult ego is a function of the ability to give and take, the infantile ego is related to the ability to take in and absorb.

Observation of infants has taught us something of their feelings. We assume that the newborn child does not recognize the breast as belonging to another person. His world is limited at first to the immediate area about his mouth. Then gradually it extends to other parts of his body. Not for a long time is it more extensive than his personal environment. And in this world he is the ruler, the all-important one; and so it should be, for his need is greatest. The inflated ego of the oral character in elation corresponds to this infantile ego. We sense its unreality in the mouth of an adult, but try and convince your patient of that. I couldn't. In the case of the girl who claimed that she was a genius, I could only bring her back to the real problems which confronted her. But at the next session, she told me, "You were right when you predicted I would get depressed."

The bubble must burst. The adult world cannot satisfy this infantile demand. Sooner or later the oral character meets with rejection. Disappointment results and a depression ensues. During the period of depression, energy movement is greatly reduced. This is followed by a period of recovery at the end of which impulse formation begins anew. Depression, as a bioenergetic phenomenon, is analogous to the remains of an inflated balloon which has burst—a piece of limp rubber. It produces a loss of self-esteem. However, I would not agree with the psychological interpretation given by Fenichel. "Depression is a desperate attempt to compel an orally incorporated object to grant forgiveness, protection, love and security." It is rather the result of the failure of such an attempt. It is easy to understand the subjective feelings in depression of loss and emptiness.

Because the need for acceptance and affection is so great in the oral character, he cannot and does not armor as does a rigid character structure. His dependence creates an extreme sensitivity to his environment. Under favorable conditions, that is, with acceptance and affection, the oral character blossoms. If conditions become unfavorable, he reacts with irritability. His tolerance of tension is very low. The reality principle is weakly developed.

Depression can be prevented by two means. If the disappointment could lead to crying, impulse formation would be maintained. This is the natural infantile reaction to deprivation. It functions in adult life, too, as an effective means of releasing certain tensions. The young infant has no other means of releasing tension. It is only much later, as muscular coordination develops, that he becomes capable of reacting to frustrations with anger. Anger and crying have two different functions. Anger is directed against an obstacle which is interposed between a desire and its object. It aims at the removal of the obstacle. Anger is not the proper reaction to the loss of a loved object. A feeling of loss calls for tears. Either reaction, however, would function to prevent the onset of a depression in the adult.

We are thus led to a consideration of the genetic factors in the development of the oral character structure. By its designation, we imply that this neurosis has its origin in traumatic experiences which occurred at a very early age. The concept of the unfilled sac can only be explained by the assumption of a lack of satisfaction during the first year of an infant's life. The infant who develops an oral character structure later is like a person who is still hungry after a meal. Obviously the meal was insufficient. Not only insufficient to give a sense of full enjoyment, but insufficient to satisfy the energy needs of the infant. The infant hungers for his mother and cries. The neurosis will not develop so long as the crying continues, for it will prevent a "primal depression." But how long can a child cry?

We can illustrate with an example from another situation which is not too dissimilar. Some friends told me how they got their baby to sleep at an early hour. He was put to bed at seven one night and his parents left the room. He began to cry and cried continuously for four or more hours, but his parents refused to respond. Finally, he fell asleep. The next night when he was put to bed at seven, he cried for only one hour before he fell asleep. After that, when put to bed at seven, he made no sound and soon fell asleep. It must be recognized that not every child is the same. Some have more energy and will put up a greater fight against deprivation. But any child who cries to the point of exhaustion stops only because the agony and pain become unbearable. When such early experiences are relived in the therapeutic sessions, the patient occasionally remarks, "I feel as if my heart would break." Most frequently, the suppressed crying is experienced as an intolerable tension in the belly. The guts are tied in knots as if they were wrung dry. One has only to observe the reactions of patients as crying deepens to realize this. The child who cries himself out gradually stifles the longing for his mother. If one agrees that the neurosis develops not from a single traumatic experience but from a pattern of repeated deprivations, one can better appreciate the power of the forces involved.

An oral character develops when the longing for the mother is repressed before the oral needs are satisfied. This sets up an unconscious conflict between the need on the one hand and the fear of disappointment on the other. In later life the repression is maintained by the structuring of this conflict into the body attitude. Psychologically, one can speak of a fear of re-experiencing the agony of the early infantile suffering, of unconscious hostility, of repressed longing. The ego has given up its conscious demand for further supplies. The child makes a brave attempt to function independently which partly succeeds. But the unsatisfied oral needs are still active on the unconscious level. They find a second opportunity to assert themselves when the genital function is definitively established after puberty. The original problem now appears as a disturbance of genitality. Disappointment on this level activates the original conflict which becomes gradually extended to embrace the whole of the individual's function.

The repression of the longing for the mother produces a child who is prematurely independent. As a consequence these children tend also to be precocious in speech and intelligence. Walking may be retarded or advanced but these children are never really secure on their legs. Their sense of balance is poor. Their mothers complain that they fall often, frequently tripping over obvious objects.

I recall a child whose mother consulted me because he had developed a coeliac syndrome. He was about three years old, rather thin and underdeveloped. When he spoke, I was amazed. He had a vocabulary and fluency of expression that was far beyond his age. I could not help but remark how intelligent he was. His mother threw up her hands. She exclaimed, "People have been telling me how intelligent he was since he could stand up." Then she added, "I want a healthy child."

Early memories and dreams of the oral character typically show feelings of abandonment or hopelessness. The following is illustrative for the memory was recalled several times in the course of the therapy. The patient related that he remembered running after his mother who was being driven down a road on a cart. He was crying desperately, then he fell down exhausted. His next recollection was that when he awoke his mother was lying beside him in his house. The latter recollection did not overcome the feeling of being abandoned.

In the case presented in this chapter, a similar memory was recalled several times. The patient was lying in a crib crying for his mother. His father appeared, leaned over the crib, and with raised forefinger and stern countenance admonished the patient not to cry, saying "shsh." The patient was very frightened. Each recollection of this memory made him furiously angry with his father.

Another patient had a recurrent fantasy which came at night when he put the lights out. He saw a single white dot in the center of a black field. This vision disturbed him very much and he tried to find its meaning. Then one night as he opened his eyes wide, he "saw" that the white dot was a scream. Then he had a picture of himself lying in a crib, alone and frightened in a dark room. He screamed. Then he felt himself "whiting out," as the white dot grew larger and filled out the field.

I cannot agree that it is ever possible to fixate a child at the oral stage through the satisfaction of its needs. Fenichel's (1945, p. 405) statement on this point is incorrect. "Regarding the factors which create oral fixation in the first place, the same holds true as for other fixations: the determinants are extraordinary satisfactions, extraordinary frustrations, or combinations of both, especially combinations of oral satisfaction with some reassuring guarantee of security."

In the oral stage of its development, the child is only less dependent on its mother than is the embryo or fetus. Logically, one can compare the nursing infant to the fruit maturing on a tree; the nipple corresponds to the stem. A natural separation of the fruit occurs when it is fully ripe. It then falls to the ground to start an independent existence by rooting itself in "mother" earth. It is only the unripe fruit which presents a resistance to its separation from the tree. Certainly the combination of "oral satisfaction with some reassuring guarantee of security" would be considered an optimum condition for the child. Extraordinary frustration would be a determinant of an oral trait. There is only one combination which could produce an oral fixation without a specific oral deprivation. Oral satisfaction coupled with a basic insecurity is one of the etiological factors in the development of a psychopathic character. The psychopathic character has a strong oral fixation. In addition, there is in most cases a masochistic under-structure. However, the dynamics of the psychopathic character structure is so complicated that it must be reserved for a separate study.

There is more to the analogy between the oral character and the unripe fruit. In the case of fruit, the more mature it is before the separation from the tree, the more natural sugar it contains and the sweeter it is. The unripe fruit is bitter as is the immature organism which loses its vital connection to its mother too soon. The oral character is bitter and this bitterness can be found in every individual who has a strong oral element in his structure.

Just as the unripe fruit fails to root itself satisfactorily, so the immature human organism has great difficulty in establishing its functional roots in reality. The physical counterpart of this problem is the inadequacy of the legs and feet. The functions of support and locomotion in the lower extremities are dependent upon contact with the ground. In the oral character the weakness of the lower extremities prevents the development of that independence and aggression which is essential to the mature adult function. Bioenergetic analysis constantly confirms the functional identity of these dynamic processes with their analogous psychological concepts.

If it would seem that a child is fixated at the oral stage by overindulgence, further investigation will frequently reveal an earlier severe lack of maternal support. No amount of toys, clothes or attention to material wants can ever make up to a child the lack of physical contact with and affection from its mother. Such children may act like spoiled brats. It would seem that they get everything they want but they are not happy. What they really wanted, contact with their mother's body, was denied; that desire being repressed, nothing will now make them happy.

The therapeutic problem posed by the oral character structure is one of the most difficult in analytic therapy if one lacks a knowledge of these dynamic concepts. One cannot supply a mother's love or even an adequate substitute for it. But even if that were possible it would not solve the problem. These patients are no longer infants and what is required is an adult pattern of functioning. Roots must be developed and strengthened to permit the full function of an independent existence. This is done on two levels. Psychologically, resistances must be analyzed and eliminated so that the patient can form adequate relationships in work and love. At the same time, physical therapy to strengthen the legs and establish good contact with the ground is necessary. The independence of all adult organisms is maintained by their dependent relationship to the universal mother, the earth.

We saw earlier that energy to fill the organism is available in the environment but that the oral character is unable to capture it. Their aggression must be mobilized and made available. This is no easy undertaking for even though the patient may feel the lack of aggressivity, many deep-seated resistances and blocks must be eliminated to mobilize the drive. The fear of rejection, abandonment and physical pain are real. We counter this with the reality of the present day misery in which the oral character finds himself. Since the oral character does not deny objective reality as the schizophrenic or schizoid character does the problem yields to patience, the consistent logic of adult reality and support.

Support for the oral character takes two forms. First, the therapeutic environment must be favorable. This is truer for the oral character than for any other neurotic problem. It requires an acceptance of the patient as an individual. He must feel that the therapist is on his side and will not abandon him. Second, the justice of his complaints must be granted. Only on this condition will he agree to the validity of the analyst's insistence upon the necessity of his acceptance of adult reality. The oral character changes to the degree that his adult functioning improves. The character analysis must be done systematically and concurrently with all work on the muscular tensions.

We start the bioenergetic therapy with the legs. These are strengthened through special exercises and more energy is brought down into the feet. The work on the legs is primary and continuous throughout the therapy. Where the direction of biological growth is from the head downward, bioenergetic therapy is oriented from the ground upward.

The muscle tensions in the back and shoulders must be released. Movements of reaching and hitting are encouraged in the sessions. The contracted throat opening should be enlarged so that a greater intake of energy through breathing is possible. All body work is functionally oriented towards the ultimate end, to increase genital feeling and the ability for genital discharge. As the genital charge increases, the charge in the head also increases, so that a better grasp of external reality is possible.

If the ego is inflated it must be gradually deflated. Not until the patient hits bedrock does it become possible to build a substantial and permanent improvement in function. Throughout the treatment, the patient must be kept in contact with reality in work and love. This may seem an obvious remark; its application is not so simple. The patient who complains about the difficulties of his job may be justified in his complaints. However, they must not serve as an excuse for drifting from one activity to another. In fighting to maintain his function even in difficult situations the oral character gains strength and assurance. Drifting prevents the development of functional roots which are so necessary to growth.

This outline of the therapeutic task is intended as a guide and not as a formula. The analytic process requires that the patient be brought into awareness of his problems and that his own energy be mobilized to effect their solution. However, there is no substitute for the analyst's intuitive feeling of each patient and no rule can determine his immediate response. No two characters are exactly alike. While the energy differences are essentially quantitative, the emotional expression in behavior of these differences have a qualitative aspect. Let me indicate the problem as it manifested itself in several different cases.

A young woman, twenty-six, who had been in psychotherapy for some time, presented more or less all the enumerated traits and symptoms of the oral character. In her physical appearance she was rounded out but the subcutaneous fat was unusually soft and her skin bruised easily. Physical activity was minimal and work on the muscle tensions was experienced very painfully. The gag reflex was very difficult to elicit and was associated with intense fear. She expressed it as a fear of what would happen to her head should she give in to the gag. It was impossible to get the patient to attempt a somersault even with my help. She was desperately afraid of losing control. She complained of fear of dying and she suffered from frightening nightmares. It was difficult for her to get moving in the morning and she was consistently late for work. The intense fear of energy movement in the body coupled with the lack of turgor in the skin pointed to a very undercharged organism. After months of character analysis and bioenergetic work, the issue was fought out on the question of lateness. She was habitually late for work. Once she accepted the rationale of the demand that she be on time to work, there was a marked change in her attitude. The necessity for physical exertion was accepted next and, with a more sustained physical effort, a considerable improvement in her condition was realized.

Another patient was a young man in his late twenties. He was tall and thin and the arches of his feet were so collapsed that his feet were turned inward. At the beginning of his therapy he wasn't working. He gave up his last job two years previously. He was living at home and supported by his parents. On the physical level he responded quickly, but there was no effort to look for work. He complained bitterly about his relation to his girl. He felt that she wasn't giving him anywhere near enough affection, support and understanding. If only she would, he could look for work.

Soon after the therapy began, he took his own small apartment and lived on some money he inherited from his father. It then became apparent that he would make no move until this money gave out. Despite all the analysis of his anxiety in presenting himself for a position, he did not make a real effort to find work. The money ran out. Now, I pointed out to him that so long as anyone would support him, he would not face the task of making himself independent. I withdrew my therapeutic help on the realistic ground that he couldn't pay for it. I did not abandon him but told him that we would resume as soon as he had a job. This is a ticklish position but it must be taken and in such a way that the patient understands the basis of the action. Meanwhile his girl friend also severed her relation to him.

I saw him six months later when he had found a job and was anxious to resume the therapy. What had sustained him was his feeling that the physical approach offered a real solution. We began on the physical work with intensity. There were no more complaints. His improvement was such that I was amazed. He gained weight, broadened out and his feet became straight. He developed a new relationship with a girl but here I had to help him realize his responsibilities in the situation. Before the year was over he had doubled his salary. He told me that he could never go back to the old way.

Is it necessary to make a character diagnosis before one can treat a neurosis? Cannot one analyze resistances as they appear and achieve the same result? Of course one should and does analyze resistances systematically as they emerge. However, a characterological change does not result until the resistances are seen as a constellation which then becomes obvious to the patient as his character structure. Without this, I doubt if there would be an end to the number of resistances which can appear. Once the character is delineated, the patient recognizes and understands his own resistances. Thus, a diagnosis is arrived at sooner or later. It is like fitting the pieces of a jigsaw puzzle together. Knowledge of the total picture greatly simplifies the task. Success is only achieved when the total picture is assembled.

There is one aspect of the oral character structure which we have commonly observed but which we have not discussed. One will frequently find that the tall, thin, asthenic individual has an oral character structure or a very strong oral element in his constitution. I do not believe that this relationship is an accidental one. If form and movement are functions of energy dynamics, growth, too, must be subject to its laws. Psychologically, the oral character is "up there," that is, above the earth. His behavior pattern is the contrary of what we call "down to earth."

Some time ago I presented a case of an oral character structure to psychiatrists and analysts attending a seminar. He was a young man six feet five inches tall with exceedingly long, thin legs. He was always tall, even as a child. The family doctor had said that "he grew up too fast" and for the first time this made sense to me. No one else in his family was of more than average height. In the discussion of his background, he said that his mother had called him "her little man" when he was still quite young.

She had always dressed him up. He was bitter towards his mother. One could interpret his over-growth as a desire to grow up fast so as to be his mother's little man, or as an attempt to grow up to get away from her. In the latter sense it could be interpreted as a growth away from the earth. Whatever the interpretation, the full understanding of this problem will depend upon a knowledge of the energy dynamics of the endocrine functions.*

Psychologically and somatically, the oral character is the result of a forced or too rapid maturation and independence of the growing organism. If the roots are weak and lack proper anchorage the energy of the organism rises upward. In plants this would produce a long thin stem or trunk with a premature development of leaves and flowers. We cut our plants back to strengthen their roots. Why should we deprive our human offspring of their naturally long biological babyhood? It is the best guaranty of health and happiness in later life. One must deplore the tendency to have young children mature too rapidly. Were it not for the fact that nursing is coming back into its own among American women, the situation of the future generations in this country would be serious. It is also encouraging to find mothers who will nurse their children for longer than one year. Their reports on the value to the child of this natural practice may induce other mothers to do the same.

To properly appreciate the nature of the oral character structure and of orality in character formation it should be contrasted with other types, especially the masochistic structure. One must bear in mind that the effects of deprivation, if they do not produce an oral character, play an important role in the formation of character structure on the higher levels of ego organization. To the extent that a child experiences a feeling of deprivation in his earliest

---

* Compare with the studies of W. H. Sheldon on body structure and temperament in *The Varieties of Human Physique* and *The Varieties of Temperament* (New York, Harper, 1940, 1942).

years, to that extent genitality, independence and responsibility is weakened.

The problem of character formation and structure
would be easy if the biological factors of oral need and
genital satisfaction were the sole determinants of character. Masochism, however, introduces a very special element. Let us now turn our attention to this problem.

10

The Masochistic Character—1

The problem of masochism has been and still is one of the most difficult therapeutic problems that faces the analytic psychiatrist. With a sympathetic and competent analyst, the oral character responds well to the analytic interpretation. While progress is slow, it is nevertheless consistent and secure. Not so the masochist. After a superficial improvement there generally is a relapse to the old symptoms and complaints, and this pattern tends to repeat itself throughout the course of the analysis. This response has become known as the "negative therapeutic reaction."

Freud's failure to overcome this "negative therapeutic reaction" in the case of masochism led him to formulate the concept of the death instinct, although the theoretical justification for the concept was based upon other observations as well. On the other hand, the clinical solution of the problem of masochism by Reich pointed the way to comprehension of the biological basis for the neurosis. Reich first published his observations in 1932 as an article, "Der Masochistischer Character." Later it became one of the chapters in the more comprehensive study, *Character Analysis*, and it remains today one of the great achievements of psychoanalytic theory and technique. Although I will quote liberally from Reich's article, the reader is advised to study it in detail for the thorough psychoanalytic presentation of the problem.

Reich's clinical refutation of the death instinct theory did not completely invalidate Freud's deductions. If we deny the existence of a primary masochism, that is, a death instinct, we still agree that clinical masochism is sadism turned against the self. The problems of the mechanism by which a drive turns inward against the self was not explained by Reich although the conditions which set that mechanism in operation and its results were fully elucidated.

Masochism was originally studied as an aberration of sexual behavior. Freud had pointed out quite early that masochism could exist in forms which lacked the masochistic perversion or masochistic beating fantasies. These he called moral masochism and feminine masochism. Reich solved the clinical problem not by concentrating on the masochistic perversion as was usual but by the analysis of its characterological reaction basis. He introduced thereby the concept of the masochistic character structure, a concept which despite the twenty years or more since its publication has not been fully understood by analytically trained therapists. In the case which follows, the absence of a masochistic perversion or of masochistic beating fantasies in no way affects the character designation.

This patient came to therapy after having been in treatment for more than five years previously. He was motivated to resume analytic therapy by his experiences during a trip abroad for business purposes. All his old symptoms came back in exaggerated form. He developed intense anxiety which almost paralyzed him, a severe lumbago, and he suffered from several attacks of the grip, and loss of weight. He could not carry on his work and was forced to return to therapy. His complaints were the same as when he first began treatment. Foremost among them was the feeling of anxiety, which would become so strong that the patient felt frantic. He complained about the almost complete lack of genital pleasure in sexual intercourse, saying that if he had this pleasure he could function better. At times he would suffer from an inertia during which he would sit for hours and brood. However, he could be easily aroused from this state. He complained, too, about negative feelings towards others: contempt, resentment, the desire to belittle. He had two physical complaints; one was the loss of his hair which was dry and greying although he was a young man, the other was the development of varicosities in the veins of his legs.

It is instructive to analyze the complaints a patient brings. The masochist suffers keenly from anxiety. We have seen, however, that the oral character too can have much anxiety. In this they differ from the passive-feminine and the rigid character types whose higher ego development has enabled them to bind their anxiety except under special circumstances. But the anxiety of the masochist differs from that of the oral character. The former experiences his anxiety when under some pressure of work or in social relations, the latter is anxious before meeting the situation. Now while this difference is slight it is important, for it is the sense of continually being under a great pressure which characterizes the masochistic ego. The inertia of the masochist is not the equivalent of the depression of the oral character. Reich's patient described it as the "masochistic bog or morass," both very apt expressions. Conscious negative feelings are never found in other character types to the degree that they are felt or expressed by the masochist.

The autobiography of this patient, written in the early part of his therapy with me, is very instructive. In addition to the fact that he had been in therapy previously for many years, his memories are quite clear to an early date. "Toilet troubles" plagued him at a very early age. He remarks, "My mother forced me under pain of hitting me to sit on the toilet for one to two hours and try and 'do' something—but I couldn't." After the age of two, he recalls that he was constipated and his mother inserted her finger into his anus and stimulated it. He received frequent enemas up to the age of seven and horribly tasting laxatives. In addition to the difficulties of toilet training, eating was a big problem. "To my mind as I look back it's not that

I didn't eat—it was that I didn't eat enough. My mother forced enormous quantities of food into me. . . . I remember, at the age of three to four, running around the kitchen table, my mother after me with a spoon full of something I didn't want in one hand and a belt in another hand, threatening to strike me which she often did. . . . One of the worst things my mother did was to threaten to leave me or to go up on the roof and jump off and kill herself if I didn't finish my food. She actually used to step out of the apartment into the hall, and I used to collapse on the floor in hysterical crying."

From the age of two and a half to four he suffered from terrible nightmares. "I awoke terrified and saw the room getting infinitely large and a man's face leering at me from the corner." This face reappeared in later years and again during the therapy. At about three or four and for a few years thereafter, the patient noticed that his penis withdrew into the scrotal sac. From five years onward, the patient had irrational fears which by the time he first began therapy had almost developed into paranoid symptoms.

Although he was physically large and strong as a boy, he was "very frightened of getting into physical combat with anyone." He did not defend his rights. He suffered many humiliating experiences of a small nature. As a child he slept in the same bedroom as his parents. He remembers being afraid when he heard them having intercourse. Of his father, he recalls little other than occasional walks together. His mother used his father as a threat but he says that he was never hit by him. At seven years of age, he saw his father's large adult penis and was awed by it.

Masturbation began at nine years; puberty at ten years. Soon after, he began to have "horrible frantic feelings" while masturbating which he wrote still plague him. Throughout adolescence, he masturbated regularly always with "horrible urgency and franticness and guilt."

It was also soon after puberty that his emotional illness showed itself fully. "The first horrible anxiety I experienced occurred about the age of eleven to twelve, and was caused by the thought of having relations with a girl. I would flush, choke up and feel anxious and frantic at the same time. I never could approach within five feet of a girl even with my tremendous longing because if I did I would be paralyzed with anxiety. This went on until I was seventeen and happens still in the present—sometimes with the same severity." He dates the breakdown of his functioning from the age of eleven to twelve, when his sexual misery began. "From then on my personality was as it is now—anxious, suffering, longing, etc." Although he didn't concentrate much at high school his average was almost 90. He was less successful in college but finished without trouble.

I quoted from the patient's autobiography at some length to show the real suffering and frustration which he experienced. Let me complete the picture with a description of his physical appearance. He was well built, rather muscular with a big chest and large shoulders. His body color had a dark hue, his hair was black but greying and thinning. The face had no special expression at rest; under emotional effort it screwed up (became contorted) in a very strong look of disgust and contempt. At the same time the back of the neck tensed in a powerful contraction. The expression of this contraction in neck and face could be interpreted as extreme obstinacy. One noted that the chest moved easily with respiration and the abdomen was soft. This, too, changed under the influence of a strong feeling. The abdominal muscles tightened into a hard knot. The buttocks contracted and the pelvis was pulled forward and upward. The shoulders were tightly held but not square. Very marked rigidity was obvious in the thighs and legs. The joints of the knee and ankle were rather inflexible so that bending was difficult. The feet were tightly contracted with a high arch. The toes had no spread.

It is relatively easy to make a diagnosis of masochism in this case from the history and the presenting complaints. We shall see that it is just as easy to arrive at the diagnosis from the structure and function of the body once its expression is understood. Let us look at this character problem more closely.

Reich summarized the main traits of the masochistic character as follows: "subjectively, a chronic sensation of suffering, which appears objectively as a tendency to complain; chronic tendencies to self-damage and self-depreciation [moral masochism] and a compulsion to torture others which makes the patient suffer no less than the object. All masochistic characters show a specifically awkward, static behavior in their manners and in their intercourse with others, often so marked as to give the impression of mental deficiency." According to Reich, only when these are all present and determine the key to the personality and its typical reactions do they add up to the masochistic character structure.

The case that follows I treated many years ago and I would like to recount that experience. At the beginning, I did not recognize the masochistic character structure of this patient. My thinking at that time was oriented along the lines of muscular tension and energy blocks and I had moved away from character analytic concepts. I began with the attempt to reduce the tensions in the back of the neck and at the base of the skull. This work together with the patient's hitting the couch produced some improvement. The patient said that his head felt better and lighter. While it lasted only a day or two it could be repeated each session. But nothing further developed. The patient was very cooperative and his complaints were sensibly expressed. Since I could go no further in this direction, I turned my attention to other aspects of his bodily function.

When the patient attempted to make a deep expiration, as in a deep sigh, the chest relaxed but the descending wave piled up into a hard knot in the middle of the abdomen. I mentioned earlier that the same thing happened under the influence of a strong affect such as crying. It made me think of someone straining at stool. The patient looked as if he were trying to push something out against a resistance. In the discussion of this attitude the history of the patient's toilet training experiences was brought to light. The autobiography from which I quoted was written later. He also said that he experienced this tension in his belly while working. Regardless of the conditions, he always felt under pressure while at work and he had to push to get some release. If the pressure in the belly became too strong, it would develop into a feeling of franticness.

A basic quality of this patient's function became clear to me. His behavior recapitulated his early toilet experiences. On the one hand his function, anal and otherwise, was blocked by an intense subconscious obstinacy which could be translated as "I won't." On the other hand, the exigencies of life required that he produce something, in work as well as anally. He had to move (bowel movement included) regardless of his holding back, but he could not move naturally. The only possible way was to push through, to squeeze it out against the resistance. Given the severe tensions, the pushing is both comprehensible and necessary. Unfortunately, pushing increases the resistance and this patient was trapped in a vicious circle. My patient perceived the tension in the back of his neck as spite and resentment but he had no control over it.

What I have described here as the typical quality of the function of this patient can be seen in all masochistic characters. They are pushers or squeezers and all of them contract the abdomen to get some emotional discharge. It is typical for masochistic patients to squeeze the penis during masturbation or at the moment of ejaculation. Translated on a broader scale, we can say the masochist does not deny reality as does the schizophrenic nor reject its demands as does the oral character. He accepts reality at the same time that he fights it, he admits the rationality of its demands at the same time that he resists them. Like no other character he is in a terrible conflict.

As I observed this regular pattern in the first two masochistic patients I treated, I felt that these were really anal characters. Neither, however, complained of constipation nor of any other anal disturbance. They had none of the other traits associated with Freud's description of the anal character: orderliness, parsimony or obstinacy. The latter could be interpreted but it was never expressed or visibly manifested. Then I thought that this was really intestinal or rectal functioning. One other consideration added support to this view. Both patients lacked a "backbone." In any situation calling for a firm stand they made an effort but collapsed soon after. This collapse, too, is typical for all masochistic character structures. Another interpretation can be made. The lack of a "backbone feeling" makes these individuals contract the gut to give them a sense of support. Of course, it cannot and does not stand up and collapse is inevitable.

At this time I worked with the patient to mobilize the spite in the back of the neck by the strong expression of "I won't." I also encouraged the hitting to develop the feeling of the backbone through the release of anger. These maneuvers had a good effect and again there was further improvement at the end of each session, but it did not carry over through the week. Upon inquiring into the patient's condition each hour, I received the same complaints. Perhaps a little less anxiety, some slight abatement of the tendency to push, but always the lack of sexual pleasure, the dominance of the negative feelings, the absence of joy. I was getting annoyed. True the complaints were justified, but I could sense a whine in the voice. Then it dawned on me that just this whining revealed a masochistic character and now, psychoanalytic and bioenergetic understanding began to flow together for me.

He had complained earlier about his depressions, during which he would sit and brood for hours. It was easy to see that this brooding was not a real depression. He would get stuck and bog down much as he got stuck in the middle of his belly during the sessions. Later he described one of these moods. It might follow a fight with his wife. He would then be caught between the desire to "patch it up" and an equally strong feeling to "wait until she comes to me." Any move on her part would bring him out of it and it is just in this that the bogging down differs from a true depression. Further, the masochist has a highly charged energy system. It may get stuck between two antagonistic impulses but the affect can be easily aroused.

It was necessary to analyze the whining. No sooner did I point it out than resentment appeared against me. I was not doing enough to help him, he felt contempt for me, but it was all expressed in a whining voice. Here was the masochistic provocation timidly uttered. "You are no good. You cannot help me." He saw clearly the connection between his wanting me "to do it for him" and his mother's action in stimulating his anus to promote its function. How would he respond if I did accede? Would he not defecate on me, figuratively speaking? What other meaning could I attach to it after I had worked hard and shown him positive results?

Reich (1949, pp. 225, 226) points out that "the masochistic torturing, the masochistic complaint, provocation and suffering all explain themselves on the basis of the frustration, fantasied or actual, of a demand for love which is excessive and cannot be gratified. This mechanism is specific for the masochistic character and no other form of neurosis." But why is the demand for love excessive? Reich says, "The masochistic character attempts to allay the inner tension and the threatening anxiety by an inadequate method, that is, by demands for love in the form of provocation and spite." Of course, it must fail. The masochistic character is close to the awareness that it must fail. It had happened many times before. He will even acknowledge the fact. One may add, then, that on a certain level he wants it to fail. Is this the need for punishment of which we read so much? It has two other interpretations. First, failure justifies his own inadequacy. The blame can be put on others. Second, success is feared for it brings the masochist into the spotlight and arouses very strong anxieties associated with exhibitionism.

For several sessions I analyzed the patient's behavior in

terms of the masochistic morass. He is like a drunk who has fallen into the gutter. He whines for help but when one's hand is extended to him, the samaritan is pulled down into the gutter to be besmirched. This is not consciously intended, it is the inevitable result of the masochistic character's pattern of behavior. To understand the problem one must conceive of the masochist as one who has been deeply humiliated and feels inferior. Their behavior, then, can be interpreted as, "See, you are no better than I am." His early history leaves no doubt as to the humiliations he had suffered.

This analytic work produced the first real emotional improvement. The patient remarked that he had experienced several periods of optimism during the past week and that this was the first time in more than a year that he had had such good feelings. This is not to say that he was free of all complaints, they were there too. Nevertheless, I was encouraged. Optimism in a masochistic character is rare for the masochistic state is founded upon deep feelings of despair and hopelessness.

During the next six weeks there was a steady improvement. The optimistic feelings continued, there was a big decrease in the whining, and the patient developed the ability to tolerate more energy in his head. This last was evident from the brightness of the eyes, the color of the face and the carriage of the head. The surge of energy into the head gives it a lighter feeling and a brighter appearance. There was no change, however, in genital pleasure.

This period came to an end as a result of a discussion I had with the patient about his attitude towards his wife. He had criticized her for a lack of aggression but she had reacted strongly to the criticism with the result that he became quite morose and upset. I had entered into the discussion because I did not feel that the solution to his problem lay in the conversion of his masochism into sadism. When the patient came to the following session, he was back in the masochistic morass. He was full of negative feelings towards me. These included hatred, contempt, the feeling that I wasn't doing anything for him, etc. Despite the fact that recently he had experienced great fear of me when he looked at me with direct, open eyes, he did, nevertheless, entertain the idea that I was a "shit" as he expressed it. After almost a year's work, the masochistic tendencies persisted strongly. I pointed out to him that despite my efforts which pulled him out of the morass, something kept pushing him back into it. Something as yet unknown. The clue came soon.

He remarked that during the past week, while listening to Beethoven's music, he had cried. Now real crying had pulled him out of the morass many times, yet this time it did not do so. And, he added, that while crying he was aware of an impish feeling inside himself which said, "You don't really want to cry, you're only doing it to fool them." Then it suddenly became clear to me. It was as if a devil inside him was laughing at him and at me and mocking our efforts to free him from the morass. I do not know if this simple observation would have made the impression upon me which it did had I not just finished reading Dostoevsky's *The Possessed*. In this story, the protagonist revealed that he was taunted by the devil. I felt that here was the mysterious something which was negating my work and the patient's efforts, and I took up the concept of the devil seriously.

To my surprise the patient told me that he felt the "devil" inside himself and that occasionally he could see him. The "devil" as the patient saw him had a man's face with a leering mocking expression, as if to say to him, "You won't succeed, you are really worthless." On the other hand, when he felt the "devil" in him, he always felt stronger and better and out of the masochistic morass. It was on these occasions that he experienced contempt for others and felt greatly superior to them. Towards the therapy, this attitude was expressed as follows: "F——you, I can get out of this myself. I don't need you. You are worthless anyway." And he recognized that it was the "devil" in him that had led him to criticize his wife the week previously.

The patient now told me that he had been haunted by the "devil" ever since he was a child of two years. During the early years of his childhood he had suffered from nightmares. While lying in his bed at night he frequently saw the "devil" in the corner of his room watching him and leering at him. At the same time the room receded from him. He was terrified by these experiences and had lived in constant dread of them.

Another thing which became clear about the patient was the meaning of his own facial and bodily expression. When hitting the couch his eyes stared, his brow raised up and two lines appeared which radiated from the brow upward and outward. In addition he leered in such a way that he actually looked like a "devil." There is no doubt that the patient saw a projection of his own expression for his description of the devil corresponded with what I saw on his face. How this occurs I cannot explain but some remarks on the nature and function of "the devil" can be made at this time.

From the patient's description of his mother and from the many things he related about her, I had no doubt that the devil was related to his mother. He has described to me the deep humiliations he suffered at her hands. She criticized every move he made, called him degrading names and said he was worthless. She leered at him and mocked him. The persistent overemphasis upon feeding and defecation undermined the child's reliance upon his own feelings. But even more disastrous to the child's developing ego was the mother's practice of inserting her finger into his anus to promote a bowel movement. By this coupling of an erotic satisfaction with a humiliation she undermined the independence of the growing personality. The father's role in this situation seems to have been a passive one. He was simply a "mysterious stranger" upon whom the child projected his own inner feelings.

In his attempt to protect his ego, the child will adopt the methods of his oppressors; I use the latter word advisedly. I believe that this is an important mechanism in the process of identification between a child and parent. We adopt the tactics of the enemy in order to defeat him. At any event this patient did beat his mother at her own game. He became more cunning, more contemptuous, more hateful, etc. Only so did he survive. If the child employs the devil's means, he in effect sells his soul to the devil who then takes possession of him. Now, the devil is in the patient. His future visions are of himself, projected upon the fact of another. "It was an adult man's face which leered at me, open mouthed, teeth glistening, eyebrows arched, face generally glistening with evil radiation. This generally happened in the dark to the accompaniment of gyration of the 'darkness.'"

That it comes from himself the patient now knows. "Just in the last session of therapy I actually called the thing 'a devil' and associated it with the involuntary 'orneryness' which is in me. What made the association was the 'leery' feeling I would get with my negative feelings and the leer on my face. Like when you say something to me about something, a leery feeling comes over me and a voice says evilly, 'What do you know about this —you piece of dirt?' etc. etc. These seem to be things I would say to my mother or she to me."

Two weeks later the patient told me that he identified the leering expression of the devil with a sneaking feeling in the genitals and in the body generally. He recognized this sneaking sensation as the basis of his attraction to women and understood its relation to pornography.

It is beyond the scope of this chapter to enter into a full discussion of the phenomenon of the devil. Reich has described the devil in the schizophrenic process. I have observed a devil function in every masochistic character structure. It is a negative force, expressing itself in doubt and distrust, the antagonist to the heart sensations of faith and love. The devil does his dirty work by blocking every expansive outgoing impulse with doubt or distrust. In the masochistic character, the distrust, founded upon early infantile experiences, is deeply entrenched and stubbornly resistant to attack. So long as it exists, a negative therapeutic reaction can be expected. It can only be dislodged through careful character analytic exposure. The position is only surrendered temporarily. At the slightest suggestion of antagonism it is quickly resumed. But the devil can be overcome if the heart feelings, love, God, eros, dominate the brain and the genitals.

The role of the eyes in the process of projection was observed in the following incident from a succeeding session. With his eyes wide open in an expression of fear, the patient remarked that he observed the devil's expression on my face. Then when I got him to continue to look at me with open but relaxed eyes the projection disappeared.

Soon after these sessions the patient reacted in a way which completely freed him temporarily from the masochistic state. He came into the session with a strong feeling of sadness. Without whining he expressed his distress at his condition. There was no frantic feeling evident. He spoke a few words and I had a very strong intuition to wait. Generally, I begin the session actively, either with a discussion or through movement. This time, I waited for him to come to me.

Within a few minutes he began to cry rather softly. The crying was not so deep as I would have liked but it was not forced. With the crying, he exclaimed "No" many times spontaneously. I could see the pulsations as the energy moved through him and down into his legs. This continued for some twenty minutes as I sat quietly.

The patient then became aware of good feelings in his chest but he felt that he could not express them. I asked him if he wanted me to help him with a suggestion. In response to his affirmation, I suggested that he lift his arms up and ask for help. He lifted his arms but all he could say was "Please, please." Later he added, "Please, help me." Could he address his plea more specifically? I had in mind a plea to God. But that he could not do. He remarked that he "trusted no one." He then began to cry softly again.

After a time I pointed out that he was like a person lost in a desert or wilderness from which he could not hope

to escape by himself. He admitted this. Was it not imperative, therefore, that he overcome his distrust and ask for
help? Yes it was, but he could not. Again more crying. I
again suggested that he offer a prayer to God. This he
immediately felt was impossible. He then told me that he
had prayed to God as a child asking God to prevent his
mother and father from fighting. He claimed that this
prayer was not answered. I countered that every prayer
was answered to the degree that it was truly felt and expressed. This is based upon the fact that prayer opens the
heart to the outside universe and so serves to release tension and gain new energy. If one prays correctly, one asks
for strength or for the release of a burden. I pointed out
that we do not know how much worse the patient would
have felt had he not prayed. The patient began to cry
again very softly but deeply. He rose from the couch and
kissed me on both cheeks. His eyes were clear and free
from distrust.

Such an emotional experience frequently proves to be the
force which loosens the character structure. It was so in
this case. Psychologically the masochistic tendencies diminished greatly. In the following sessions, there was an almost complete absence of the whining and of the contempt
and a marked decrease in the deep-seated distrust. However, the physical tensions and blocks which form the
basis for the masochistic character attitude are not removed by such analytic work. They no longer function in a
unitary fashion as a masochistic character structure, and
so each energy block can now be tackled individually. The
job of strengthening the flow of energy into the head and
genitals had to be continued and until this was more advanced one could anticipate further relapses into the masochistic morass. But now the patient knew the way out and
a relapse was only momentary. The therapy continued
for several months with slow but marked improvement.

Positive attitudes towards the therapy and the therapist
gained increasing ascendence as the patient asserted
himself more easily in the sessions. The mobilization of

the shoulders through hitting the couch gave the patient a feeling of strength in action. On the other hand, the spastic condition of the thighs, legs and feet required more work.

At this stage in the patient's treatment, the technique of bioenergetic therapy developed to include more intensive work on the tensions of the lower limbs. A strong ego structure can be built only upon a secure foundation and such a foundation was lacking in this patient. Further, as long as his sexual dissatisfaction continued, one could not count upon a permanent improvement. Energy discharge either as a genital function or in terms of movement depends upon contact with the ground. Neither the collapsed arch of the oral character nor the tightly contracted arches of the masochist afford sufficient stability. In addition, the masochistic character generally has an overdevelopment of the calf muscles and of the muscles at the front of the thigh. At the same time, the hamstring muscles at the back of the thigh are quite tense. The result of this condition is an inability to execute a normal pelvic thrust.

The masochistic character pushes his pelvis forward, he cannot swing it. He pushes the pelvis forward by squeezing the buttocks together and contracting the abdominal muscles. One can understand the small amount of genital satisfaction he derives. The very act of genital discharge in the masochist creates the tensions which prevent an effective discharge from occurring. Normally, the pelvic swing in sexual intercourse is controlled by the legs. Where the legs are weak, as in the oral character, or immobilized, as in the masochistic structure, a natural pelvic movement is impossible. We shall inquire into the reasons for this immobilization in the next chapter.

We noted that the tendency to collapse, that is, to fail and to sink into a morass feeling, is typical of the masochistic character. But he does not completely collapse physically; he does not fall to the ground. It is countered by the tension in the muscles of the calf and of the front of the thigh. Movement is sacrificed for security. I mention this now because this was the problem which I attacked in this patient during the next phase of his therapy. Then, for the first time, I got the positive results I wanted.

As the pelvis was gradually freed and its forward movement developed, the patient reported new feelings of genital pleasure in sexuality. True, they were inconsistent, but an important step had been achieved. And the patient recognized the validity of this approach immediately. Still, an important step remained. At each session, the patient waited for me to tell him what to do. Although he knew the specific exercises we used and the results they brought him, he did not assume the responsibility for initiating the movements. One might say that he still wanted his mother "to insert her finger into his anus" to get things going. Only after this was worked out analytically did a consistent improvement ensue.

Bioenergetic therapy is fundamentally an analytic procedure. The analysis is done on both the psychic and somatic levels. The expression of feeling verbally and in movement is employed to bring about a release of the blocked affect. A statement of the therapy with this patient would be incomplete without at least a mention of the analytic work to free the patient of many of his minor masochistic traits: the compulsion to overload himself with work, his anxiety in the face of pleasure, his inability to buy nice clothes, his difficulty in the expression of affection.

When the therapy with this patient ended he felt satisfied with the results. He had gained insight into his disturbance and he felt he could meet the normal situations of life without fear or failure. Above all he had gained control over his body and he knew how to prevent or overcome the collapse of his ego and sexual drives. However, one must bear in mind Reich's (1949, p. 246) admonition: "One also should not forget that a definite dissolution of the masochistic character cannot take place until the patient has led an economic work and love life for a considerable period of time, that is, until long after the conclusion of the treatment."

We are in a position now to discuss the more important features of the masochistic character structure. The central problem of masochism is the seeming need of the masochist to suffer or to derive satisfaction and pleasure from pain or from experiences which others regard as unpleasant. In the usual case, this need to suffer finds expression either in masochistic fantasies which accompany sexual excitation or in provocative behavior which leads to the castigation of the masochist and his humiliation. In the former case the fantasy, such as being beaten or tied, is a necessary condition to the ability to reach a discharge in the sexual act. The provocative behavior must be viewed as having a similar function. The humiliation leads to sadness which opens up the deeper feelings. After a fight with his partner the masochist functions better sexually.

Analytic studies had revealed that the masochist has a very severe superego. The need to suffer was interpreted as an attempt to assuage the superego, to allay the pangs of a guilty conscience. Underlying the masochistic behavior is spite and hatred. This latent hatred in the masochistic character would fully justify the severity of the superego or conscience. But these observations do not resolve the difficulty. The question remains, how is it possible for an impulse (hatred) which is originally directed outwards towards the world to turn inward upon the self?

Freud's (1950a, pp. 74–75) answer to this question was the assumption of a death instinct, that is, a primary instinct of destruction which is originally directed against the self. Under the influence of eros (love) this instinct is directed outwards towards the world as sadism mixed with love. According to this concept, masochism results from a condition which produces a defusion of these two instincts so that the death instinct is now free to resume its original direction against the self. "We should not be astonished to hear that under certain conditions the sad-

ism or destruction instinct which has been directed outwards can be introjected, turned inward again, regressing
in this way to its earlier condition." This masochism he
called "secondary masochism" to distinguish it from a part
of the original death instinct which is not included in this
displacement "outward" and which he called primary
masochism.

The existence of a death instinct is highly debatable.
There are, however, in man and in animal life, two streams
of energy which give rise to impulses which may be designated as instinctual. In our discussion of this problem in
chapter 5 we described these instinctual impulses as aggression and tender feelings; the latter can be equated
with eros. As Freud says, under certain conditions these
instinctual tendencies may defuse and become antagonistic. Let us see how this happens.

When we study the physical structure of the masochistic
patient we are impressed with several features. Structurally, they all tend to be heavy set with a strong muscular development. And both male and female are physically
strong. It is not the physical strength of the lithe, agile
athlete; it is more like the crushing strength of the gorilla.
In their physical appearance too, they remind one of a
gorilla for their back tends to be rounded over, their neck
short and thick, the arms and thighs well muscled. Every
true masochistic character shows the condition known as
"musclebound" and this accounts for their ataxic behavior
in movement and expression. When tracing the energy
movement in such a structure with its severe tensions
at the back of the neck and in the lower lumbar region,
one finds an explanation for the masochistic behavior. Figure 14 (*left*) is a diagram of the energy movements in the
normal individual. Contrast this with the condition in the
masochistic character (Fig. 14, *right*).

In the masochistic structure the aggressive drive is bent
inward as if huge pliers had been applied to the two ends
of the organism. As a result the tender feelings are compressed between the arms of aggression and bound. Eros,

represented by the single line, struggles to break out of this binding, but fails and collapses. It would seem that it is the failure of eros to keep the arms of aggression directed outward which accounts for the aggression being turned inward. Such an interpretation would support Freud's thesis of a primary death instinct. This, however, would not explain the genetic development of masochism

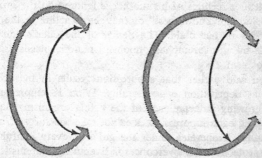

FIG. 14. Energy movements in the *(left)* normal and *(right)* masochistic individual.

nor do justice to the fact that, in the normal individual, the two instincts are not antagonistic but complementary. Each needs the other.

This case is particularly illustrative for the study of the genetic factors which produce the masochistic character structure. First, we must recognize that the masochistic character does not complain of feelings of inner emptiness. Rather, he complains of feelings of bursting, internal pressure, and the inability to release the tension. He shows no signs of deprivation. Each masochist feels that his mother loved him. It is the way that love was expressed which created the disturbance and not the lack of it. The expression "smothering" applies to the mother of the masochist and not to the mother of the oral character.

The ego of the masochist is crushed as if caught in a vise. This is almost literally true. At the upper end it is the forced feeling, at the lower end it is the imposition of a strict training to excremental cleanliness, which constitute the two major pressures. To turn the aggression inward the pressure must be applied before the aggression is anchored to reality in the genital function and in the mental function. The child reacts to these pressures very strongly. He cries, he fights back, he withdraws. By look, by gesture and through movement he appeals to his mother for sympathy and understanding. This appeal to the tender feelings of his mother is ignored on the ground that "mother knows best" or that she is acting in the best interests of her child. The denial of the child's spiritual needs by an overemphasis upon his material needs creates masochism.

We said earlier that suppression results in masochism just as deprivation causes orality. What is suppressed is the growing independence of the young organism, the developing ego. Suppression does not take the form of overt hostility. It operates under the guise of overwatchfulness, overprotectiveness, overconcern. Eventually, submission is achieved and the masochist becomes a good boy. Strong measures are employed: nagging, punishment, appeal to the child's love for the mother and, finally, the threat of deprivation of the mother's love if the child does not obey. It ends in a state of terrible confusion for the child: his tender feelings are called upon to block his aggression, the blocked aggression prevents the expression of tenderness. In no other character structure is the ambivalence so marked, the conflict so great.

In the development of this character structure, the muscular system of the growing child is subverted from its natural function of movement to the neurotic function of holding. The muscles overdevelop to hold back negative impulses and to control natural ones. Forced feeding tends to cause vomiting which then is held back causing severe tension in the neck and throat. Premature insistence upon excremental cleanliness forces the child to employ the levator ani muscles, the gluteals and the hamstrings to gain anal control since the external sphincters have not yet come under voluntary control. The severe muscle tensions in the shoulder girdle hold back the hatred and rage against the mother. While masochism develops from practices begun during the second year of life, the masochistic structure does not take definitive form until later. There generally is an intervening period of struggle, temper tantrums and rebellion, and not until this resistance finally subsides is the masochistic structure fully jelled, usually after puberty.

Can we give another answer to the question of how and why being beaten or the fantasy of being beaten can be experienced pleasurably? Reich's (1949, p. 217) answer to this question was one of the masterpieces of analytic investigation. He showed that the masochist does not strive for the beating but for the pleasure of the sexual release like any other person. "The specific pleasure mechanism of the masochist consists in the fact that while he strives for pleasure like any other person, a disturbing mechanism causes this striving to fail and causes him to experience as unpleasurable sensations which the normal person experiences as pleasure when they exceed a certain intensity." This specific disturbing mechanism is the spasticity of the musculature which on the genital level prevents the tender feelings from strongly charging the organ of discharge. The result is the pile up of energy in the pelvis; tender feelings in the belly, aggression in the buttocks and thighs. At this point, in severe cases, the masochist experiences sensations of bursting, he becomes frantic, and a release must be achieved. In this situation the masochist is like the tense, cranky, irascible child whose annoyance of its parents finally results in its being beaten after which the child cries, quiets down and falls asleep. The parents frequently sense the need of the child to cry, and they may even sense the mechanism. The beating in the case of the child increases the tension to a point where holding is impossible. The blocked energy breaks through in convulsive crying and sobbing. It is the crying and sobbing which discharges the tension and produces the relaxation, not the beating.

The situation in the masochist is similar. The fear of strong genital excitation causes a holding of the energy in the pelvic organs and buttocks. Here it bogs down, not being able either to move outward in discharge nor inward in retreat. An intolerable state of anxiety results. One of two alternate mechanisms may be employed to reduce the tension. By squeezing the thighs together very strongly and by compressing the buttocks, the energy may be forced into the genitals and discharged. This is the common masochistic practice in masturbation and intercourse. Of course, the pleasure of the discharge is considerably reduced. What the masochist has done here is to adopt an anal practice to the genital function. The other way would bring about a stronger discharge but it requires the application of force to increase the tension to a point where holding becomes impossible and a breakthrough to discharge occurs. The masochistic beating or beating fantasy serves this purpose of increasing the tension.

It is not always necessary to have a beating fantasy. It is necessary that the fantasy be sufficiently powerful in the given individual to produce a strong reaction, to mobilize the additional energy needed to overcome the block. The fantasy would tend to repeat the infantile situation which originally produced the fear and tension and it thus mobilizes the aggression which is frozen in the holding attitude. Here the compulsion to repeat is shown in its clearest form, but the reason for such behavior is also evident.

The psychoanalytic interpretations of the same actions view the situation from the surface in contrast to the dynamic interpretation on a bioenergetic level. "The deepest meaning of the passive beating fantasy" seems to be: "Beat me so I can get the relaxation without being responsible for it." Psychologically, it is true that there is a "shift of the responsibility to the punishing person." The role of the nates has a double psychological interpretation. Freud had pointed out that the "nates are the special erotogenic bodily regions which have preference in the anal-sadistic stage." Reich showed that the beating on the buttocks has the function of protecting the vulnerable genital region.

The spasticity of the pelvic floor in the masochistic character extends to the genital apparatus too. In this patient there was a tendency for the penis to withdraw into the scrotum. I have seen the retraction of the penis in other masochistic characters. Psychologically, there is very strong castration anxiety. The masochist is afraid of intense pleasure sensation in the genitals. The inhibition of increased excitation changes it into anxiety. Then the lack of pleasure increases "the longing and suffering which underlies the masochistic character reactions." Reich's patients described the fear as a feeling that "the penis would melt away," or that the penis might "burst if it went on getting increasingly taut." One of my patients experienced pain in the penis as the excitation mounted. He had an uncontrollable urge to squeeze the penis and hold back the ejaculation. Masochistic fantasies of fire are related to this fear of genital heat.

The masochist transfers to the genital function a pattern of response derived from his experiences with the anal function. He is afraid of the involuntary discharge and acts to control it. This control reduces the pleasure to a point where it is unsatisfactory. His increased longing drives him to seek more genital satisfaction. As the longing increases, so does the excitation and the holding. It is a vicious circle and the masochist is trapped in it. Too frequently the analytic therapist gets caught in the same circle. In the following chapter we will study further aspects of this problem and the therapeutic measures necessary to handle it.

11

The Masochistic Character—2

The masochistic character shows typical behavior patterns in all aspects of his function. In a bioenergetic analysis these behavior patterns are observed, consistently analyzed and changed. Reich noted some of these traits. We can enlarge upon them both psychologically and bioenergetically.

Foremost among the qualities which distinguish the masochist is the subjective sensation of suffering and unhappiness which expresses itself objectively as a tendency to complain. The suffering is real and the complaints are frequently justified. It is difficult to convince the masochist that the two are not related, that the satisfaction of his complaints would not relieve his suffering. A young woman with a masochistic character structure complained that her husband was cold. He expressed little desire for her sexually although she knew he loved her. The complaint was valid but one knows that with her structure she would derive little satisfaction from sexuality. The most frequent complaint is that the therapy isn't really helping. The masochist always feels that he is making a maximum effort which is not appreciated and doesn't succeed. If so, the fault must lie elsewhere. This poses a difficult problem for the analyst since one must concede that the masochist is really trying.

218

It is characteristic of masochism that the bigger the effort the more hopeless the situation. The masochist is in a trap and the more he struggles the more bound does he become. Since his aggression is directed inward, the self-destructive nature of his activity must be kept in mind. It is just this trying that constitutes the masochistic pitfall. His effort is not rationally directed towards the needs of the situation. He tries to win approval, to gain love and affection by the sincerity of his effort. This is clearly demonstrated when one asks a masochistic character to strike the couch. He puts everything he has into the action without regard for its meaning, its purpose or its consequences. He is not angry although he may put on the appearance of anger. One must convince the masochist that his efforts do not express his own feelings, that he is doing what is expected of him; that he is trying to please the therapist, to win his approval.

To make progress in the treatment of the masochistic character one should begin by asking him to express his negative feelings. Such expressions as "I won't," "I hate you," etc. come easily. The held back aggression constitutes the negative feeling. Here, too, one must be careful that the action is genuinely felt. To be sure, I ask against whom the negative attitude is directed. If the reply does not include the therapist, one should distrust it for every masochistic character has a specially negative attitude towards the therapy or analysis.

This work of exposing the negative character of the masochistic behavior pattern may take considerable time but it should be diligently pursued. It is impossible to afford any substantial relief to the suffering so long as this basic negative attitude persists. Enclosed within this layer of negativity, the masochist distrusts the world, reality and the therapist. No love or approval can penetrate the barrier and no positive feeling can be expressed through it. This is also the reason for the masochistic suffering. He wants to come out but dares not, he wants you to release him but he does not trust you. Dostoevski makes an observation which is particularly appropriate to the masochist. In *The Brothers Karamazov*, Father Zossima remarks, "Hell is the suffering of those unable to love."

What makes the treatment of masochism so difficult is the deep distrust through which the masochist regards the world. We saw that it is even difficult to get a sincere expression of negative feeling from him. Everything is so tainted with distrust that the masochist ends up distrusting himself, his action and his improvement. Since this distrust is based upon experiences in early life which would justify such an attitude, one cannot expect the patient to give it up quickly. In the face of this resistance, the analytic therapist must gain the patient's confidence and good will if he is to achieve a positive result. But it is like scaling the sheer face of a cliff. The analyst matches the strength of his positive attitudes supported by his understanding against the obstinate negativity of the masochist. To those who have grappled with this problem failure is no surprise and no deterrent. Sympathy for the real suffering of the masochist and approval of every positive expression must underlie the analytic and bioenergetic work.

The tendency to complain is, as Reich pointed out, the objective expression of the masochistic suffering. But it is the manner of the complaint more than its substance which stamps it as masochistic. Given the efforts and the failures, the longing and the lack of satisfaction one must concede to the masochist the justification for his complaints. It is the whine in the voice, the constant repetition, the implication of blame, which arouse one's suspicions that the complaint is not meant to set forth a problem. Sooner or later it will arouse the therapist to anger and, strangely enough, after such a reaction one notes an improvement in the masochist's feeling and behavior. One realizes that this is typical provocative behavior motivated by the same need which produces the masochistic fantasy or beating. The masochist provokes, bringing the situation to a boiling point, so that he can get some emotional release.

It is important to know the bioenergetic dynamics of the suffering and the whining. The energy of the organism is trapped by the inwardly directed aggression which closes up the outlets. The longing, contained within, creates the suffering. But the outlets are not completely closed. That would be death. Rather they are severely constricted. A small trickle of energy flows out. Vocally, this small trickle of energy or air produces the whining sound. If the masochist really opened his throat and let his voice out he would not whine. Neither would he be masochistic.

Tendencies to self-damage and self-depreciation are another masochistic quality. These have been analyzed psychologically to mean: "See how miserable I am. Why don't you love me?" Very frequently these tendencies are not vocally expressed. They manifest themselves in the clothes and care of the body. Masochistic patients often come to their sessions unkempt and with dirty clothes. One patient told me that whenever he feels inadequate, he puts on a shirt with a frayed collar. The contempt which the masochist feels for others is also turned inward upon himself. Here, too, a provocative element enters: "Do you love me dirty and unkempt as I am?" The other side of the coin is seen in some characters who have an exaggerated feeling of cleanliness. This is, obviously, a defense reaction against strong masochistic tendencies to self-depreciation.

What are the energy dynamics of such tendencies? What is their genetic origin? I mentioned in the preceding chapter that the masochist functions on the intestinal level. We noted, too, the lack of backbone feeling. Now, we can say that, on the unconscious level, the masochist feels himself as a worm or snake. His tendency to wriggle can be observed both psychologically and bioenergetically. Again, on the unconscious level, he feels that he belongs on the ground. It is very difficult for him to maintain his body strongly erect and the tendency to collapse to the ground is characteristic. This quality results from the collapse of the longitudinal energy swing which we have described as the basis of the reality principle. The masochist fears a strong assertion and a strong genital erection. In terms of his body bearing the severe muscular tensions prevent the development of erect posture which comes from a strong energy surge. As a consequence of the blocks to the flow of the energy, the stream is tentative and hesitant. Movements are not direct and forcefully expressed, they are wild, tentative and indirect. It is the perception of this phenomenon which makes the patient feel like a worm. The self deprecatory feelings of the masochist are expressions of this perception. I take them literally as descriptive of the true state of affairs.

If we look for the common denominator of those early experiences which produce masochism, we will find it in the feeling of humiliation. The masochist is an individual who was deeply humiliated as a child. He was made to feel inadequate and worthless. What experiences would produce such a feeling? In the case discussed in the preceding chapter they consisted of forced feeding in disregard of the child's feelings and training to excremental cleanliness which invaded the child's feeling of privacy about its own body. These seem to be the most important mechanisms. The use of the enema which was and probably still is in current practice in some homes is only slightly less damaging than the mother's insertion of her finger into the child's anus. Overwatchfulness robs a child of his privacy. The old fashioned spanking in which a child's buttocks are exposed acts in a similar way.

The humiliating nature of these experiences lies partly in the forced exposure and interference with functions which every animal organism regards as personal. Try to force food into a dog or cat and see the reaction. The concern which some parents show over the bowel functions of their children stems from their own neurotic feelings of shame about those functions. It is almost impossible to find a masochist who does not have the feeling that the functions of discharge—anal, urethral and genital—are dirty. As a child, the masochist was forced to expose himself in the face of an attitude that the exposed region and function was unclean and disgusting. The insistence upon eating can create a similar problem. The child who is pushed to eat frequently reacts by throwing up the food. This action then brings forth a reaction of disgust from the mother.

The young child, just as the animal, puts up a strong fight against this interference with its natural functions. And this fight must be suppressed before a masochistic character structure will develop. However, only rarely is physical force used to achieve compliance. These mothers believe that they are acting in the best interests of their children and do not as a rule hit them. Rather compliance is rewarded with approval and rebellion with marked disapproval. Once the child submits and the pattern becomes established, all future actions of the individual are oriented towards winning approval. All masochists show an inordinate need to be approved. They strive to please hoping that approval will bring love. In this, of course, they are constantly disappointed. We do not judge those we love and we do not love those we must judge. It is humiliating for an organism to feel that its security and acceptance depends upon its servility. For the masochist in the long run becomes servile.

In the history of every masochistic character the analyst will find a period of rebellion highlighted by temper tantrums and spite reactions. At this stage the aggression is still directed outward. Masochism as we see it clinically in adult patients does not develop until after puberty. The rebellious child may show many masochistic features but there is no feeling of suffering. The tender feelings are suppressed in favor of defiance and rebellion. It is only after the sexual need strongly asserts itself that the trap is sprung. For the conflict between need and spite, conformity and rebellion, intensifies to a point where no solution is possible.

Attention to the material needs of the child with disregard for its tender feelings or spiritual needs create a masochistic problem. It is not surprising that later the masochist will talk of spiritual values but act on a material level. He tries to gain love in exchange for work and effort. He denies the importance of material things yet possessions mean much to him. He is confused in his desires, embarrassed to express his wants and doubtful that he can achieve any satisfaction.

Because of these early experiences the tensions in the masochist center about the two openings of the intestinal tract. In his throat there is the conflict created by the fear that food will be forced in or that he may throw up. In the anus and rectum there is the fear that he will move his bowels or that something may be pushed in. The shoulders are held tight to guard the throat; the buttocks and thighs are tense to guard the anus. Behind both tensions lies impulses to evacuate the contents of the alimentary tract.

The masochistic character is a pregenital structure. The problem has its inception before the genital function is established. It can also be considered one aspect of the oral problem for it prevents the natural progression to independence, although it does this not by deprivation but by the suppression of the child's feelings. Since the masochist grew up in an environment inimical to the expression of tender feelings, he can only react to any one else's tenderness with distrust. Did not his own mother play upon his sympathy and love to humiliate him? Were not his appeals and entreaties ignored? Of all this the analyst must be aware in his approach to the patient.

Given the severe tension at all outlets, the masochist can obtain discharge only by pushing or squeezing something out. Both his work and his sex functions are stamped by this quality of response. He pushes in work so that while this function can be carried on to a degree which is impossible for an oral character, it is not a relaxed and easy activity. He works with his guts but not with his heart. As a consequence spontaneity and creativity are generally lacking from his endeavors. Since the masochist puts his guts into everything he does, he is a hard worker. This is related to his strong need for approval. In the long run this pushing ties up the guts to a degree that collapse is inevitable.

This tendency to obtain discharge by pushing and straining is more evident in the sexual function than in work. But here it is more disastrous. For while pushing may produce something in a work process it inhibits the pleasure of genitality. The result is a feeling of resentment against the partner. The pattern is one of strain and recrimination, effort and resentment. Overriding the whole problem is the guilt associated with sexuality, the shame of genitality and the fear of ego assertion.

Analysis of the masturbatory practices of masochistic patients always reveals the same story. Masturbation was not practiced in the normal way. In both sexes, build-up and release were obtained by rubbing the thighs against the genitals at the same time that the buttocks were squeezed together. Sometimes the genitals were pressed against the bed but one notes the restraint in the use of the hands. It is as if touching the genital was forbidden and so it probably was. This type of masturbation produces a very weak energy discharge. The masochist cannot stand a strong discharge. One patient told me that at the moment of ejaculation he had to squeeze the penis tightly to prevent the strong ejaculatory squirt. Reich pointed out that the masochist transfers to the genital function an anal type of release which has a flat curve of energy excitation and release. Behind this behavior is the fear that a strong energy discharge would rip through the severe tensions causing great pain. There is no doubt in my mind but that it would.

It has been observed that the masochist in his intercourse with others may appear quite stupid. Even a superficial analysis would reveal that this is due to a confusion of which these patients frequently complain. They suffer from a block in the ability to express an idea or feeling. This contrasts with the fluidity of expression characteristic of the oral character. Despite this apparent clumsiness in expression, the masochist is very intelligent and sensitive. His perception and understanding of the behavior of others is penetrating and accurate. Par contra, he ignores those forces which determine his own conduct. His intelligence is used in the service of his distrust and thus it plays a sinister role in his personal life.

Just as the tendency to cyclic swings of elation and depression marks the oral character, so the energy pattern of masochism is characterized by an alternate between anxiety and collapse into a morass. Theodore Reik described it well when he wrote: "It is like sinking in a quicksand where every effort sends one deeper." It is not an impasse but a constant struggle, not a static state but an intensely dynamic mobile condition. Every movement forward is made in the face of increasing anxiety until exhausted the masochist falls back into the swamp. Here he broods until new impulses, a new day or new conditions call forth another effort. The way out is through genital release but this way is blocked for the masochist by an unaccountable terror. An external force must be applied to enable the masochist to force the barrier. Sometimes literally, but always figuratively, he must be whipped forward.

If the confusion which the patient presents superficially is penetrated one finds in the deeper layer good insight and resolve. On this level the masochist knows his problem and his underlying impulses. Here again is a point of contrast with the oral character. The latter with weakened impulses is really confused, the masochist is aware of the ambivalence of love and hate which determines his condition. This explains the crushing guilt, the terrorizing superego which torments these individuals.

The problem of masochism can be understood and treated only as a characteriological disturbance. Ambivalence, vacillation and uncertainty stamp every aspect of masochistic behavior. Every aggressive impulse, every movement or gesture shows this basic disturbance. Before an impulse can be completely expressed it is overtaken by doubt and uncertainty and will be either restrained, pulled back or pushed through against the resistance. We tend to see only those impulses which emerge; it requires a depth analysis to reveal the blocked anger and fury.

There is no inner emptiness in the masochistic character, rather there is always a sense of inner tension and anxiety. He feels that he has much to offer in the way of love or work if only he could get it out. He is more independent than the oral character but this independence is undermined by the strong need for approval. The masochist is the analyst's most willing patient but he is also the one who shows the poorest therapeutic result. To better comprehend the dynamics of this aspect of the masochistic problem, let us compare bioenergetically the oral character structure with the masochistic character structure.

The oral character is determined by a lack of aggression which is due to the underdevelopment of the motor component of his energy system. It appears as a relatively weak, uncoordinated and immature muscular apparatus. One should not make a diagnosis of oral character if this muscular weakness and impotence is absent. The schizoid personality shows, superficially at least, many traits and attitudes which resemble those of the oral character, but these individuals have a muscular strength which is not found in oral character structures. There is an imbalance in the oral structure: a high degree of spiritual development with an infantile motor function. This explains his being "up in the air." We can portray this imbalance by the use of the Hebrew symbol. One triangle is expanded to the degree that the other triangle is reduced (Fig. 15, *left*). This shows the tendency on the part of the oral character to elation, megalomania, grandeur and omniscience.

The masochistic character shows an overdeveloped musculature with a reduced spirituality. It is as if the muscular system overwhelmed the spiritual side of the organism and crushed it. The masochistic is earth-bound, heavy, and his aggression is reduced. As we learned earlier, the overdevelopment of the musculature is not related to movement but to the holding back of movement. It is not surprising then that it results in a reduced aggression.

The small triangle in Figure 15 (*right*) portrays the tendency to self-depreciation, feelings of worthlessness and inferiority. The imbalance is as clearly shown in the masochist as it is in the oral character. The problem posed by the oral character is due to his lack of a muscular development strong enough for sustained adult effort. Once the resistance to the acceptance of reality is broken, rapid progress follows a good bioenergetic physical therapy. For muscular development proceeds apace with physical movement and exercise. The oral character has a real interest in the outer world though he is afraid and incapable of reaching out to it. And this is true despite the superficial narcissism which marks their behavior, just as it is true of the child despite the egocentricity of his demands.

In masochism, however, we have a double problem, for the natural instinctual drives have been turned against each other. If we encourage the aggression, it acts against the tender feelings and produces no real satisfaction. To liberate and free the spiritual feeling when the very motor power needed for such liberation is itself the jailor

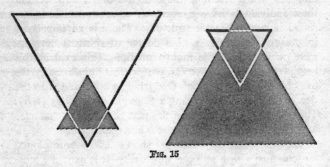

FIG. 15

seems well-nigh impossible. It is not easy to reach the spiritual center of the masochist imprisoned as it is in the deep dungeon formed by his tight and overdeveloped muscular system. Yet the cry of the spirit for liberation, feeble as it seems and in the form of a whine, is continually heard.

The therapeutic approach to the problem of masochism is a many-sided one. Some contact must be established with the imprisoned spirit to sustain and maintain it in the arduous struggle which lies ahead. That is, at all times the sympathy, understanding and support of the analyst must be held out to the masochistic patient in the face of his repeated failure, hopelessness, distrust and antagonism to the analytic therapist. At the same time, he must not be allowed to throw the burden and responsibility for his condition on to the therapist. Difficult as this is, to maintain a rational balance between sympathy on the one hand and critical analysis of his behavior on the other, it is only the framework within which the therapeutic work is undertaken. The spasticity of the muscular system must be dissolved. Movement which has been blocked must be freed. The ambivalence between aggression and tender feelings must be eliminated and some degree of instinctual fusion must be achieved. The latter is a genital function.

We are forced to concur with the masochist that the solution of his problem lies in the development of increased sexual pleasure and satisfaction. But here, it is his own energy function which will control the result and the therapist can only guide the patient and show him how to overcome the difficulties which he faces. We are potent only in our knowledge and faith, impotent to do it for him. If that knowledge and faith is stronger than all the distrust and hostility the patient can muster, the therapy will succeed. But knowledge without its successful application is worthless. Have we the means to prove our contentions and to demonstrate the possibility of a different function?

The dissolution of muscular tensions and spasticities depends upon a knowledge of the dynamics of body movement which is beyond the scope of the present study. However, several suggestions relative to the treatment of the masochistic problem may be made at this time. The masochistic structure is based upon an overdeveloped and contracted musculature. To overcome the severe contractions, movements involving stretch and elongation are required. In striking the couch, for example, a feeling of rearing up in the head and body with wide extension of the arms is suggested. Deep tensions which bind the scapula and upper arm are thus brought to consciousness. The whole action is one of strong ego assertion. In a similar way movements which will open up and release the deep tensions in the pelvic girdle must be used. The contracted thigh muscles must be stretched and the mobility of the pelvis developed. Further the means to achieve and maintain a feeling of relaxation and fullness in the pelvis must become part of the conscious knowledge of the patient.

Perhaps the most outstanding feature of the masochistic body structure is the bull neck. Masochistic patients show a thick, muscular neck without much rigidity. The rigid neck is an expression of pride which is absent in the masochistic structure. The severe spasticity which shortens the neck is located in the deep seated muscles which are not reached by ordinary conscious movement. These muscles hold the unconscious spite and block the upward moving impulses from expression. When one uses the gag reflex with these patients, one finds that the wave moving upward which is the impulse to vomit is caught and held in the throat. It is not blocked by the rigidity which one finds in the throat of hysterical characters. Rather it is caught and suppressed by a contraction which proceeds downward from the head and stops the expansive movement. It is as if the head says "no" to the impulse to vomit. This condition is identical with the one which develops in the lower part of the body. But with the use of the gag reflex we have a means to bring the mechanism to the consciousness of the patient and to show him how to overcome it.

In the lower half of the body the tendency to pull in the belly and to raise the pelvic floor to stop the downward flowing wave of excitation is another aspect of the same mechanism which we observed above. The problem of masochism cannot be solved unless this tendency to pull in and contract the belly is overcome. This can be consciously worked on but it must be remembered that this contraction is based upon a fear of pain should the strong wave of excitation reach the spastic pelvic floor and tight genital apparatus. The active contraction has the function of forestalling an experience which would be painful. This pain must be faced and an ability to tolerate it developed until the patient loses his fear of it. Several means to achieve this based upon the stretch of tight muscles are available. What is involved is the operation of the pain-pleasure principle. As the tolerance to pain increases, the possibility of pleasure is likewise increased. For the masochistic character structure has a pregenital pattern of behavior which is not firmly anchored in adult reality.

Where the oral character lacks contact with the ground because of weak foot arches and undercharged peripheral structures, the masochist's contact with the ground is limited by contracted foot arches and spastic foot and leg muscles. In both cases, though for different reasons, the foundations are insecure and the base for movement is sharply limited. It is as necessary to overcome these tensions in the masochistic structure and to ground his feet as it is to strengthen the legs and feet of the oral structure.

At the opposite end of the body expressive facial movements are also limited. I mentioned earlier that the typical facial expression of the masochist is one of innocence or naiveté. This may take the form of wide-eyed innocence, good-natured smiling, or an expression of grinning stupidity. Underneath is the fear, the contempt, the expression of disgust and, even deeper, the frightened child. These expressions should be brought to the surface and made conscious and the fright opened up and abreacted. No single maneuver is more rewarding than the release of these frozen expressions.

No bioenergetic therapy is effective if a depth analysis along characterological lines is not carried out at the same time. This may be overlooked by those who are impressed by the physical aspects of this therapy. In the treatment of the masochistic problem, this consistent analytic work is of primary importance.

Analytic interpretations, however, suffer from the general fault of all psychologizing: Do I run because I am afraid or am I afraid because I run? Not infrequently, the same action is susceptible to two different interpretations.* Let me illustrate.

A female patient who had a strong masochistic character structure related this incident from her youth. When she was called upon by her teacher to recite she deliberately gave the wrong answer and would appear stupid although she knew the correct answer. The patient offered this explanation. She said that she could not bear to be outstanding and have the class look at her. Reich had interpreted such behavior as a fear of exhibitionism. On the other hand Theodore Reik interprets such behavior as negatively exhibitionistic. The masochist calls attention to himself by his failures and complaints. Actually both interpretations are correct, one is merely the reverse side of the other. The masochistic character has repressed exhibitionistic tendencies. On the conscious level we find a strong fear of exhibition and exposure. Inevitably, then, the blocked impulses will find some means of expression, if indirectly, unconsciously and in a typical masochistic fashion. It may be that a wrong answer from a normally intelligent pupil will draw more attention than a correct answer would have done. But one brings the attention on the level of being sorry for the individual while the other makes the patient outstanding in a positive way. To avoid this difficulty we make our interpretations on a bioenergetic basis as often as possible. Bioenergetically, we would explain this behavior then as a fear of self-assertion and of the accompanying pleasure and expansive feelings.

* Compare with Freud's remark about "Dostoevski's famous 'knife that cuts both ways.'" "Female Sexuality" (1931) in *Collected Papers V*. London, Hogarth Press, 1953, p. 258n.

In masochism we are dealing with a personality in which indirection, ambivalence and manipulation of situations are the characteristic qualities. In the autobiography in the preceding chapter the patient described how his penis withdrew into the scrotum. This tendency of the penis to shrink is just the opposite of the normal exhibitionistic tendencies in children. Yet the masochist maneuvered this situation to some good for he went to his mother, showed her the condition and asked her to redress it.

Exhibitionism in the young child is a testing of reality. Mostly it takes the form of athletic accomplishments but it may be overtly sexual. The child expects approval and admiration which strengthen its ego and assure it of the support of its environment. A positive response enables the child to move on to higher levels of ego functioning. A negative response undermines the assurance needed for self-assertion and makes the individual dependent upon approval in adult activities. Masochism stems from attitudes of disapproval and derision in these early days. It is for this reason that masochism is associated with humiliation.

There is one more aspect to this problem which we must consider. The discharge which is achieved through the masochistic maneuver is pleasurable although it by no means releases all the available excitation. This poses a difficulty for the masochist since he would like to retain the pleasure yet be relieved of the price he has to pay for it. In many cases, therefore, it can be expected that as the patient gives up the pushing and provocation sexual potency will be diminished. But the way is then open for an exposition of the underlying spite and a dissolution of the deep spasticities. I had occasion to observe this phenomenon clearly: I had made excellent progress during several months of therapy with a patient who had a masochistic character structure when suddenly one day I found that he had relapsed into a very severe state of masochistic morass with marked accentuation of all symptoms. He could recall nothing to account for the relapse. I inquired into his sexual activities during the preceding week. He then remembered an act of intercourse which he had with his wife the night before the relapse occurred. He then told me that he had been highly excited sexually during the act but that the penis had slipped out of the vagina just before the acme. This could be interpreted as an expression of spite. The patient denied sexual satisfaction to his partner even at the expense of his own gratification. Since there was no other act of intercourse following this incident, it was clear to both of us that the undischarged energy had then stagnated producing a true internal morass.

From a knowledge of the dynamics of the character structure one can deduce the form of the transference problem and the nature of the resistances. We can anticipate the attitudes which the masochistic character would present. First he looks to the analyst for approval convinced that once he gained that approval everything would be all right. When this fails he expects the analyst to "do it for him" and in this the analyst is regarded as the knowing and protective mother. On the negative side there is the contempt, the disgust, the hostility and the spite which was originally felt towards the parent. The masochist transfers his dependence to the analyst as an unconscious demand that the analyst "do it for him" and he resists every rational demand that he take the responsibility for his own behavior.

It is necessary in the treatment of masochism to demand the expression of some positive feelings. Only so can the nature of the spiteful holding be fully exposed. It can be expected that such a demand will be strongly resisted. The masochist is very much afraid to open up. To say that he fears to be rejected in his offer of love is to put it mildly. He had been humiliated as a child and he will not risk it again. The doubt and distrust are deeply engrained. Can he find joy and happiness? Will it not lead to further suffering? It will. He will cry deeply and feel his anguish keenly. But only after the crying will he feel peaceful and, to some extent, joyful. The masochist *must* suffer. As soon as he gives up the pushing and forcing, sadness overwhelms him. If the spite which blocks his submission is released, a most unhappy child confronts the therapist. But the specific masochistic character is overcome.

Let us look again at the dilemma of the masochist in terms of this problem. His longing to love and be loved is caught at each end of its pendular swing. Above, in the brain, is the distrust and doubt. These prevent the flow of feeling (as in sobs) through the throat. The spite at the back of the neck is as effective against the masochist as it was against the mother. The "I won't" originally directed outward now prevents the giving in to the self. And the "devil" in the mind always has cogent, rational reasons to justify this attitude. Below, the flood of tears are bound by the deep tensions in the belly. Only as long as the masochist holds the pelvis and the belly tightly contracted is he safe. A trickle may break through now and then but it is not dangerous. If the pressure becomes too great, steam is let off either by whining or by some other provocative behavior. The value of this function as a safety-valve must not be ignored.

What would happen if this safety valve were denied to the patient? For this is what we do when we stop the patient's whining and provocative behavior. What possibilities present themselves?

If we force the patient to face his unsatisfied longing, his sadness and sorrow, we risk his collapse into hopelessness. It is against this hopelessness that the masochist struggles. It creates in him an unconscious fear which may express itself as a fear of drowning or of being overwhelmed by the sea of misery within himself. Yet only the acceptance of this hopelessness will break the pattern of pushing, provocation, frustration and failure. If it is hopeless what is the sense of struggling? We must recognize, however, that just below the hopelessness is faith, under the sorrow is joy, and beneath the spastic pelvic floor is the genital apparatus and the way to freedom. Can it be doubted that the masochist wants to suffer and is afraid of suffering at the same time? I do not doubt it. You may recall the verse of a popular song of some time ago which expressed this masochistic state well. It was: "(I am caught) between the devil and the deep blue sea."

In the foregoing study I sought to present the main aspects of masochism as a characteriological problem. The masochistic character structure is the foundation of all forms of masochism—sexual, feminine or moral (to use Freud's categories). Within this characterological type individual variations exist which determine the specific personality. The patient I described in the preceding chapter was distinguished by the leer on his face which was masked by an expression of seriousness. Character-wise he was a leering devil who mocked you and derided your efforts. Let me describe two other patients.

The first was a young man who had a typical masochistic character structure. His face was round and puffy. He had an habitual grin which, with his small eyes, gave his face a very stupid expression. He was far from being stupid as his excellent professional attainment proved. The facial expression also impressed me as being piglike. The pig quality is not unrelated to the masochistic morass and every masochist was in his childhood at least a so-called "good eater." In this case, the stupid expression was the key to the specific personality. As a boy this patient organized small gang raids upon the neighborhood stores. They stole fruits, vegetables and candy. Whenever he was caught, the patient turned on his "silly, stupid" expression to disarm his captors and mask the malice in his actions. At home, too, under this guise, he could get away with deeds and behavior which otherwise would have brought a severe punishment.

The other patient, a young woman with masochistic fantasies, had a very bright smiling face. Her eyes were wide open but near-sighted. A little smile gave her countenance an expression of surprised innocence. Behind this expression was a calculating mind. I did not succeed in her analysis until I discovered and exposed her tendency to maneuver people into situations in which she was always the innocent injured party.

The oral character is afraid to reach out to the world. The masochist reaches out to reality but with such doubts that the reach is withdrawn before it attains its objective. Yet both types are related in being pregenital energy structures, in their lack of independence and security, and in their need for a favorable environment. In the broad sense masochism is a form of orality, as opposed to organisms which function on the genital level. In the oral character, energy production generally is low so that despite tensions and spasticity in the genital apparatus there is little sensation of suffering. The masochist has a high energy production with a low genital capacity. This leads to strong feelings of frustration and misery. The more highly organized ego structures with sexuality anchored on the genital level show a better balance between excess energy production and the ability to discharge it, between the sensory and motor components and between the spiritual and material sides of their natures.

Before we begin our study of the character types within this group it is important to recognize that masochism is a tendency—to contract, to doubt, to fail and to whine. It derives, as we saw, from experiences in which the active suppression of the child's independence and assertion constituted the trauma to the personality. If this tendency is the key to the personality and determines its basic pattern of response we speak of a masochistic character structure. This is not to say that it is a pure type but rather that we can thus categorize its fundamental energy relationships. Rare, however, is the child, in our culture at least, who can escape some active interference with his independence and assertion. Equally rare is the individual who does not show to some degree or other this masochistic tendency to withdraw, to doubt, to complain. If it is not the dominant tendency we describe it as a masochistic trait. It may be weak or strong. In the more highly organized ego structures it is compensated by ego defenses on the psychological level and by rigidity on the somatic level.

The analysis of masochistic traits is carried out in the same way as the analysis of the masochistic character structure, with due regard for their role in the total personality. How adequate are the compensating mechanisms? How much of a threat to the ego is there in the underlying masochism? These factors must be evaluated in an appraisal of the individual character structure. If the masochistic tendencies are obvious, the character analysis proceeds from that point. On the other hand, where the compensations are highly effective, the masochistic tendencies will not appear until the dominating rigidity has been loosened characterologically and physically.

We can summarize the problem of masochism by comparing it again with the oral character. Orality is the result of feelings of deprivation suffered in early childhood and infancy. Masochism results from the active suppression of independence and assertion at the age when the child becomes conscious of its oral, anal and genital functions. Maternal interference and domination of the child's oral and anal functions is especially responsible. Where the oral character is characterized by an unconscious "I can't," the masochistic character is determined by the unconscious "I won't." Both are ego deficient structures deriving from the dominance of pregenital drives. Fortunately, the recognition of self-demand feeding and the knowledge of the physiological basis for training to excremental cleanliness should help greatly to reduce the incidence of masochism in future generations.

12

The Hysterical Character—1

In chapters 9–11 we discussed two character types which can be considered to be ego-deficient structures. They merit this description because the pendular energy swing which constitutes the basis of the ego perception is not fully extended so as to be firmly anchored in brain and genital function. They may also be considered impulsive types as opposed to those character types which show a predominance of affect block. Further, because energy production generally is in excess of the ability to discharge that energy in work or sex, both types of character structure are subject to frequent anxiety attacks. In this chapter, I shall discuss a character type distinguished by little anxiety, more or less affect block, and an ego structure anchored in an established genital function.

While the concept of the hysterical character is a late development in psychoanalytic thinking, hysteria and hysterical symptoms were the subjects whose study led Freud to the initial constructions of psychoanalysis. It would be interesting and valuable, therefore, as part of the analysis of this character type, to relate the dynamics of hysteria to the bioenergetic basis of the hysterical character. To do so we must first analyze the psychology and biology of the hysterical character structure.

Fenichel (1945, p. 527) describes the problem as follows: "Considering the mechanisms of hysteria, it is to be expected that traits are manifested that correspond to the conflicts between intense fear of sexuality and intense but repressed sexual strivings." To this is added a list of traits which while applicable in these cases are too vague to delimit the type. "Hysterical characters have been described as persons who are inclined to sexualize all nonsexual relations, toward suggestibility, irrational emotional outbreaks, chaotic behavior, dramatization and histrionic behavior, even toward mendacity and its extreme form, pseudologia phantastica."

In problems of character analysis, on a psychoanalytic level, it is Reich's work which offers the best insight into the nature of the character structure. On the hysterical character Reich (1949, pp. 189–191) tells us, "Its most outstanding characteristic is an obvious sexual behavior, in combination with a specific kind of bodily agility with a definitely sexual nuance. This explains the fact that the connection between female hysteria and sexuality has been known for a long time. In women, the hysterical character type is evidenced by disguised or undisguised coquetry in gait, gaze and speech." The basis of this character structure is "determined by a fixation on the genital phase of infantile development, with its incestuous attachment." Reich's interpretation of this exaggerated sexual behavior is classic. "The hysterical character has strong and unsatisfied genital strivings which are inhibited by the genital anxiety; thus he feels constantly exposed to dangers which correspond to his infantile fears; the original genital striving is then utilized for the purpose of feeling out, as it were, the nature and magnitude of the threatening dangers."

Analysts who are well acquainted with Reich's character analytic theories and techniques can recognize this type rather easily. However, since the dynamics of the structure have not been thoroughly worked out either psychologically or bioenergetically, deep reaching changes in structure and function are not easily achieved. Let me add one word of caution. The description of the overt behavior of the hysterical character is derived from observation of individuals whose development took place twenty, thirty or more years ago. Further, European culture differs in many respects from that in America. The coquette, the flirt, the vamp are not our current types. Hysteria, as it was known around 1890–1900, when Freud investigated its mechanisms, is rare today. Far reaching changes in our sexual mores have altered the superficial aspects of character types.* In the same direction, a well studied character structure common to the culture out of which psychoanalysis arose is infrequently seen in practice today. This is the compulsive character as described extensively in psychoanalytic literature. If, however, the external characteristics of the hysterical character structure are less evident, the libido structure is fundamentally the same. Let us study a specific case.

A young lady in her early thirties came to therapy with one complaint. Her love relationships failed to grow and develop. She had been married once to a boy she knew for many years but this marriage was a failure and lasted less than one year. In the succeeding years she had a number of affairs but, for one reason or another, each one broke up. One man proved impotent, another was too young, a third was financially dependent on his family, etc. The counsel of a friend and her own realization that something was wrong made her seek professional help. She had a good job, was interested in the dance, and suffered from no physical disabilities. Actually this patient was symptom free and the complaint was a very general one.

Examination of the patient revealed several very interesting observations. Most evident was the fact that the

---

* Otto Fenichel comments, "Classic hysteria worked with the defense mechanism of repression proper, which, however, presupposed a simple prohibition of any discussion of the objectionable drives. . . . The change in the neurosis reflects the change in morality." *The Psychoanalytic Theory of Neurosis.* New York, Norton, 1945, p. 464.

area of the face extending between both cheek bones and across the bridge of the nose had a dead appearance. The skin was fairly taut and dry and looked cadaverous. The eyes had a frightened look. The mouth was tight but the lips reached forward. The shoulders were high, straight and very stiff. The arms were thin giving the shoulders a bony appearance. The upper half of the body above the pelvis was thin and very stiffly held. The chest was rather soft but the back was very rigid. The color of the skin of this part was white. In contrast the part of the body from the pelvis downward was full and soft. The skin here had a tan coloration and the legs were quite hairy.

Several bioenergetic interpretations were possible on the basis of this body structure. The split between the upper and lower halfs made one think of a child's body sitting in a woman's pelvis. Certainly where the lower part appeared to be sexual and yielding, the upper half was rigid and holding. From the neck upward, the expression was one of deep fright. The thin arms and bony shoulders looked impotent and this impression was strengthened if one asked the patient to make an aggressive movement with the arms such as reaching out or hitting the couch. One further deduction could be made which bore upon the failures in this patient's love relationships. The lack of aggression in the upper part of the body made one surmise that her sexual behavior was marked by submission with the hope of thereby gaining the love of a man and at the same time to avoid the terror expressed in the eyes. Such an attitude never realizes its hope as this case will illustrate. The patient understood this immediately when I pointed it out, but that changed nothing. She admitted, too, her lack of aggression in her relations with people at work and also that she was afraid to stand up for her rights.

In the sexual act this patient generally reached a climax, and while the pleasure varied with the circumstances she did not feel unsatisfied. This accords with the absence of anxiety and contrasts with the feelings of the masochistic character. She did not whine or complain about her condition except to remark that she was often tired after a day's work.

The history of the patient adds to our understanding. She was an only child. Her father had died of tuberculosis before she was born. She was nursed as an infant but weaned because her mother had to go out to work. She had cried all day when this happened but the next day she took a bottle without protest. She lived with her aunt for awhile, then her mother had to board her out. When she was two she had pneumonia. At about three she was placed in a Catholic convent. An early memory from this period is that of seeing a dog killed by a pitchfork. The discipline at the convent was very strict. She told me many times of a Sister who tried to choke her and hold her head under water while she was being bathed. She was lonely, yearned for her mother and suffered frequently from illness.

When she was seven her mother remarried and took the patient to live with her. She was afraid of her stepfather who was strict and stern. When she was an adolescent her mother went away during a summer. The patient kept house for her stepfather and recalled that he insisted on her sleeping in the same bed with him. He made no sexual attack upon her although he tried to hold her close to him. She was taught how to masturbate by a cousin but she told her mother about it and was warned that it leads to vice and insanity. She masturbated after this but only following a struggle and with much anxiety.

Her home life was far from a happy one. Her mother and stepfather quarrelled often, mostly over money, but also because he wanted children of his own which were not forthcoming. Her mother tried to commit suicide once. She was always afraid of her stepfather and although she sympathized with her mother she also tried to win the love of her stepfather and to be the good girl he wanted her to be. The prevailing impression was that he had to be pacified at all costs. The neighborhood she lived in was a very tough one and she did not get along well with the other kids. More than once she was backed up against a wall by some other girl and beaten without making an effort to fight back. She felt it was no use to strike back because she always closed her eyes when fighting and never landed a blow.

She recalled her adolescent years as a period during which she was determined to achieve some independence. She was serious and quiet, did not joke much and did not go out with boys. She wanted to be an actress but upon graduation from high school she decided to get a steady job and prove that she was capable of earning her living. In the succeeding years she was able to work well but the problem of establishing a satisfactory love life seemed more and more difficult. She had her first act of intercourse at twenty with a boy she had known for a year and she was very much afraid. She wanted above all to be loved and protected. Her sexuality was for the man who would marry her. As we learned earlier she was married, but it ended in a quick divorce. All other affairs proved equally disappointing.

From this short history it is easy to see that fear ran deep in this patient. Her outstanding emotional states are two: being scared and lonely. An analytic therapy which aims at a *reversal* of the deep-seated pattern of submission present in this case would have to be dynamic. I began it with a concerted attack: character-analytic on the one hand and muscular on the other. I would like to sketch briefly the development of the treatment for it reveals more of the nature of the problem than I could convey otherwise.

Early sessions were directed toward mobilizing energy and overcoming the immobility of the shoulders and the deadness of the face. Respiration was without difficulty but the neck did not yield and the back did not bend. In view of the ease with which the chest moved I did not anticipate much difficulty in resolving the tensions, but I underestimated the very expression which was so charactersitic. Further, the back was exceedingly rigid. Nonetheless, these early therapeutic sessions (first two to three months) produced a noticeable change in the patient's appearance. The muscles of the face relaxed somewhat, especially when they were subject to gentle manipulation, and with that the skin of the face took on a better color and looked more alive. The patient became aware that she carried her shoulders high and she made an effort outside of therapy to drop them. Pressure upon any of the tense muscles was too painful and could not be maintained. The patient felt better too. She became slightly more aggressive though not to any marked degree.

Following this early period there was no significant improvement in the condition of the patient for nine to ten months. At the beginning I was surprised at the lack of results. I have since learned that this is to be expected. It does not mean that the therapy is unproductive. The surface problems are resolved and penetration is made into the depths. Analysis of form and movement is carried on and this is integrated with the general character analytic work. At the same time muscle tensions are worked on and energy is mobilized through movement. There is some improvement. At times it was quite noticeable but one does not have the impression that it is substantial or more than a temporary phenomenon. If it should persist so much the better. One should not count upon it. This phase of the therapy ends when the character, both in its psychological and biological expressions, stands fully revealed, naked as it were, as the central disturbance of the organism. At this point, both therapist and patient become completely aware of the patient's way of being and acting, i.e., her character structure. Now, for the first time it becomes concretely possible to effect those deep changes for which the patient hopes.

In the present case every effort was made during these nine months, to bring the energy into the head.* The

---

* This present case was analyzed and treated during that phase of my work before I began the systematic bioenergetic

shoulders were mobilized through reaching and hitting. In response the neck had developed increasing tension, especially in the nuchal region. The tensions of the neck and of the shoulders stood out as the main block in the upper half of the body. It was obvious that if the energy could pass through the neck and into the head, the latter would lose its cadaverous expression. Work on these tensions produced some crying and occasional screaming. The patient felt very much the need and the desire to scream but during this period of therapy the screams were not experienced as a satisfactory release. We both felt that there was more, but we couldn't get at it.

The tension of the back of the neck gripped the base of the skull. One felt that the patient was holding on "for dear life." The jaw also was quite tense. Work on these muscles was so painful that it was impossible to do much to relieve the tension. The eyes were dull, occasionally they even looked lifeless. When the patient opened her eyes wide she experienced considerable fright, but she was not aware of what caused this fright, nor did this action produce any involuntary scream of terror. The terror was there; at the moment, however, it was beyond reach.

As I mentioned above, concomitant with the intensive biological therapy to bring about the flow of energy, I carried out an extensive character-analytic study of the patient. We saw, earlier, the interpretation of the general body structure. Now, besides the evident deadness of the face, the expression about the mouth was significant. I could not get away from the impression that it resembled a fish's mouth in the way the latter opens to draw in water.

---

practice of working from the ground up. I am sure that with the newer principles and methods the whole history of the therapy would be different. But that was not possible until I had fully explored the segmental tensions and had arrived at a deeper understanding of character structure. This case is included here because it was part of that process of exploration and added much to my understanding of the hysterical character structure.

It was also a sucking motion, but it had to be interpreted in the character of the patient. I made the following correlation. Here was a fish which wanted to be caught and was afraid of it. This is the typical behavior of the hysterical character structure and is especially evident in her sexual relations. As Reich described it, "when the sexual behavior seems close to attaining its goal, then the hysterical character regularly retreats or assumes a passive, anxious attitude."

All of this came to a climax one session when my irritation at this attitude made me take a sharper tone to the patient. I pointed out the deadness of her emotional life. She wanted to love and be loved but all she did was submit passively. She wanted to be respected but she would not stand up for her rights. I reviewed many of the circumstances of her life to show her that she was afraid of the very thing she wanted. She was a poor fish, indeed!

The patient made a few feeble attempts to defend herself against my remarks. She did not become angry at me which was a reaction I hoped to produce, rather she shrank back on the couch in an attitude of resignation. This, too, was pointed out as part of the general submissiveness and as her typical reaction in the transference situation. Here is evidence that what we designate as resistance to psychoanalytic interpretation, or as transference in the analyst-patient relationship, is nothing but the specific character attitude of the patient as determined by his structure. At this point, one could have beaten the patient into insensibility and she would not or could not have made an outcry. Despite this, I could not soften my attitude towards her. Of course, she did not cry. She left the session in a state of shock.

Immediate events were to prove that such strong action was both opportune and necessary. It served to expose the deeply rooted emotional illness. In this respect the therapist is like a surgeon and, as in surgery, there is a risk. If the indications exist and the conditions are right, such action may also be life-saving.

At the following session, one week later, I attempted to relieve the effect of the impact somewhat. If anything the deadness of the facial expression seemed to have deepened. I continued the muscular work as before. When I saw her one week later she looked grey. I was alarmed. She then told me that while she was undertaking a new project she felt no enthusiasm for anything. But she had also arrived at an important realization. She knew that her attitude as she expressed it was that: "I would rather die than fight back." I had hoped that this realization might prove crucial in the fight to break up the character armor and I was not disappointed. At the moment, however, there was the problem of overcoming the actual dying which was taking place in the patient. In my turn, I realized that I had underestimated the problem. The patient's deadness went much deeper than I had imagined. The expression of the face and head could not be taken lightly.

I had several techniques available to halt and reverse the dying tendency. For one thing, I felt encouraged by the patient's awareness of the problem, for that could represent a mobilization of her available energies. The most important of these techniques was the use of the gag reflex. I knew its worth from long experience with its use. One could also mobilize energy by work upon the long muscles of the back especially in the region of the diaphragmatic crura. This is as close as one can get to the energy centers of the body. The muscular work upon the important tensions of the neck, both at the base of the skull and at the apex of the thorax generally produces some positive feelings. The spasticity of the muscles at the base of the skull is especially responsible for feelings of hopelessness. I continued this work for several weeks and the improvement in the patient was noticeable but gradual. It was an uphill fight at the moment but we were succeeding.

At this point the first spontaneous movements broke through in the patient. They developed as a result of work upon the scalene muscles and appeared as a wave moving from the chest to the belly where it stopped. It was an attempt to unite the upper and lower halves of the body, the separation of which was an important factor in her character structure. I became deeply aware of another facet to this problem. Too many of the patient's movements and actions seemed mechanical. I had the strong impression that she forced herself through the daily routine of living, and through her therapy too. The inner impulsion to action seemed weak. While the "forcing" was and is necessary so long as the spontaneous flow of energy to the outside is blocked, the "forcing" itself is part of the block. Mechanical, forced movements translate an inner attitude of isolation, of lack of contact with life and the world, of emotional deadness. I was very encouraged, therefore, to see the spark of spontaneity become visible in this patient.

Despite the experiences of the past weeks, I still felt that I needed a better grasp of the character armor of this patient in order to produce a major improvement. I was prevented from applying pressure on the muscles because the patient experienced it as too painful. Her body, especially the back and shoulders, had a brittle feeling as if it could break under force. How could I get the patient to take a little more pain so that I could soften the extremely tight and tense areas? To some extent, the pain was compounded of fear which could be decreased analytically. But if I could get the patient to accept the necessity for the pain as a part of her therapy more could be accomplished.

The element of brittleness became the basis of a new interpretation. She was afraid to be hurt because she had a feeling that any injury could crack her. Something about her seemed to be made of glass.

Another aspect of her character was the sense of isolation, of lack of contact with life. This was conveyed by a type of movement which seemed to fit reality but was void of any emotional relation to it. We said earlier it was mechanical, automation-like, lifeless. It is as if the movements took place in a vacuum.

The expression of the mouth was characterized as that of a fish. This had a double meaning. On the one hand, she reached out for life with her mouth, on the other hand, she was very much afraid to be caught. It was now possible to fuse all these aspects into a composite portrait. She was a fish in a glass bowl. The moment this idea occurred to me, I saw that it could explain everything: the brittleness, the isolation, the deadness despite apparent movement and life, the being caught and her fear of it. It would be necessary to hurt her, to break the glass bowl which isolated her from the stream of life, and she had to accept the pain of it. At this point I became aware of how much fear lay under the pain. The patient agreed that she reacted with a grimace of pain before she experienced any really strong physical hurt.

This interpretation made sense to the patient. It did not, however, have the dramatic effect I hoped for. She agreed that the pain was "somewhat necessary," but the barrier persisted. For my part, I recalled Dostoevski's remark in the closing paragraphs of *Crime and Punishment*: "He did not know that the new life would not be given him for nothing, that he would have to pay dearly for it and that it would cost him great striving, great suffering." To make the patient more willing to accept pain, almost to the limit of physical tolerance, I introduced the idea of sin and expiation. I suggested to the patient that she was a sinner. Now, for the first time, I met with a reaction of anger from the patient. Why should I call her a sinner? What had she done? I replied, could not one say that it is a sin to walk upon this earth without love, without expressing love? And is not this the greatest of sins? Her reaction was very strong. She cried bitterly and then remarked that she had lived for years under the spectre of sin. With effort she had freed herself from its weight and now I pushed her back into it. Rebel as she would she had to admit the justice of my observation. Her crying deepened and continued.

Let me enlarge upon the concept involved here. If a child can only survive the agony of a difficult childhood situation by substantially deadening itself no one can blame it. Certainly the background of this patient was such that a reaction of this kind could be expected. Under given circumstances the action is rational. However, as soon as the independence of adulthood is reached and the intolerable situation no longer exists, every effort should be made to overcome this disturbance. To do this it is necessary to reverse the process, to return to the agony, to reexperience it and to resolve it in another direction. Of course, the patient will suffer but the suffering here is rational and necessary. It is the heat which melts the rigidities and permits the rebirth of a new ego.

Following the above analytic work, I undertook to release more energy. I began to work again on the muscles at the root of the neck, the scalenes. I worked these over well and proceeded forward to the chin. Then, by massaging the mental muscles, I softened the thrust of the chin. This last maneuver produced an outburst of crying which became gradually more intense. Energy flowed upward through the neck. An expression of deep hurt came into the face and eyes and I sensed the agony which underlay the deadness of the facial expression. The crying lasted for some time and I comforted the patient. As it subsided, a dramatic change came over her. The whole face was alive: skin, eyes, mouth, etc. There was an expression of joy in the face which I had never seen there before. The patient felt radiant. I did not expect this condition to last more than 24 hours. However, it pointed the way to the future.

Succeeding sessions saw the gradual extension of the patient's awareness of her body and its functions. Physical pain and the feeling of brittleness slowly decreased. The patient herself made increasingly strong efforts to mobilize her energy through hitting the couch and through other movements. Her arms became stronger; her shoulders filled in. Crying became easier but the deep tensions yielded slowly. From this point on the general improvement in the patient was continuous and lasting. Her aggression became more available. Her work situation substantially improved. She formed a love relationship with a young man in which she no longer used sexual submission as a means to gain love.

The therapy with this patient continued for about a year after the significant interpretations mentioned above. It terminated when the patient became engaged. She felt that she could go on alone secure in her new feeling of strength and courage. I was able to follow her for several years after the termination of the therapy. She had married and had borne a child to her husband. Despite problems which inevitably arise in the wake of new responsibilities this patient has more than held the gains she made in the analytic work.

On the basis of our study of this patient, it is possible to define the important characteristics of the hysterical structure which we can then check against other observations and cases. As we saw, Reich named the "obvious sexual behavior in combination with a specific kind of bodily agility" as the "most important characteristic." The evidence upon which Reich based this conclusion was much in force in the early part of this century. Today such attitudes are uncommon, except for the manifestation known as the "sweater girl." But if the obvious sexual behavior of the flirt or coquette is rare, the use of sexual activity as a defense against sexuality or love is as true today as it was then. If the flirtatious behavior had the function of "feeling out, as it were, the nature and magnitude of the threatening dangers," the sexual submission of the hysterical character of today is subject to the same interpretation.

We had interpreted the sexual behavior of this patient as one of submission with the purpose to win the favor and love of the male. The bioenergetic meaning of the body structure was similar. While the lower part of the body from the pelvis down was soft and yielding, the upper half was rigid and holding. If the genitals gave their assent, the heart said "no." But, you may ask, "Where is the threatening danger?" Of what is the patient afraid since intercourse is accepted? The threatening danger is deep emotional involvement. Should the heart pour its great feelings into the genital apparatus, the latter would develop severe anxiety. For the hysterical character is determined by genital rigidities or spasticities which permit the discharge of only moderate amounts of energy. The accepted psychoanalytic explanation is the "fixation on a genital phase of infantile development, with its incestuous attachment." So long as this incestuous attachment is not resolved, love is split into two incompatible emotions: tender feelings and sensuality. The hysterical character cannot combine these two emotions, to any important degree, into a unitary feeling towards one person.

Fenichel (1945, p. 527) bases the hysterical character upon the same conflicts which underlie hysteria. "Considering the mechanisms of hysteria, it is to be expected that traits are manifested that correspond to the conflicts between intense fear of sexuality and intense but repressed sexual strivings." What distinguishes this type of character structure from the oral or masochistic character? In the latter, the conflict between sexual striving and sexual fear is even more intense, so much so that the masochist may be in a real state of panic at times. In the hysterical character, the sexual strivings are repressed; that is, they are to a large extent unconscious. In the masochistic character, the desires are highly conscious but the holding back is repressed; that is, the masochist is not ordinarily aware that he is holding back sexual feeling. The masochistic squeezing, rolling and pushing to obtain a discharge is not felt as a maneuver to overcome a resistance. The masochist is surprised if you point out his holding; the hysterical character is surprised when you point out the sexual meaning of her actions.

Let me put it another way. The masochist comes to therapy because he wishes to be free; he identifies with his impulses. The hysterical character comes for help because something has gotten out of control, she wishes to reestablish that control. Was not that the fundamental problem presented by the hysterical symptoms which Freud was called upon to treat in those early days? Still, we must ask how is it possible for the hysterical character to identify consciously with restraint and control, while the masochist identifies with the impulse, and with freedom of expression? This question can be answered on many levels. I like to compare this problem to a similar one existing among peoples and nations. The have-people are all for law and order, the have-nots are the revolutionists. The hysterical character is a genital structure; the oral character and the masochistic character are pregenital. Once the genital function has become firmly established, an adult energy economy is operative in the organism. The pendular energy swing which is the reality principle and constitutes the basis of the ego perception is now anchored at both extremities: brain and genitals. It is conceivable that regression can occur under very unusual circumstances. So long, however, as these two anchorages remain secure, the organism will be able to regulate within limits the amount of energy production to the amount of energy discharge. And so long too as this balance is maintained the hysterical character will be able to avoid anxiety, to remain in control and to have some contact with reality at all times.

I said in the preceding paragraph that the hysterical character comes to therapy because something has gotten out of control. This means that anxiety has developed. The neurotic regulatory mechanism has failed. One should ask, Why has this happened? What circumstances bring it about? Before I answer those questions, I should point out that today an hysterical character may also undertake an analytic therapy because the control is too effective. Energy production and impulse formation may be decreased to a point where a satisfactory function under the conditions of modern living is impossible. Our competitive society demands a fairly high degree of aggression. In more advanced circles it also expects of the woman an ability to enjoy the sexual experience. These are new cultural factors which have changed the psychoanalytic picture of the neurosis and which are, in part at least, due to the dissemination of psychoanalytic ideas. Let us return to the questions posed above.

Two factors can upset the balance of energy production and energy discharge. An increased production of energy without a corresponding increase in the ability to discharge that energy will produce anxiety. This frequently happens to young girls at the beginning of adolescence. It occurs during a good analytic therapy when the freeing of the repressed affects increases energy production before a corresponding change in the ability to discharge that energy has been achieved. It happens when the level of emotional charge is raised to a very high level as at the beginning of a love relationship when the opportunity for discharge is not immediately available. This is the normal anxiety of love, it can become pathological if it brings the patient into conflict with strong repressive forces. The problem of hysteria is related to this process. On the other hand, any marked decrease in the discharge of energy without an equal change in its production produces anxiety. As early as 1894 in a discussion of the anxiety neuroses, Freud pointed out that the forfeiture of satisfaction in sexual intercourse through the practice of coitus interruptus always resulted in anxiety. Similarly any interruption of a normal sexual life can lead to severe somatic anxiety if alternate means of energy discharge are not available.

The problem of hysteria and of the hysterical attack is related to the first condition. A sudden sharp increase in energy production produced by the release of strong repressed affect results in great anxiety. This anxiety is bound or converted into a somatic symptom and the conflict is transferred to the psychic level. The hysterical attack is the psychic counterpart of the attempt to repress a strong anxiety state. Freud recognized the corollary of this proposition when he said (1894a, p. 105) that, "aspects come to light which suggest that anxiety neurosis is actually the somatic counterpart of hysteria." This specific condition, however, can happen only to this character type. Anxiety is a common experience in masochism, it leads either to provocation and discharge or it ends in the stagnation of the masochistic morass. In the oral character, anxiety is countered by withdrawal. In neither of these structures does the condition become explosive. The fluidity of the energy processes, the lack of anchorage, the absence of rigidity prevent an explosive situation from developing.

The hysterical attack is an explosive phenomenon. The sudden development of an excess of energy can overwhelm the ego in a so-called hysterical outburst, or it can be funneled into one part of the body and isolated, their producing an hysterical symptomatology. Immobilization will result in the striking picture of an hysterical paralysis. If the energy cannot be effectively immobilized it will produce involuntary movements (clonisms, tics, etc.) I shall have more to say about the problem of hysteria in another context. What is important in this process is the fact that the explosive situation depends upon the build-up of a force within a closed, rigid system or container. Now it is just this systematic rigidity which is the essential nature of the hysterical character structure. It is not merely a specific tension or spasticity such as is found in the oral or masochistic structures; rather, the rigidity of the hysterical character is a total body process which surrounds the organism as with an armor. Earlier, I had described the hysterical character as belonging to the rigid type of character structures. At this point, one can say that this is also the armored type of structure.

The concept of armoring was introduced by Reich to describe a state in which anxiety is "bound up" in a protective mechanism which has the definite economic purpose of serving on the one hand "as a protection against the stimuli from the outer world, on the other hand against inner libidinous strivings." One immediately thinks of the armor of the knights of old which served as a defense against certain external forces. Later, Reich showed that the character armor had its somatic counterpart in a muscular armor which has the same function bioenergetically as the character armor had psychologically. While we use the expression "character armor" as being synonymous with character resistance, we should not confuse the *armor* with the *character* itself. Every neurotic individual attempts to armor against the dangers and threats both from without and within. Actually, the oral character and the masochist are only partially successful at best. Both types are, therefore, subject to anxiety attacks and have developed other mechanisms to cope with this anxiety. The oral character withdraws from reality either to fantasy or to depression; the masochist retires into a brooding solitude. Basically, these are essentially unarmored types and they are in consequence very sensitive to their environment. The ability to armor is available only to character structures based upon a genital function.

In the case presented in this chapter, the character armor had the interpretation of the glass bowl within which the fish swam. The armor provided protection but exacted isolation. And it limited the internal motility of the organism. We have seen that the armor is represented somatically by muscular tension and spasticities. A distinction must be made, however, between armoring and muscular tension. All armoring is based on muscle tension. But not every muscle tension is an armoring. The latter depends upon whether the spasticity serves to protect against outside stimuli and effectively binds anxiety. The severe muscle tensions found in schizophrenics, the oral character and even in masochism do not constitute an armoring. Individuals who suffer from these disturbances are both sensitive and burdened with anxiety. What, then, is the exact nature of a true muscular armor?

The bioenergetic study of the hysterical character structure shows that it is based upon a total body rigidity. The back is rigid and unbending. The neck is tight and the head is held erect. The pelvis is more or less retracted and is tightly held. More important, the front of the body is hard. It is the rigidity of the chest and abdomen which is essential to an armor. The front is the soft and vulnerable aspect of the body, its sensitive aspect, the realm of the tender feelings. If this aspect is unprotected, all the so-called armoring of the back would serve for naught.

One can hypothesize that man's erect posture, exposing this aspect of the body, required the development of an armor for its protection. This might appear to be the case except that the freeing of the forelimbs for aggression in the human animal, as compared with their use for support and locomotion in the lower mammals, balances the scales. As long as the arms are available for attack and defense, there is no need for armor. Genetically, the armor develops through the immobilization of the aggression in the child. The aggression is not turned inward against the self as in masochism but it is used defensively. Psychologically, the armor is the expression of the attitude of stiffening to meet an attack rather than striking back. Dynamically, the tension in the front is produced by pulling back the shoulders and pelvis, thus putting all the front muscles on the stretch at the same time that they are contracted. When the front and back of the body are thus encased in a rigid sheath of tight muscles we can say that the organism is armored.

How does the armor serve to bind anxiety? Is the energy locked in the contracted muscles? I had thought so for a long time for some energy can be mobilized by the relaxation of the contractions. Practical therapeutic experience forced the realization that no great change is accomplished in character structure simply through the release of muscle tension. This is a necessary part of the job but only a part. The change in structure develops through a change in the dynamics of the character structure; it is the release of aggression from its defensive function which changes the hysterical character. No armor can be removed without setting free repressed anger which then flows strongly into the arms and hands. As the shoulders gain motility, the chest wall relaxes; respiration deepens and energy production rises. This would result in the appearance of anxiety unless the analytic work has prepared the way for its discharge through analysis of the sexual function. With the use of the bioenergetic technique of grounding the legs, the channel for discharge is prepared before the anger is released.

We are in a position now to understand the mechanism whereby the armor binds the anxiety. It does so by reducing respiration through an unconscious control over the muscles of the front of the body. Although the diaphragm is relatively free, the rigidity of the total structure limits the intake and output of air. This explains why the first step towards the biological treatment of the neuroses was a technique based upon the establishment of full and free respiration. An increased oxygen uptake increases energy production and strengthens impulse formation. Under that technique impulses could develop sufficient force to overcome the repression and reach the surface as awareness and action. While this technique is generally applicable it is particularly valid for those character structures based upon the maintenance of a balance between energy production and energy discharge. In bioenergetic therapy, however, the function of respiration is coordinated with the total behavior of the organism and is not treated as an isolated function.

Although the relation of energy production to energy discharge varies with different individuals, it is relatively fixed for each hysterical character. This type comprises individuals who might be called "adjusted" persons. The danger in the structure lies in the fact that there are strong unconscious drives to break out of the armor, to free one's self from its limitations, to become fully alive. Many hysterical characters will unconsciously seek situations which excite them and increase their inner charge. This is the bioenergetic explanation of their flirtatious behavior. Under such circumstances strong anxiety may result and a typical hysterical reaction may become evident.

If, as a result of early experiences, the structure contains strong oral or masochistic traits, the rigidity which finally develops will be strong enough to compensate for these underlying weaknesses. That was the situation with the case presented earlier in this chapter. The reaching of the mouth which I interpreted on the genital level in accordance with character analytic principles manifests at the same time oral wishes and can be regarded also as an oral trait.

The rigidity one meets with in analytic work varies greatly. As an armoring process, it begins with the surface muscles, in contrast with the spasticities of oral and masochistic structures. Under circumstances, however, where frustration is severe and the life situation unfavorable, the organism may become more rigid, less flexible and the process then may extend into the depths. While the loss of elasticity leads to brittleness, the extension of the freezing process into the depths may actually touch the core with its icy fingers. If a permanent diminution of impulse formation results, a real dying has occurred in the organism. The case cited earlier was particularly illustrative of this condition. The other extreme is an organism in which the armor is very superficial and light. Such individuals show a degree of health and grace that is frequently the envy of others. But it is difficult to conceive how in our culture an organism can completely escape without some disturbance of its biological functioning.

In this chapter I have endeavored to explain the nature of the hysterical structure. The rigidity of the body structure is the terrain in which the hysterical attack erupts. Other questions remain to be answered about this character type. They will be the subject of the following chapter.

13

The Hysterical Character—2

Psychoanalytic writers have related the hysterical character to the genital conflict which arises out of the unresolved Oedipus situation. In *Character Analysis*, Reich (1949, p. 190) said, "The genital incest wishes are repressed but have retained their full cathexis, they are not replaced by pregenital drives." Every hysterical character approaches sexuality with an unconscious attitude derived from the Oedipus situation. This attitude expresses itself in an ambivalence towards the sexual object which, through analysis, can be shown to correspond to the girl's attitude towards her father.

If we do not debate the origin of the Oedipus situation but accept its occurrence as a fact in our culture, we must recognize that the female child's first genital object is her father. This flow of libido to the adult male occurs however only after the genital function has become fully established in the child; that is, about the age of two to three. Prior to that time, object attachment is on the basis of the infantile ego with its strong oral, narcissistic demands. In the Oedipus situation, much depends on the actual role played by the father in the childhood and youth of the girl. A strict authoritarian father can produce great fear of the male in the young girl. In such a case not only is the genital desire inhibited but the anger which arises as a result of the frustration is blocked and repressed in turn. The inhibition and repression of anger towards the male is not sufficiently appreciated in the hysterical character. More importance has been placed upon the conflict with the mother whom the young girl regards as a rival for her father's affection. So much of this is well-known that I hesitate to go over these basic insights were it not that an important clarification could be achieved through a change in the interpretation of the problem.

If we recognize that an ambivalent attitude towards the male is the basis of the hysterical character structure, much can be explained. On the one hand, desire is blocked by a fear which has its roots in the original rejection of the child's sexuality by the father; on the other hand, anger is inhibited by the repressed longing. One could simplify the problem by saying that longing is blocked by repressed anger, as the anger is blocked by repressed longing. The stiffening produced by the repression of these antagonistic impulses, one acting on the front, the other on the back of the body, creates the rigid armor of the hysterical character. Each repression acts as a defense against the antagonistic impulses. The anger cannot be released so long as sexual desire for the father or father-surrogate (the analyst in the transference situation) is suppressed. Repressed anger and pride block the approach to the suppressed longing.

In this situation, how does the hysterical character function? Repressed longing prevents a direct approach to the male. Obvious sexual gestures involving a certain motility of the hips and the use of the eyes, though generally unconscious, serve to entice the male into a sexually aggressive action. The character structure of the average male, as we shall see, fits him well for this role. What follows is the typical pattern of pursuit which generally leads to the submission of the female for this was unconsciously intended by her all along. Sometimes a show of resistance is overcome by force. In the Italian motion picture, *Bitter*

Rice, this was dramatically portrayed. A young girl, coquettish and aware of her sexual charms, flirts with the boy friend of another girl. Her action seems intended simply to win him away from her rival. As she follows him into the fields one day he turns upon her suddenly and beats her severely with a stick which he picked up for that purpose. She then yields to him sexually and becomes his subservient mistress. It is typical of the hysterical character structure that it yields to force, direct or indirect. This then adds to the latent anger against the male. In the film mentioned it led the girl to kill her lover. Not every pursuit ends in the surrender of the female. Occasionally, a cornered female will turn on the male and express her rage with the fury of a hellcat.

What is the psychological meaning of this behavior? The submission of the female is not an act of love. To the degree that love enters into the sexual relation, the stigma of neurosis disappears from it. Since the submission was unconsciously intended, it serves the purpose of shifting the responsibility for the sexual act upon the male. This would seem masochistic were it not for the fact that the hysterical character is not passive. Under the apparent submission is an aggressive attitude which leads to sexual discharge. The pursuit by the male tends to repair the narcissistic injury suffered by the father's rejection of the young girl's sexual love. If the tease can be carried out further it serves to revenge the original injury at the hands of the male sex. And just as the neurotic male may think of his action as a conquest, so the hysterical character regards her behavior and its result in the same light. Sexual submission re-establishes the Oedipus relation but in a way satisfactory to the female. By his aggression, the male shows his interest and desire, by his pursuit he proclaims his strength and power, in taking the submission he accepts the responsibility. We noted in the case discussed in the preceding chapter that sexual submission was a means employed to obtain the protection of the male.

Sexual submission which covers an aggressive attitude

is the distinguishing mark of the hysterical character. The pattern of response seems to be: teasing, resistance, and then submission. In this respect we are far removed from the flirtatious behavior of the hysterical character of fifty to thirty years ago which excluded genital contact. However, the sexual submission in no way changes the fundamental problem. Submission is based on fear, the same fear which underlay the behavior of the hysterical character of earlier times, although not so great or intense. It is fear of strong genital excitation, of being overwhelmed, of losing control. Strange as it may seem, sexual submission has the function of preventing too great a genital excitation which would result if the sexual desire was overtly and directly experienced and expressed. In this respect genitality is in the service of a defense against sexuality.

It is a characteristic of the hysterical character that despite the rigidity and armoring of the body, the pelvis is more or less soft and sexually alive. The specific tensions of the hysterical character are superficial: the main ones are located in the vaginal muscles and the adductors of the thigh. The oral characters and the masochistic characters lack the sway of the hips which gives a girl what is described as "sex appeal." Now in some cases it is easy to descry an exaggerated motility which is undoubtedly flirtatious and definitely a mark of the hysterical character. But such cases are rare today. If anything, the girls of our present day culture seem to have less pelvic motility than one would expect in a naturally alive organism. Nonetheless, the first statement holds true, that the hysterical character has a body structure in which the rigidity of the body is coupled with a sexually alive pelvis. In this way, sexual discharge is provided for at the same time that the rigidity limits the genital charge. Given this limited charge, the pelvis can move with apparent freedom. The superficial tensions, however, may be quite strong. They necessarily limit movement and fullness of discharge.

The hysterical character functions without symptoms

so long as the balance between energy production and discharge is maintained. But so long as this balance is maintained at a level other than one close to full capacity, life is relatively unexciting and meaningless. The lower the relative level of energy production and discharge, the closer the individual is to death. Where energy production stops, impulse formation ceases and movement comes to a final arrest. We saw in the case discussed in the preceding chapter that when energy production is greatly lowered, an expression of death is actually visible in the countenance of the person. To return to the question of excitement. The person is not always consciously aware that he is functioning at reduced energy levels, but feelings of boredom, of being in a rut, of dissatisfaction are common. To judge from the intensity with which people search for excitement in one form or another we can assume that their daily lives are quite dull. All this, of course, is known. It is important in our present study because it explains why the balance referred to above is at best precarious. The hysterical character constantly seeks to upset it in the direction of more energy and deeper feelings. It is this desire and need which drive them to flirt, to seek romance, to engage in extramarital relations.

It is not too difficult for the hysterical character to increase the level of energy production; anything which increases the feeling of excitement does it. The most common way is through a new liaison. The problem then changes into how to discharge the extra energy. Genital tensions and spasticities are not removed in the flush of the increased excitation. The inhibition of pelvic motility has not been resolved. True, the increased excitement consequent upon the novelty of the new experience and on the feeling of conquest in the new affair results in greater sexual charge, heightened aliveness and a feeling of joy. Since the ability to discharge has not kept pace with the increased charge, the energy economy must return to its previous level. Excitement decreases, energy production drops; the novelty of the affair is gone and a new liaison must be sought.

The forces which operate to maintain the status quo are powerful. It is never sufficient that the patient be made aware of the problem. First, energy production must be raised to a higher level, and, second, the individual must learn to tolerate and discharge this increased energy. Since more energy is made available than can be discharged some anxiety is to be expected. When both energy production and discharge are handled as a common problem this anxiety is kept at a minimum. Further, the disturbance of the energy balance has another effect. The pelvis which can move with some facility at one level of energy and feeling becomes paralyzed at a higher level. A genital apparatus which can discharge a certain quantity of energy fails to function when that quantity is significantly increased. Thus we expect that when the love feelings of the heart are mobilized in the sexual impulse, the resulting anxiety may kill the sexual desire, prevent any sexual discharge, or turn the woman against the man. It is a common experience in the treatment of the hysterical character that successful work both analytically and bioenergetically leads to a falling off of the sexual drive. If this is watched for and controlled the reaction is temporary.

These observations teach us that the hysterical character of today is not so much afraid of the genital aim as they are of the deep love feelings originating in the heart. Theirs is a sexuality limited to the genitals and which does not embrace the total organism. We find a split in the personality between the loving, tender feelings and genitality. Our modern hysteric has identified with her genital strivings in contrast to the hysteric of thirty years ago who, according to Abraham, rejects the normal genital aim. The hysterical character of those days was a romantic dreamer. In either case, the identification is only with one aspect of sexuality: submissive genitality or romantic love. The neurosis consists in the antagonism of two aspects of a single impulse. As long as the identification is with the genital function, the hysterical character is spared the symptomatology formerly seen. Only when genital discharge is blocked do conditions become favorable for the development of the typical hysterical symptoms.

If one attempts to reach the heart of the hysterical character, to mobilize the deep feelings of love, one will meet with a most determined defense. Bioenergetic study shows that this defense is localized in the neck and jaw in the form of muscle tensions which give these structures a stiff, set quality. The whole neck feels stiff and the jaw is set. Analysis of the expression tells us that it is one of pride and determination. I have not seen the hysterical character who did not have these traits of pride and determination, and in whom this determined pride was not the key to the character. The oral character and the masochistic character structures definitely lack this quality. One could say that in them the lack of pride is apparent as a fault in the character. There is, of course, a natural pride, but the pride of the hysterical character is more or less set, inflexible and determined. Further, one can correlate quantitatively the intensity of this stiff pride with the degree to which there is a tendency to hysterical symptomatology in the character.*

I do not like to refer to characters in literary fiction to maintain the ideas I have advanced here. The material presented in this study is derived from clinical cases. On this question of pride and hysteria, however, it is worth mentioning the names of some female figures in the novels of Dostoevski. One thinks immediately of Nastasya Fillipovna of *The Idiot*, Lizabeta Nikolaevna of *The Possessed* and Katya Ivanovna of *The Brothers Karamazov*.

---

* Sometimes, however, the energy production of the hysterical character is so low that the head cannot be maintained stiffly erect; the neck is not so rigid and pride is not so evident. This was the situation in the case analyzed. If the pride is latent, it is nonetheless a potent factor. As soon as the energy level mounts it comes to the surface.

In each case we have a beautiful and proud woman who has suffered some deep insult at the hands of a man. In each case pride goes before a fall. It is worth mentioning these names because few clearer examples of the hysterical character structure can be found.

Just as one cannot find a hysterical character without this sense of pride, so too will one always find in these character structures a deep sense of hurt. This unconscious sense of having been hurt is so strong that it determines the behavior in terms of an unconscious attitude not to suffer a hurt again. Actually, the pride and determination are aspects of this attitude—not to be hurt again. Let me explain why this is typically hysterical.

The oral character has suffered a much deeper hurt than the hysterical character yet lacks the pride of the latter. The reason for this is very simple if one recalls the description of the oral character as a "have-not" structure. The oral character's need for love is so great that his feeble attempts at defense collapse quickly. This is one mark of an oral character structure. The masochistic cannot be proud because he feels inadequate. He is masochistic because he seeks to suffer. The hurt which the oral character suffered was a deprivation on the oral level and at an age when no defense was possible. Masochism develops out of humiliating experiences which crush the ego. Its counter-aspect is sadism which, psychologically, can be interpreted as a revenge mechanism. The injury which the hysterical character suffered is a rejection of her love on the genital plane. This happens because this love is first proffered to the father who is, of course, unable to respond to it. It is not a question of a single experience but of the fact that the girl child is caught between strong impulses of sexual love and fear of rejection because of the oedipal situation.

At this point, the tender feelings which derive from heart sensations and the genital sensations are unified in a single current or feeling. The young girl does not differentiate between love and sexuality. At this age, such a differentiation is unnecessary. If this distinction is forced upon the child it produces a splitting of the unitary impulse. It is my conviction that as the child matures it will make this distinction in a more rational way, that is, according to the situation. The healthy adult is capable of love for many people, yet the same love in its fullest expression, which includes genital longing, is reserved for one partner. The damaging effect upon the child is the result of an awareness that one must not have both tender feelings and genital sensations for the same person. The latter, then, are repressed and this repression of genital sensation in the growing child is responsible for the latency period.

With the very strong sexual surge at puberty, genital sensation is reawakened. Since this new genital sensation seems to give added meaning and excitement to life, the girl will strive to guard this genital feeling at the expense of the deeper love feelings associated with heart sensations. In all hysterical characters there is a double sense of hurt: one that relates to experiences dating to early childhood and another from the period of adolescence. Freud had recognized this double determination of hysteria in his study "The Etiology of Hysteria" published in 1896. Of the two determinants, the earlier is the more important. The later one, however, determines the characterological aspect and must be consistently analyzed.

The sense of hurt which is carried over from late infantile or early childhood experience and which leads to the inhibition of genital sensation is responsible for the analytic concept of a castration complex in the female. I have no hesitation in stating that no female in whom there is not a prior disturbance of genital function would feel penis envy. It must not be taken for granted that the repression of genital sensation which occurs in the young child from the age of three to six is due solely to the conflict of the Oedipus situation. An hysterical character structure can and does develop in girls who grew up in homes without a father during their earliest years. Of course, even in such homes, a male is never completely absent, either physically or in spirit, but the absence of a father rules out the Oedipus conflict as the sole factor. The other factors derive from the sex-negative attitude of our culture. There is the frustration of infantile masturbation, the restriction upon sexual play of children, the denial of infantile sexual curiosity, etc., etc. The growing child faces the fact that the reality of social life is antagonistic to his sexual drive. The child reacts to this situation the same as if the frustration of the sexual impulse stemmed from the father. Depending upon the severity of this frustration, the child represses genital sensation until puberty. Among the most severe cases of rigidity I have seen are girls whose childhood years were spent in a convent. The lack of privacy which prevents the continuation of infantile masturbation, the strong discipline based on fear and the separation of the sexes, create a situation which is extremely frustrating to the child.

The frustration of the child's sexual impulse is not experienced by the child as a denial of genitality. Since this impulse flows directly from the heart to the genital, the rejection is felt as a rejection of love. It is this which accounts for the deep sense of hurt. Actually this perception of the child is correct, for love that does not manifest itself in physical contact fails to satisfy the basic needs of the organism. All physical contact between the parents and the child is experienced by the child as a sexual contact. Only after the unity of tender feeling and genital sensation is disrupted does the relationship between parents and children lose its sexual quality.

Having been hurt through the expression of love, the child gradually learns to decrease its vulnerability to such injury. It does this by "stiffening up," as if to say, "I won't give in to my feeling of love for you, then you can't hurt me by your rejection of me." Pride is the attitude which expresses this feeling. The "stiffening up" occurs in the back from the base of the skull to the sacrum. As part of this process the neck stiffens so that the head is held very erect. Since the analysis proceeds in the reverse direction to the development of the character structure, the first major resistance one will encounter in the therapy of the hysterical character is this pride. The hysterical character cannot give into the analytic or therapeutic procedure so long as this pride is not exposed and analyzed. Of course the fact that the patient comes to therapy is an indication that she wishes to overcome the rigidities which disturb her function. The analyst has to show the patient that he is aware of the underlying hurt before he can expect the patient to let down her defense.

Let me summarize the main features of the hysterical character structure. The ego function is grounded in reality as the sexual function is grounded in genitality. But these are overdetermined in the hysterical structure. They are maintained by the stiffening of the aggressive motor component which is made to serve a defensive function. The pride manifested in the stiff neck and the determination shown by the set jaw are ego aspects of this character attitude. The tightness of the lower back and the retraction of the pelvis are the sexual analogues of the ego attitude. Aggression becomes antagonistic to the tender, sensitive and spiritual side of the personality. The hysterical character is afraid to fall in love. They are afraid to fall in general, and this fear of falling manifests itself in the rigidity of the legs. Falling anxiety and dreams of falling are more clearly evidenced in the rigid structures than in the less highly developed ego structures.

We saw, too, that this antithesis of aggression and sensitivity is reflected in a splitting of the sexual function. The aggressive component is permitted expression while the tender feelings are repressed. The hysterical character is capable of discharge, that is, of reaching a climax. If the rigidity is at all marked, the amount of feeling is greatly reduced. Since the aggression is used defensively it is not overt sexual aggression but sexual enticement of the male. This dominance of aggression in the sexual function is a phenomenon of puberty. It was preceded by a period of more or less sexual latency in which the opposite was true: tender feelings dominated the personality. The typical tomboy behavior of pre-adolescent girls belongs to a type of structure which we call masculine-aggressive and which is a mixed type.

Within this broad pattern of response, individual differences are present which determine the specific character of the individual. The persistence of oral traits derived from early deprivation are easily discerned. In the case discussed as illustrative of this character type, the interpretation of the expression in the mouth can be made on both the oral and the genital level. It expresses an oral trait within the framework of a genital structure. Similarly, masochistic tendencies are to be found in the hysterical character. They must not dominate the picture else we would have a masochistic character. The rigidity itself may be slight or severe. This will depend upon how much aggression the child had when it reached the genital phase of its development and how much frustration it suffered at this stage. Orality and masochism are tendencies which decrease the available aggression. Rigidity immobilizes the aggression by making it serve a defensive function.

The examination and analysis of several different hysterical characters would reveal the fundamental similarity of their bioenergetic structures despite important differences in their superficial aspects. A young mother came to therapy because of a lack of satisfaction and happiness in her relations with her husband. She complained further that she was irritable with her children and not a good mother. These are vague complaints yet they were sufficiently disturbing to this patient to motivate a serious study of her problems. She was rather small and dainty in her body but she had a big head and a large expressive face. The eyes were alive, the nose small and regular, the mouth slightly uneven with a large lower jaw. A small neck joined this head to a petite body which was evenly proportioned except that the shoulders were noticeably narrowed. I mention these details of her physical appearance because they made an immediate impression upon me as I observed her on the couch. She looked like one of those "kewpie dolls" one can see at Coney Island. Not only were the shoulders narrowed but they were held tightly forward so that in movement they looked as if they swung upon artificial joints. Somewhat the same impression was given by the legs. It was surprising, therefore, that with this evident lack of strength in arms and legs she ran a house and two small children.

Everything I learned about the history of this patient bore out this interpretation of her character as "doll-like." She was an only child and a spoiled one as she herself said. As an infant she already looked like a little "angel." In her autobiography she described her mother's attitude as follows: "She wanted everyone to like me. I should always be sweet and kind and never get angry or they *won't* like you." Her mother nagged both her and her father. She remarked that her father had a set jaw. At the age of eight years she had an attack of poliomyelitis in which the neck, jaw and legs were involved. It is also interesting to note that as a child her defense against other children's attacks was to bite.

When I pointed out her doll-like character, the patient immediately felt that I was right. Later in the autobiography she recalled that a teacher had called her a "doll." For all her doll-like appearance this patient had a fair sexual discharge, a good contact with reality and a good work function. The rigidity of her body, chest, back and pelvis supported the diagnosis of hysterical character. In line with this diagnosis I interpreted the set jaw as an expression of determination to be "the nice little girl" her mother always wanted her to be. A slight twist to the mouth while smiling plus a twinkle in her eye made me suspect the imp behind this façade. These observations enabled me to analyze her problem quickly. She was doing an adult job in managing her household yet she tried to be the "nice, little girl," to "do things right," and to be "well-liked by everyone." Her determination was directed towards these objectives. Little wonder then that she was irritable. I was more astonished that she had done as well so far. Despite the weakness of arms and legs, this patient had a basic ego strength which was visible in the set and determined jaw.

In the first session I made an effort to soften the jaw. It brought an immediate reaction: the patient cried bitterly. I had no difficulty then in getting her to express anger. Both intellectually and emotionally she recognized the validity of my interpretations. This enabled me to proceed more vigorously with the bioenergetic work in succeeding sessions. At each session the "doll" became more alive, the "imp" in her receded progressively, and the physical appearance of the patient changed accordingly. Arms and legs strengthened, the shoulders broadened appreciably and the face developed more signs of maturity. The complaints for which she began therapy were gradually eliminated. In the course of this work the hysterical attitude towards sexuality and the male was exposed and analyzed.

While this patient, with her doll-like hysterical structure, was very amenable to bioenergetic analysis and therapy, the case of the girl mentioned in one of the earlier chapters, with the mannequin-like character, proved much more difficult. For one thing, this latter patient had a waxy quality to the skin of the face which indicated a much weaker life force than in the case just discussed. Mannequin-like or doll-like, this quality suggested the wax museum. This was further borne out by an obvious gesture: that of lying on her back with her arms crossed on her chest. One needed only to put the lily in place! Yet here too, despite the rigidity and lack of life, we were dealing with a character structure organized on the basis of a stable genital function.

Two aspects of this latter case are very interesting. Although this patient had reached a point of fairly satisfactory sexual discharge, this was a late development. As an adolescent she had passed through a period of frequent and promiscuous sexual activity of a genital nature. It was as if she submitted to almost every demand for intercourse made by a young man. None of these acts led to a satisfactory discharge although she was not frigid. Later when a satisfactory sexual discharge resulted her sexual promiscuity ceased. I have seen this change in behavior and for the same reason in a number of cases. It supports Reich's contention that satisfactory sexuality is the best guarantee for a naturally moral sexual behavior. If one wishes to interpret the promiscuity one must consider it as a search through different partners for a lost condition, one in which the individual had experienced the pleasure of sexual release. At the same time sexual promiscuity is always passive and represents a submission which must have its basis in fear of the male. Continued analysis in this case brought to light the memory of several violent physical fights with her father around the age of puberty. He struck the patient forcibly for staying out with boys.

I did not have the opportunity to complete the therapeutic work with this patient. Analysis had revealed that her passive attitude was a waiting for a man who through his love for her would awaken the dormant life. She was the "sleeping beauty." When, however, in the course of therapy, the life stirred within her, marked anxiety developed. It was experienced as an "icky" feeling which made her very uncomfortable. "Icky" could be related to sticky, that is, it could be regarded as a manifestation of the binding power of eros. This patient was afraid to become attached in an emotional way to the male. The problem of the transference could and did serve as the vehicle for the working through of this attitude. As I said, I did not complete the therapy. She left to get married and moved to a distant city. This, in itself, was a big step forward. Before leaving, the patient told me that she had greatly benefited by the therapy.

Frigidity in the sense of the absence of any genital sensation is purely a hysterical problem. It can almost be called a conversion symptom or an expression of hysterical anesthesia or paralysis.* Females with an oral or a masochistic character structure are never frigid. They may fail to achieve genital discharge but sensation is never absent. Frigidity is not the absence of sexuality. The frigid female may reveal in her behavior obvious sexual gestures. She will be unaware of these, of course, since she has no genital sensation. The problem is an interesting one and it is analyzed from a bioenergetic point of view in the following case.

The patient was a girl eighteen years of age. She came to therapy because she felt that her lack of sexual response to the male represented a disturbance in her personality. This awareness was not based on any emotional experience in which her frigidity was perceived as a serious fault. For one thing, she was young. Coupled with this was the hope that if the right young man came along she would not be lacking. Yet she was intelligent enough to know that her present function was pathological. There was another element to this particular problem. If she went out with a boy she frequently had the fear that her father was following her. This was not an hallucination but a fear.

One can find several comparisons in psychoanalytic literature between the problem of frigidity and the fable of the sleeping beauty. There is little question in my mind but that the comparison is a valid one. In fact, the hope that an ideal lover will come and liberate the repression-bound female sexuality can be found in every hysterical character. The fantasy life of the individual will always

---

* Otto Fenichel, writing about the same problem, says: "Finally, there are the cases of total frigidity, whose genital erogeneity is entirely blocked. In these cases 'not to feel anything' expresses the idea: 'I do not want to have anything to do with it,' which is a special case of the general type of defense of estranging oneself from one's own body. This estrangement is the same as that in the sensory disturbance of hysteria." *The Psychoanalytic Theory of Neurosis.* New York, Norton, 1945, p. 173.

compensate for the neurotic disturbance. But this really tells us little about the problem of frigidity, that is, if we define it as the absence of any genital sensation. We must regard it then as one aspect of the larger problem, which is the inhibition of sexual sensation in general.

Would you expect to find frigidity associated with a high energy level in the organism? Strange as it may seen such was my experience. Where the energy level is rather low due to severe rigidity, this very rigidity acts as a hollow tube to funnel sensation into the genital. Clinical observation of patients with a low energy economy, such as the one of the preceding chapter where death had touched the countenance, never reveal this genital anesthesia which is the mark of total sexual frigidity. This young lady, then, was a girl with vivaciousness, an expressive manner, a warm pleasing personality and a quick smile. Her face was attractive, her body of average height, her figure trim and well proportioned. She was physically strong and agile. Members of the opposite sex would certainly find her exciting. There was nothing in her work function nor in her relations with people which would in any way give us a clue to the meaning of her disturbance.

What makes this problem very interesting from a bioenergetic point of view is precisely this seeming contradiction between high energy production with a good grounding in reality and the lack of genital sensation. It is our basic postulate that the genital function expresses the reality principle, and we have attempted to show that any individual's character attitude to reality is manifested in their genital function. The hysterical character is a genital character, being in contrast to the pregenital types. We have seen that the ego swing is securely anchored at both ends of its trajectory: genital function and realistic thinking. Is this case of frigidity an exception? Can we explain this seeming contradiction?

My answer to this problem is that there is no contradiction here. This patient has a genital function in the sense of charge and discharge although she does not perceive it.

The situation is analogous to the one which Reich faced in his attempt to comprehend the masochistic problem. Reich wrote that it was, "Only when I began to doubt the correctness and precision of the patients' statements did the light begin to dawn." There it was a question of how the fantasy or the act of being beaten can be experienced as pleasurable. Despite all reports by masochists to the contrary, we have seen, following Reich's analysis, that the fantasy or act of being beaten is not the source of pleasure. So in this case of absolute sexual frigidity, according to the statements of the patient, we must doubt both her statements and the possibility of such an absolute frigidity. We can agree that whatever genital excitation does occur is repressed below the level of conscious perception. When such repression exists, the function against which it is directed is reduced to the level of the involuntary autonomic processes of which one is generally unaware. But so far in this analysis we have not resolved the problem of frigidity, rather the contradiction is eliminated and the question must now be rephrased.

What is the mechanism by which a strong libidinal flow fails to produce a genital excitation of sufficient intensity to lead to perception? When the problem is thus expressed, it can be seen that it is the central question of the hysterical symptom, or more accurately of the chronic symptom or condition of hysterical anesthesia. The psychic elements in this problem were analyzed by Freud in the preceding century. Compare Freud's article in 1896, "The Etiology of Hysteria," or even his first article (with Breuer) in 1893, "On Hysterical Mechanisms." In the earlier paper Freud pointed out that hysteria develops on the basis of a splitting of consciousness into a hypnoid consciousness and a normal consciousness. "During the (hysterical) attack, control of the entire somatic innervation has passed to the hypnoid consciousness." The hypnoid state contains the repressed memories "with full affective tone for a long period." In the later paper, further elements of this mechanism are elucidated. The "repressed memories" are infantile sexual experiences which, ineffective in themselves, can "exercise a pathogenic influence only later when they are roused after puberty in the form of unconscious memories." The symptom is determined by the effort of defense against a painful idea of more recent experience which has associative and logical connections with the unconscious infantile experiences. Freud emphasizes that the infantile experiences must have occurred before the eighth year of life for hysteria to develop. While no precise statement is made as to the nature of this temporal limit, other than its relation to the development of the second dentition, we can assume that if consciousness is not affectively split prior to that time no later experience will produce such splitting. Freud's brilliant insights throw into relief the essential problem which is the mechanism of the unconscious itself.

We started this discussion on a bioenergetic level. Let us return to it. Here, too, we can obtain some help from Freud. Writing on "The Anxiety Neurosis," Freud (1894a, p. 105) said: "In each of them [anxiety-neurosis and hysteria] there is a psychical inadequacy as a consequence of which abnormal somatic processes come about. In each of them there occurs a deflection of excitation to the somatic field instead of psychical assimilation of it." This means that hysteria is fundamentally a problem of anxiety. The hysterical predisposition is the tendency to anxiety based upon an energy economy in which energy production is maintained at the level of energy discharge. Anything which would increase the energy production above this level could lead to hysteria (the hysterical attack as an anxiety reaction). Any situation which would cause a decrease in the amount of energy discharge below the level of energy production could produce an anxiety neurosis. This is the essence of Freud's observations made in 1896 on anxiety. The specific situations he referred to were: abstinence, coitus interruptus, anxiety in the climacteric, etc. In the case of maturing girls first meeting the sexual problem the "anxiety neurosis is typically combined with hysteria."

In the hysterical character the quantity of energy which reaches both the genital apparatus and the brain with each oscillation is reduced. The very nature of this swing requires that no more energy can charge one end than the other. We can go further than to equate the genital apparatus with the brain. The genital organ, which is only part of the total sexual apparatus, corresponds to the fore-brain. Psychical inadequacy corresponds, therefore, to genital inadequacy. One does not exist without the other. The process involved is a restriction at each end of the swing. If energy production is high, this diminution at the ends of the swing can only occur if energy is deflected from the swing into paths away from the cortex or genital; some "abnormal somatic process" results. This remark by Freud recalls Reich's statement that the hysterical character has a "specific kind of bodily agility with a definitely sexual nuance." From this study we may deduce that when a strong libidinal flow fails to produce an equally strong genital excitation a deflection of the excitation has diverted energy away from genital and cortex.*

If we return to our case of so-called absolute sexual frigidity, in which the energy production is fairly high, we should expect to find manifestations of the diverted en-

---

* One further corollary of this theory can be mentioned here although its full elaboration is reserved for another occasion. The unconscious must be related to this decrease of charge in the forebrain. In the hysterical character it is precisely genital experiences which are repressed and genital sensation which is inhibited. Therapeutic results confirm this relation. As the genital charge is increased memories return of pubertal or infantile sexual experiences. It is not necessary to postulate that the memory is locked in the muscle tension to explain this phenomenon. The extension of the energy swing always affects both ends. As it extends further downward so it also extends upward. It is not surprising, therefore, that the representation of the body in the motor area of the cortex is in the form of an inverted man: the lowest point of the body occupies the highest point in the cortical representation. The unconscious has both a psychic and a bioenergetic meaning.

ergy in the form of body movement. Among the most obvious of these manifestations is a kind of smiling, occasionally laughing, over which the patient has no control and which is provoked by a glance or a touch. More striking are the constant small movements of the body which, if suppressed, produce immediate anxiety. The general impression is that these bodies are very alive and unrigid. Yet they are obviously armored both psychologically and muscularly. The jaw is quite strong and determined. But one does not find the platelike armor on the chest or back which characterized the previous cases. Muscle tension exists everywhere but it is surprisingly flexible. One must think of it in terms of mesh or net or chain armor which is very much more efficient that the platelike armor of the more rigid structures.

This flexible, meshlike armor makes possible the shifting of tension within the armor. It is more difficult to attack therapeutically than the more rigid platelike armor. For example, if respiration is mobilized through work on the chest, the defense can take over in the neck to prevent release of the energy. The big advantage of this type of armoring is that it permits of more movement within the armor. In addition, its meshlike structure functions as pores through which a certain amount of the energy can be discharged. Such an armor permits a greater energy production at the same time that it functions to bind anxiety and prevent injury. Nonetheless it reduces sensation and limits the expression of impulses. Only such an armor can decrease genital sensation below the level of perception in a highly charged organism. The greater part of the energy is deflected into the musculature where it sets up a series of small movements within the armor and eventually is discharged through the pores. It is in this sense that, in the hysterical character, genital libido floods the whole organism like a "flexible" or shifting masochism.*

* Compare this with Ferenczi's observations on the same problem: "These apparently harmless activities can easily become hiding places for the libido . . . should the patient notice

There is another aspect to the problem of the meshlike flexible armor. Since the unitary swing of the energy is broken up to prevent strong genital sensation, the form of movement which results is segmental rather than unitary. One patient with such an armor told me that she felt that her pelvis moved with a side-to-side motion in intercourse. She described it as a "squirming." Given a meshlike armor close to the surface, segmental movements in the nature of squirming, and a strong jaw, one is reminded of a snake. Reich evidently refers to this type of armor as the hysterical character for it accords with his description of this character as having "a specific kind of bodily agility with a definitely sexual nuance." On the other hand the orgasm reflex bends the body in one arc from shoulders to pelvis.

The problem of frigidity, as absolute sexual frigidity, is the problem of the avoidance of genital excitation by means of squirming movements which in themselves are an expression of negativity. Squirming is a natural reaction to pain or unpleasure when the means of escape are blocked and the organism does not "freeze up." Undoubtedly the squirming developed under circumstances which did not permit the escape from unpleasant excitation. Such circumstances are those in which an adult carries out a sexual aggression against a young child. The combination of sexual excitement and fear keeps the child rooted in a situation which is full of anxiety. The child squirms. So we come back to Freud's earliest statements on the etiology of hysteria. However, an important distinction must be kept in mind. Freud studied the hysterical attack and the hysterical symptom. The hysterical character struc-

---

that these possibilities of satisfaction escape the analyst, he attaches all his pathogenic phantasies to them, short-circuits them constantly by motor discharge, and thus saves himself the irksome and unpleasant task of bringing them to consciousness." "Technical Difficulties in the Analysis of a Case of Hysteria" (1919). *The Theory and Technique of Psychoanalysis II.* New York, Basic Books, 1953, p. 193.

ture which forms the basis for both symptom and general behavior has a broader etiological origin.

Squirming in relation to sexual excitement is not limited to those experiences in which a child suffers a sexual aggression by an adult. Consider the case of a child of five years who is masturbating with great pleasure and is then surprised in the act by an irate mother. Should the child experience intense fear she could "freeze up" as we say. This reaction tends to produce the rigid platelike armoring. If there is less fear because the mother is less threatening, but the child is subjected to the unpleasant experience of having to explain her actions, the combination of excitement and anxiety can make the child squirm. This type of reaction becomes the basis of the flexible meshtype of armor.

Both types of armoring have the function of limiting energy production. They accomplish this by decreasing motility and respiration. The platelike armor is more restrictive and less efficient. Since it is an expression of a process of "freezing," it develops in organisms which lack a very high charge. The more highly charged organisms do not freeze-up so easily. Heat is a function of energy charge. These distinctions must not hide the characterological similarity of these two structures. The very nature of the armoring process must make us aware that the sexual aggression is used defensively.

From the case of frigidity discussed we must not draw the conclusion that the hysterical character with a flexible armor is necessarily frigid. The contrary is much more common. The flexible armoring is generally associated with a high degree of genital potency. It is my contention, however, that so-called absolute genital frigidity can develop only in this character structure.

The tendency to squirm which underlies this type of structure helps explain a phenomenon which analytic writers have related to genital excitation. Many girls and women have a marked reaction to the sight of a snake. This has been interpreted as a fear of the penis for which the snake is a symbol. Actually, the individuals involved have no such reaction to the penis itself. The live snake especially produces in these females a feeling which is a mixture of fascination and repugnance. Can we not say that it is the peculiar movements of the snake which re-activate in these persons repressed sensations of squirming together with associated feelings of sexual excitation and fear? And that these derive from very early sexual experiences which have been repressed? I believe that it can be shown that this reaction to the snake is limited to this type of character structure.

In the analysis of the individual, we cannot always characterize the armoring as rigid or flexible. Some degree of squirming can be detected in all rigid structures. Character analysis is based upon dominant tendencies. This is not to say that other traits are overlooked. They form part of the constellation which is the individual character. We must regard the hysterical character structure as a classification in which we include female personalities with a rigid ego structure, armored with either a flexible, meshlike armoring or an inflexible platelike armor, and who use aggression defensively. The more inflexible character uses genitality to ward off deeper sexual feelings, while the flexible character uses superficial sexual movements to diminish genital excitation. In both cases we have a mechanism of defense which limits feeling or energy charge and discharge.

The pattern of the armor conforms to the total muscular system of the organism. Where the armor is inflexible it defines a tube, broader or narrower, softer or harder. Occasionally a patient perceives this internal structure. One patient saw herself enclosed in a "stainless steel sheath" located just below the surface of the body. Within this tube the energy streams along the length of the body. The tube recalls the wormlike pattern of our internal structure. As the tube becomes more rigid, respiration, feeling and emotional expression are correspondingly reduced. But by virtue of the fact that the head and the genitals are always linked, the functions of reality and genitality are consistently maintained.

Rigidity of ego structure depends upon this process of muscular armoring. It differs from the specific tensions of the oral character or masochist in that it is total and coextensive with the muscular system. It prevents the collapse which characterizes the masochist and provides an anchor to reality which is lacking in the oral character. But it is a neurotic defense mechanism which creates in the female an hysterical character structure.

Rigidity of ego structure and armoring is a consequence of genital frustration. Deprivation leads to inner emptiness and orality, suppression to severe inner tension and masochism. Genital frustration in the oedipal period produces a stiffening up. It is as if the child said, "Since you reject my love, I shall bind myself not to offer it to you again. In that way, I cannot be hurt."

Since neither the oral nor the masochistic character develop on an ego level to the genital stage, they are in no position to offer their love. Rather, the oral character wants to be loved; the masochist seeks to be approved. Of course, every individual will show some oral traits and some masochistic traits. To the degree that they are present in the structure, they weaken whatever rigidity the child may subsequently develop. In the character analysis of a patient these elements must be defined in the general structure. The presence of oral and masochistic traits does not produce a mixed character type. We must emphasize again that character analysis is based upon dominant patterns of behavior. Yet it is not uncommon to find that either the oral element or the masochistic element is as strong as the rigidity. In such cases we have real mixed character types. These will be discussed in Chapter 15.

Rigidity of ego structure is a quality of reality functioning which includes genitality. While it results from genital frustration, it can only develop in an ego structure which has substantially advanced to the genital level. Should we say that rigidity is pathological per se? We must say that since frustration is and will be an experience of life, the ability to stiffen up to take the frustration is a natural defense reaction of the organism. It becomes pathological only when it becomes characterological, that is, where it is the only response of which the individual is capable. The rigid ego is inflexible; it denies the healthy give and take, it suffers from a lack of adaptability. In a similar way, we can say that the collapse of the masochist is pathological only because it is his only response to pressure. The masochist lacks the ability to stiffen up in situations of pressure. The oral character is not pathological because he wants to be loved. The structure is neurotic because this is the only response. More appropriate attitudes to meet the various reality demands of life have not been developed. In this light character neurosis is seen as the limitation of behavior to specific reaction patterns to the exclusion of the broad range of emotional reactions which should mark the adult and mature ego.

Let us turn now to the study of the problem of characterological rigidity in the male.

14

The Phallic-Narcissistic Character

Character types are differentiated psychologically by their ego structure, that is, by their attitude towards reality. Bioenergetically, they may be differentiated by their genital function. The oral and masochistic characters are classified as pregenital types: their contact with genitality is insecure, their attitude towards reality is infantile or childish. Both are unarmored structures. Accordingly, we must group in one category all character forms which are grounded in genitality, more or less armored, and more or less secure in their relation to reality. To the degree that a genital character structure is neurotic, the neurosis will manifest itself as rigidity psychologically as well as somatically. For this reason, we describe this type of neurotic character structure as rigid. We saw that this category comprises the hysterical character which is the form of this disturbance in the female. The male counterpart of the hysterical character, that is, the form which rigidity takes in the male, is called the phallic-narcissistic character.

Before proceeding to study this character type, it would be well to understand why a distinction is made between the male and female types of rigid structure. In the discussion of the oral and the masochistic character structure, no distinction was made between the sexes. The problem of orality and the problem of masochism do not differ in the two sexes. This follows also from the fact that these are pregenital structures. On the other hand, the genital problem is different for the boy and for the girl. While the basic disturbance caused by rigidity affects the function of each sex similarly, the manifest pattern of behavior will differ according to the sex.

Reich (1949, pp. 200–201) said that the phallic-narcissistic character was formulated to provide for a type which would "stand in between the compulsion neurosis and hysteria." Hysteria, however, is not a character type, it is a symptom. While the symptom is generally associated with the character this is not necessarily so. Hysterical paralysis does occur in the male sex. Symptom formation depends upon special conditions whereas the dynamics of character structure are persistent phenomena. The distinctions which Reich drew between the compulsive character, the hysterical character and the phallic-narcissistic character were based upon traits and not upon the dynamics of the energy processes involved. "While the compulsion character is predominantly inhibited, self-controlled and depressive, and while the hysterical character is nervous, agile, apprehensive and labile, the typical phallic-narcissistic character is self-confident, often arrogant, elastic, vigorous and often impressive." My experience with many patients has shown that these traits are not so sharply limited. Arrogance is frequently the mark of individuals with strong compulsive traits. Elasticity and agility can be confused. This confusion is apparent in the following remark by Reich. Speaking of the phallic-narcissistic character, he wrote, "The facial expression normally shows hard, sharp masculine features, but often also feminine, girl-like features in spite of althletic habits."

Reich and other analysts used the designation "hysterical character" to describe both male and female character types. I prefer to limit the hysterical character to the female structure. The reason for this is that the description of the male hysterical character resembles the passive-feminine type of structure which is a mixed type and more closely related to masochism than to the genital type of structure. The passive-feminine type may be considered one of the subdivisions of the masochistic problem, what Freud called the feminine type of masochism. We shall discuss this type in the following chapter. The phallic-narcissistic character describes a personality structure which is grounded in reality and anchored to genitality by means of ego defenses which are absent in the pregenital structures.

As to the distinction between the compulsive character, which is essentially a European type, and the phallic-narcissistic character, I shall show that it is merely one of degree which does not merit a separate designation. This is not to say, therefore, that the concept of the compulsive character is invalid. From a symptomatic point of view, one can differentiate a compulsive individual from the typical phallic-narcissistic character, and when analysis is carried out as symptom or resistance interpretation such a distinction has value. Bioenergetically, both are rigid, armored structures which differ only in degree. However, let us first look at a typical phallic-narcissistic character; then such variations as lead to compulsion will be more readily understood. This is a case which I treated some years ago.

A young man in his early thirties came to therapy because of premature ejaculation. Friends had told him about my work and he hoped that I could improve his sexual function. He reached a climax about one minute after penetration and as this was always much sooner than his partner reached her acme this disturbed him. In addition, he had read Reich's *The Function of the Orgasm* and he felt that he should experience more pleasure in the sexual act than he was getting. He was an attorney by profession, fairly successful in his work and confident of his future. At the time he began his treatment, he was planning to be married. The fact that his fiancee had been under analysis also influenced his decision to come for treatment.

I mention these facts in detail because it is not often

that the typical phallic-narcissistic character does come
for analytic therapy. They are generally successful in
their work function, fairly well adapted to their social
milieu, and sexually attractive to the opposite sex. As Reich
points out, one of their most important traits is "aggressive courage" which frequently leads to success in achievement. On the other hand this "aggressive behavior itself
fulfills a defense function." If we accept this fact, Reich's
concept of the "genital character" is an idealization; the
phallic-narcissistic male character may range from almost complete health to severe neurosis. Reich recognized
this for he wrote: "In relatively unneurotic representatives
of this type, social achievement, thanks to the free aggression, is strong, impulsive, energetic and usually productive, the more neurotic the character, the more peculiar
and one-sided the achievement." This description applied
to the individual under consideration and therefore his
submission to an analytic therapy was somewhat unusual.

In manner this patient behaved with the aplomb one
would expect from a rather successful attorney. He was
self-confident, outspoken and yet on guard. Of average
height, his body was well-developed and well-proportioned.
He told me that he had always engaged in sports and had
continued his athletic activity into the present. His face
was expressive, the eyes lively and open, the mouth easy
and tending to smile, the jaw rather set and determined.
On the couch, one noted the wide shoulders, full chest,
narrow hips and rather tight legs. Respiration tended to
be abdominal; the chest was held in the inspiratory position.

I began by pointing out to the patient the immobility
of his chest. I encouraged him to try to let the chest move
with the respiration and after some time he was able to
do so. His face now showed a slight apprehension. Occasionally, it is possible to produce a dramatic effect in the
first session. That happened here. I asked the patient to
open his eyes wide; to raise his forehead and then to let
his jaw drop down. He screamed as if with terror. The

reaction was instantaneous. He told me that he felt that he would see a very frightening object. When the patient repeated the expression the same scream ensued but no object was visible. This impressive experience demonstrated that the self-confidence of the patient covered a deep-lying fear and was itself a defense against this fear.

Succeeding sessions were rather highly affect charged. For a time breathing produced strong streaming sensations in the patient which manifested themselves as currents and tingling in both arms and legs. On one occasion, the currents became so strong that his hands froze into a Parkinsonian contracture. Hitting produced strong feelings of anger against someone who, later, was revealed to have been his father. At the time when the patient experienced the anger as being directed specifically against his father, he recalled having been spanked by him for leaving the vicinity of his home. These early sessions, as in so many cases, produced a marked improvement in the patient. He felt more alive and in a better mood than he had for a long time. This improvement generally is temporary for it represents the release of tension which is superficial to the main character armor or blocking. However, it provides the motivation for the difficult task of character restructuring which follows.

The first phase of this therapy was very encouraging. The patient himself was enthusiastic. He envisaged the elimination of all his difficulties in short order. We resumed the therapeutic work after a summer vacation which the patient spent most agreeably. The specific work continued as before. This time the breathing did not produce any sensations. The hitting was just as determined as ever but there was little feeling of anger and no memories. In contrast to the first phase, months passed without any progress. At the time this therapy was undertaken I had not fully worked out the dynamics of character structures. The analysis was carried out on the patient's attitude and on his experiences professionally, socially and sexually. Although it was obvious to both of us that the patient did not give himself fully either in work or in love, still my efforts to change his character and unlock the feelings in the core of his being were unsuccessful. And so the months passed, six of them.

When one meets with an impasse of this nature in an analytic therapy, the reason frequently is that while the broad pattern of behavior is understood, the underlying dynamics of the behavior and the specific quality of the individual structure are not comprehended. In this case both the patient and I knew that he was ambitious. We knew, too, that he was afraid of deep involvement with a girl and that he suffered from some prematurity in ejaculation. All the elements of the phallic-narcissistic character structure were clearly delineated. Yet the rigidity of body and mind could not be altered. The one emotion which was not expressed was crying. And I could not bring about the release of this emotion. The clue to the personality was revealed when it appeared as if the therapy might not succeed.

I asked the patient if he thought it was possible that the treatment might fail. His answer was "no." When I questioned him about this answer, he said that he had never failed in any endeavor. He had never failed an examination in school; more, his grades were far above average. Socially and professionally he had always managed to achieve what he wanted. How did he accomplish this? Through persistence. If he strove for an objective that was very important, he could not rest easy unless he felt that he was doing everything necessary to insure the success of his efforts. So far as I could learn after discussing this point in some detail, it was not an obsession. The idea of failure was intolerable to the patient, but only if the objective was an important one. In such a case the thought of failure produced intense anxiety and the patient redoubled his effort to insure success. The determination to succeed was based as much upon the fear of failure as upon the rewards of success. This framework of behavior was broad enough to permit much flexibility. A considerable amount of failure could be accepted without producing anxiety through a mechanism which shifted the importance of objectives. This mechanism was operative, moreover, in the more important areas of endeavor.

Now I understood the reason for the failure of the therapy to advance during the preceding half year. Acting in character, the patient was working to achieve a spontaneous feeling. It is the same contradiction which is inherent in the remark, "Try and relax." This patient was determined to love; that is, to give in to his tender feelings. But the determination meant a set, hard jaw, braced shoulders, stiffened back. This very attitude was the major resistance to the therapy, the main character block and the expression of the most important muscular tensions. If the drive and determination of the patient were the factors responsible for his social and professional success, they were, in turn, responsible for the major aspect of his neurosis.

My reaction was to tell the patient simply, "Don't try. This isn't a school, with demerits and stars for behavior or performance. My job is to take the pressure off you not to add to it. You are accepted here as you are, not on condition that you do what I want." I was astonished at the effect these words of assurance had on the patient. His eyes filled with tears and he began to cry softly. Here was the spontaneous expression of a tender feeling for which we had been working. It came as a release phenomenon. I do not believe that this patient would have cried so long as he felt under pressure in the therapy. This follows from the nature of the rigid structure. Pressure, responsibility and struggle produces a stiffening or increase in the rigidity. Since crying, which involves the body in sobs, is a convulsive release of tension, rigid organisms will exerience considerable difficulty in crying. It follows as a general principle that one can produce crying in a rigid structure only by increasing the pressure almost to the breaking point and then quickly withdrawing it. Under these circumstances the crying is frequently a very pleasurable experience.

In succeeding sessions the patient was able to elucidate

some of the psychological factors and genetic experiences which led to the block in crying. He did not feel that crying was a sign of weakness or femininity. Many men do express these sentiments and we are familiar with them. He wanted to cry but it was painful. The pain was felt in the throat as a severe spasm. After crying had begun, deepening of the crying was accompanied by painful and spastic sensations in the guts. The patient said that he felt the problem was a specific difficulty in expressing his sorrow. The thought then came that there was so much unhappiness in his childhood home that he could not add his misery to the suffering of his parents. Actually both his father and mother had expressed their unhappiness to the child on very many occasions and each time he felt such pangs of pity that he resolved to do his best to bring them some happiness. He recognized immediately that he labored under this sense of responsibility even in the present although it was coupled with an underlying resentment.

The meaning of the wide shoulders also became clear. Raised and squared off shoulders are a sign of premature responsibility. It is as if the shoulders were braced to support an extra heavy load. Bioenergetically, the throat block diverts some of the energy horizontally into the shoulder muscles. In the back, the flow of anger into the arms and head is similarly blocked at about the level of the seventh cervical vertebrae with a resulting contraction of the muscles of the shoulder girdle. When these blocks are very severe they lead to the passive-feminine character structure. Once this interpretation was grasped by the patient, it became possible to release gradually the shoulder tensions. During session after session, anger and resentment were expressed, especially against his mother for having imposed these burdens upon him. At the same time, he was able to give in more and more to fuller and freer crying.

The fear of failure is related to this sense of responsibility. The patient, himself, was aware that his desire to succeed had as its ultimate goal the satisfaction of his parent's desires and as its deepest motivation the desire to gain the approval and love of his parents, especially that of his mother. In addition to this general motivation to succeed, the patient recalled that on one occasion during his early school days his father had expressed the disappointment he would feel if the patient did not receive the best grades. The patient recalled how shocked he was by this statement, so much so that he resolved not to return home if he failed in school during that term. I am analyzing these factors in some detail here because the question of ambition in the phallic-narcissistic character has been in the forefront of the study of this type of structure. Abraham, for example, relates the ambition of these character types to urethral erotism and suggests that the phallic structure and urethral traits are synonymous. Fenichel (1945, p. 139, 233) also ties ambition to urethral erotism via the feelings of shame. "The aim of ambition based on urethral eroticism is to prove that there is no need to be ashamed any more."

There can be no doubt that there is a relation between urethral eroticism and the ambition which marks the phallic character. One is reminded of the practice of boys standing at the curb and seeing which one can urinate the farthest. The function of micturition can take on an aggressive quality and it does so in the phallic character. Enuresis, for example, may have an "aggressive, spiteful significance aimed at hurting the parents' feelings," according to Fenichel. Perhaps the best specific illustration of this function is the action of some apes in the zoo who will express their anger at the on-lookers by urinating upon them. This patient remembered an incident from his fifth year of life which confirms these analytic observations. His father had reprimanded him rather severely for exposing his penis. The next day when the family was away and he was alone in the house, he walked through the rooms and urinated on the floor with a feeling of revenge. However, even if some connection can be demonstrated, this is far from proving a direct cause and effect relation between ambition and urethral erotism. We are under the necessity of finding the link and establishing the exact nature of the relationship.

The phallic-narcissistic individual is characterized by his drive, i.e., by his aggression. This is a dynamic factor based upon an energy function. Reich was cognizant of this factor at the time he wrote *Character Analysis* in 1933. He observed, "Constitutionally speaking, there seems to be, in these types, an above average production of libidinal energy which makes possible an all the more intense aggression" (1949, p. 206). If this statement is true, we are forced to inquire what is neurotic in the process. Or the statement is true just because it describes an appearance and the neurosis lies in the fact that the reality is other than the appearance. In other words, the phallic-narcissistic character acts as if he were very potent sexually. Such individuals brag about their conquests and powers (the latter measured as the number of acts of intercourse per evening). Actually, orgastic potency, that is, the ability to experience pleasure, is proportionately diminished. The reason for the frequency of the sexual act is in fact the failure to achieve satisfaction in one experience. In the same way the aggression of the phallic-narcissistic character is exaggerated to make up for a constitutional weakness. If we equate aggression with reaching we can describe the character types as follows: the oral character is afraid to reach, the masochist reaches then withdraws, the phallic-narcissistic character grasps. This grasping is based upon a fear of failure or loss. But if the sexual libido is less than the pretense, and if the aggression is weaker than its appearance, how can we account dynamically for the drive, the ambition and the seeming "above-average production of libidinal energy"?

We have classified the phallic-narcissistic character as a genital type. This means that the energy swing is securely anchored in brain and genital function. It also means that this type of structure is not undercharged like the oral character nor guilt-ridden like the masochist. Since the character determining disturbance occurs at a comparatively late age, roughly around three years, the mechanism of defense or reaction to the traumatic experiences is different than in other types. Once genitality is reached, pressure in terms of frustrations or punishments results in a stiffening of the organism. It is the same process which we saw in the hysterical character structure. The musculature contracts to support the ego structure forming a tube around the body. Another patient described it as follows: "I had a sudden vision of a shining steel tube, large like a manhole, which enclosed my body. Inside this tube, I felt myself alive." When I analyzed her perceptions and sensations, she added that previously she had felt herself on the outside of her body. The inside felt imprisoned and she could not reach it. Now, she had made contact with her innermost being and she was highly thrilled and excited. What I have categorized as the rigid structures all have this tubelike armor, either platelike or meshlike. The depth of the armoring and the width of the tube are inversely related. A wide tube is related to a more superficial armoring. A narrow tube results from spasticity of the deeper muscle layers and is more rigid and inflexible. I need not emphasize the value of this hollow tubelike structure as a physical support against pressure which would tend to collapse the energy swing.

Once we comprehend the nature of this armor most aspects of the phallic-narcissistic character structure can be explained. The rigid tubelike structure funnels the energy current into the brain and genitals, frequently overcharging these structures. At the same time the rigidity decreases the flexibility of the organism psychologically and somatically. The overcharge results from the failure of the energy stream to broaden out into the natural lakes before it reaches the outlets. These lakes or reservoirs are the pelvic region below and the head above. Following the narrowing of the waist and neck, there are the enlargements of the head and pelvis. The development of a natural reservoir just upstream from the genitals, prevents them from overcharging and discharging too soon. In the same way, the brain acts as a reservoir to restrain an impulse in order to subject it to the critical appraisal of the ego. It is impossible to conceive of a reality function without these reservoirs. Precisely the same principle is used to control the surge of rivers swollen from heavy rains or spring thaw.

We would expect then that the rigid structure, because of the narrowing of these reservoirs, would show a greater impulsiveness than the pregenital character types. In one sense, this is so. In his genital aggression, the phallic male shows stronger impulses than any other neurotic character. And the same is true in terms of the drive for material success. This aggressiveness, however, is obtained at the expense of flexibility and spontaneity. The very rigidity of the structure favors genitality and reality at the same time that it limits these functions. We see the picture of an individual who is genitally aggressive and yet premature in ejaculation. The genital discharge occurs long before all the excess energy has been brought down into relation with the penis. A single act is therefore insufficient to discharge the tension. The phallic male considers himself potent because he is capable of many acts of penetration and discharge in a single evening. However, the strength of the aggression is not to be measured by its appearance. Further, since satisfaction depends upon the degree of build-up of the tension prior to discharge, the phallic male frequently derives little pleasure from his sexual experiences.

The ambition of the phallic male must be explained by these dynamic processes. Given a constant funnelling of energy into the outlets at the same time that satisfaction from discharge is limited, one can understand the persistence of the drive. It is easy to explain, too, why the phallic male seeks feminine conquests. Since sexual satisfaction is incomplete, a feeling of dissatisfaction with the sexual partner arises. There is the hope, conscious or unconscious, that a new partner may provide greater pleasure. In the flush of excitement evoked by the chase and by the new relationship, this often happens. As these conditions disappear, the old situation is reestablished, sexual pleasure declines and so the pursuit is resumed. This process, which occurs on the genital level, is typical or characterological. The phallic male finds no deep satisfaction on any level of activity and he is forced into continued pursuit and conquest. We must distinguish this ambition from the growth and creative activity of healthy individuals.

If this is so what is the relationship of phallic ambition to urethral eroticism? Any increase of energy within a rigid tubelike structure is immediately transmitted as an increase of pressure to the two ends of the tube. The bioenergetic shape of the mammalian organism is tubelike and concave forward. This is only to say that we are built on the principle of the worm: the tube within a tube. In its natural, soft and flexible form, the two ends of the tube are the genital below and the face above, specifically the region around the glabella which includes the eyes and the root of the nose. In health this tube is quite soft and flexible and capable of expansion and contraction in its segmental diameters. As the tube loses elasticity and tends to become rigid it straightens out. The loss of elasticity accounts for the fact that the pressure of the energy is immediately transmitted downward and will be felt by the organs below. The straightening also causes a fixation of the pelvis backward. With both rigidity and retraction, the pressure is felt on the bladder and produces a desire to urinate. This accounts for the fact that the phallic male feels the need to urinate before and after the sexual act. Urethral eroticism is thus associated with sexual excitement. And since the pattern below is duplicated above, the relation between drive, ambition and urethral eroticism is seen to be one which derives from the dynamics of the body structure.

These conclusions are supported by the observations of

these patients. In the case presented above there was the incident when the child, prevented from masturbating, urinated on the floor. This could not be considered a premeditated act. Rather the energy, blocked from access to the genital, charged the bladder. Just as the retraction of the pelvis brings the bladder into the line of energy flow, so, too, the pelvis can be brought forward in such a way that the bladder is free from pressure. Another patient who had a very blocked and immobilized pelvis recalled that he was able to control the problem of eneuresis by locking his pelvis forward. In this way he could sleep through the night undisturbed by fear of wetting the bed.

There is another relation between urethral eroticism and the phallic character which should be elucidated. The laws governing the flow of blood are derived from the laws which govern the flow of liquids in a tube. These laws also explain some of the dynamics of bioenergetic processes in the organism since all bioenergetic phenomena occur within a fluid medium. Liquid flowing through a rigid tube under pressure will move continuously and be discharged at the outlet uninterruptedly. If the flow occurs in an elastic tube, the flow is pulsatile and the ejection intermittent. The flow of urine partakes of the former quality. The movement of blood and seminal fluid, that is, of highly charged fluids, is pulsatile. When the ejaculation in the male takes the form of a continuous flow of semen and lacks pulsation, it feels like the act of micturition. This lack of pulsation in the ejaculation is characteristic of many rigid, phallic men.

The problem of prematurity is one of the main symptoms of the rigid male structure. There is another which is less common but which must be explained on a similar basis. The phenomenon of obsession, so far as I have ever observed, is limited to rigid structures. It is experienced frequently as a tension in the forehead and represents, dynamically, an overcharge of the frontal lobes. In this symptom the close parallelism between genital function and mental function can be studied.

I had occasion to treat an engineering student for insomnia who also suffered from an obsession. The obsession was not the main symptom yet it provided the basis for the psychological understanding of the character. In addition to the obsession the patient had a phobia of crowds and of people sitting behind him. Another symptom was attacks of marked involuntary tremors of both legs for which he had consulted several neurologists. I must admit that during the early part of this treatment I had not linked all symptoms to one bioenergetic structure which would permit the explanation of each aspect of this single problem. I conducted the therapy on the basis of resistance analysis which while effective is neither so efficient nor so consistent as the character analytic approach.

What was the obsession in this case? The patient could not free himself from the vision of a young lady who had been his sweetheart during their adolescence. The relationship was terminated after seven years when the girl fell in love with another boy. During the seven years of their relationship, sexual activity though frequent never led to intercourse. With her new boy friend the girl did have intercourse. She then told my patient that their failure to have intercourse led to the breaking up of the relationship. His obsession with the girl had a double emotional quality. At times he saw her with feelings of remorse that he had not known her more intimately and at others with intense rage that she had left him. The patient's background was unusual in that it was extremely puritanical for this day. The cinema was regarded as the temptation of the devil, and pleasure in general was looked upon as sinful. His home life was dominated by a severe paternal authority.

I must mention that there was another symptom in this case which moved to the foreground in the later part of the therapy. The patient was subject to fairly frequent attacks of jaundice with pain in the upper right quadrant, malaise and weakness. These attacks generally followed some emotional upset or, as the patient was convinced, a change in the weather marked by increased humidity and falling pressure. The patient was more upset by these attacks than by any other aspect of his condition. They were accompanied by feelings of hopelessness and despair. While such an attack might confine the patient to bed for the day, they did not incapacitate him for any length of time. No x-ray examination was made of the gall bladder or biliary ducts, but in view of the *transient* nature of the attack, occasionally accompanied by clay-colored stools, I diagnosed the condition as biliary dyskinesia or spasm either at the sphincter of Oddi or elsewhere in the ductal system.

In spite of the pressing nature of the patient's complaints the early phase of the therapy was marked by such resistance that the patient interrupted the treatment twice. When we resumed the third time I made the therapy conditional upon the fact that there would be no more interruptions. This, of course, did not change the resistance which continued in the face of evident over-all improvement. The patient experienced the therapeutic work as a threat and it required my best analytic effort to overcome his fear. His conflict over the therapy and his fear of it and me continued until a simple occurrence suddenly changed his attitude. To encourage his aggression I engaged in a tug-of-war with him using a towel. He reacted with a determination and energy which surprised me. I used my greater strength to make him exert himself and then I let him win. He beamed as if he had achieved a significant victory over me. From that time on his fear of me and of the therapy disappeared. Not all resistance disappeared but now the patient was cooperative where before he was overtly hostile.

Despite this hostility, the patient was continuously drawn to the analytic therapy by my specific insight into his problems. I mentioned earlier that the patient had consulted several neurologists about the trembling of his legs. No one could find any organic lesion to account for the phenomenon. It is not so rare a condition and most patients will exhibit such trembling in the course of the therapy. It can be interpreted as an expression of anxiety but the only real explanation is a bioenergetic one. Energy flowing down into the lower half of the body will be discharged either genitally or through the legs into the ground. If the genital outlet is blocked or closed, the legs will carry an extra load which they can only discharge through motion. This trembling of the legs is energetically similar to the trembling which occurs in strong emotional states of fear and anger. In each case the trembling serves to discharge energy which is not released in purposeful action and in each case the trembling acts as a safety valve. When I explained this to my patient he was greatly relieved.

In this patient, the conflict over genital feelings was very intense. A very strict religious upbringing opposed a very strong sexual drive. When the feelings of guilt were dominant, the patient was most tormented by his obsession. If the genital impulse broke through to discharge in masturbation, both the guilt and the obsession were greatly decreased. Later in the course of this therapy, as the patient developed a continuous and satisfactory sexual relationship, the obsession disappeared completely. The oral character has no conscious conflict with his genital impulse for the reason that the genital is flooded with oral libido. Penetrating analysis of every case in which the oral element dominates the character shows that the genital impulse has the meaning of reaching for closeness with the partner, of wanting to be loved and to be warmed. He may question his promiscuity or his lack of discharge or deep satisfaction, but in my experience he never doubts his right by any standard to genital activity. Masochistic characters, too, are not in conscious conflict over their sexual impulses. This may seem strange to those who are accustomed to think that masochists are overwhelmed by conscious guilt. The masochist identifies with his impulse at the same time that he questions his environment or himself. Morality is an issue only with the phallic male or with the hysterical female.

Now let me describe the structure of this patient. You

will see that all of his problems can be explained in terms of the dynamics of this structure. The patient was a little below average height, thin and rather wiry. His face, too, was thin with an intense look and lively eyes. His shoulders were rounded and he carried his head and neck bent forward as if he were carrying a yoke across his back. There was no doubt that he had a lot of energy: his movements were quick and determined. He did not complain of tiredness. Despite the apparent thinness of the body structure, the musculature was well developed with good tone so that his appearance gave one the impression of narrowness rather than of asthenia. The distal parts of the extremities, wrists, hands, ankles and feet, were quite strong. The musculature of the back was much more tense and unyielding than that on the front of the body.

Psychologically and bioenergetically, the character structure of this patient would be diagnosed as phallic-narcissistic. On more than one occasion the patient expressed his conviction that women were attracted to him. He also told me that he felt that he had a large penis. At the same time he had fantasies of clubbing women or piercing them with his penis. He showed the usual ambition and aggression for this type of character. He was rather graceful in his movements and adept at sports. Yet there could be no question about the rigidity of the body structure. It was not massive as some rigid types are, rather the musculature formed a tubelike structure from head to genital so that the energy was piped directly into both end systems. When, as in this case, the rigidity is marked and the tube narrow, the charge at both ends is exaggerated. The obsession results from the continuous charge of the frontal region at the same time that discharge is blocked or limited. The patient experienced the obsession as a constriction or tension in the forehead. In a similar way, the over-excitation of the genitals results from the inability to fully discharge the tension so that the penis is easily recharged and tends to retain its rigidity. The healthy genital function is distinguished from the phallic type of genitality by the fact that in the former the emphasis is upon the fullness of discharge rather than upon the strength of the erection. More precisely, it is the difference between orgastic potency as opposed to erective potency.

Here then is a phallic male narcissistic in his overvaluation of his sexual potency with his obsession, his insomnia and his attacks of biliary spasm. The first two are obviously related to the overcharge at both ends of the tube plus the conscious holding back of the discharge. He was constantly sexually excited and he looked at every female as a possible sexual object. He was tormented by guilt which manifested itself in the obsession. How could he sleep if he didn't discharge the excitation in his head and in his genital? But how can we explain the attacks of jaundice? For the moment we must content ourselves with a psychological interpretation. He was envious—envious of men who had girls with whom they could have relations. The prototype of this man was his father who, while he forbade sexual pleasure to his son, enjoyed the marital state as a patriarchal possession. This patient was full of anger against his father which he dared not express. It showed itself in the transfer of hostility to the analyst. And it explained why our fight was so significant. Having vanquished the analyst, he dared face his hostility towards his father. Now the attacks of jaundice must be interpreted as a result of the attempted repression of his envy and hostility. He never had an attack when he was aggressive. If he became overtired or when the weather changed in the direction of lower pressure his aggression collapsed and he had an attack. As these problems were analyzed, he began a more active sexual life. His removal from his home environment facilitated his therapeutic progress. I could open up and release more and more real aggression. It is interesting to note that after a period of intense sexual activity, he fell in love and got married. And at this stage all his symptoms had disappeared.

The problem of obsession is closely related to the larger

problem of compulsion. They have been linked in the phrase obsessive-compulsive behavior. Compulsion is more pathological than obsession though less disturbing. Analytic writers regard the compulsion as a defense reaction against the obsession. We should expect to find them related bioenergetically. Actually, compulsive behavior is the extreme form of rigidity on the psychological level. This same excessive rigidity characterizes the somatic structure and enables us to comprehend the bioenergetic basis of such behavior.

As the natural tube of the body becomes more rigid, it tends to straighten and to shorten. I believe that this is a biological law which can be demonstrated in a single hair. When hair loses its natural curl, it becomes shorter and straighter. This straightening of the natural curves of the body produces a regression of the outlets. The ends of the energy swing recede somewhat from their normal outlets in the genital and in the forehead and overcharge the top of the head and the anus. Since these are not natural energy outlets the energy must be held and not discharged. The compulsive character holds back his impulses to a degree which is found in no other structure. He will lose his hair at the top of his head because of tension and have a very tight anus below. He will be extremely constipated and show the typical traits of pedantry, avarice and orderliness which have been so well described. "In his outward appearance he will show marked restraint and control . . . [which] in extreme cases becomes a complete affect block."

The character analytic problems of the compulsive character have been well studied and analyzed by Reich. From a bioenergetic point of view the compulsive character will pose the same problems as those of any rigid character to a degree, that corresponds with the severity of the rigidity. The shift from aggression to holding illustrates in an advanced state the fundamental tendency of all rigid structures to use aggression defensively. The phallic male shows his holding in the attempt to control his ejaculation and maintain his erective potency. For this reason, the compulsive character is grouped within the category of rigid male structures.

It would be an error to think that the compulsive character has given up his genitality much as he shows anal traits. Reich (1949, p. 196) recognized the fact that "in the typical compulsion neurosis, the development proceeds, nevertheless, into the phallic phase." He believed that genitality "was activated but soon relinquished again." Bioenergetically, one can say that genitality cannot be relinquished without a withdrawal from reality. Actually the compulsive character may decrease the charge at the genitals to a point where that function no longer dominates the behavior of the individual. This is a matter of degree which is not basic to the main categories of ego structure. Within the broad category of rigid character structures, one can oppose genitality to anality so that the more genital the character, the less compulsion is found in the structure.

Reich (1949, p. 198) described the rigidity of the compulsive character well. "The affect block is one great spasm of the ego which makes use of somatic spastic conditions. All muscles of the body, but particularly those of the pelvis and pelvic floor, of the shoulders and the face, are in a state of chronic hypertonia. Hence the hard, somewhat masklike physiognomy of the compulsive characters and their physical awkwardness."

We are now in a position to describe two varieties of the rigid character structure in the male. These are both neurotic types and, therefore, they are more evident in their extreme manifestations. One is the small, rather narrow body structure with an intense emotional life, i.e., highly affected charge. In these organisms the ratio of free energy to physical mass is high, genital activity is strong. The patient described above belonged to this variety. By contrast, there is a rigid type of body structure with a larger bony frame and a much heavier musculature. These individuals have a solid jaw which is aggressively set forward; the shoulders are broad, the waist rather narrow, the hips tightly contracted. This body structure gives one the impression of strength and hardness. The ego is equally hard, inflexible and cold. Since the hardness represents the repression of emotional expression, these individuals are characterized by their affect block. One can say that the affective life is frozen in the structure. The first of these types is typically phallic-narcissistic, the second is compulsive.

In the extreme, the compulsive character has a rocklike solidity. One such patient whom I treated for some time gave me the impression that he was like the Rock of Gibraltar. This is a different type of rigidity than we find in the phallic male; it is much more severe and penetrates more deeply towards the center. It is easy to understand the dynamics of the compulsive behavior in these individuals. The solidity of the structure does not permit any spontaneity in movement or expression. Every aggressive movement requires a great effort (on the unconscious level, of course) to overcome the resistances implied in the hardness and solidity of the structure. Little variation in expression is possible, so that the body movements have a mechanical, driven quality. Genital activity will show this same forced quality but it will lack the charge which characterizes that function in the phallic character.

These descriptions portray two extreme types of rigidity in the male. One tends to be obsessive, the other compulsive; in the one case genital activity is very strong, in the other it is weakened by severe anal tension. This type of compulsive character has few compulsive symptoms for the reason that compulsion dominates every action. It is a way of being not a symptom. Between the extremes will be found cases where both tendencies exist in a state of conflict. These are the true obsessive-compulsive characters in whom the obsession with sex and genitality is countered by marked compulsive traits. In these cases, the compulsive symptom is a defense against the underlying obsession with its concomitant anxiety.

Depth analysis permits us to make one further interpretation of these structures which leads to insight into the genesis of these types. The true compulsive character shows both passive tendencies and tendencies to unconscious homosexual behavior. The phallic male is more aggressive and has a stronger identification with his own genital function. Since both types have reached the genital stage in their development, we may ask what factors determine the different evolution. So far as I can determine, this depends upon which of the parents exerts the greater frustrating influence. If the father poses the main threat, the child will develop an acute castration anxiety in which a high genital charge is blocked by fear of punishment. The desire of the child to overcome the father becomes another psychological factor in the genesis of his ambition. The phallic male identifies with his father whom he regards as his enemy. If, however, the main frustration proceeds from the mother, the resulting repression of sexuality is more severe. The child faces a more threatening situation. Genital activity is blocked by fear of loss of love and support from the mother. Since these are mothers who wish to dominate their children, one also finds in these cases a previous active interference with anal functions. Further, the father would tend to support the mother's attitude and to add his power and authority to force the child from its genital position. On the surface, there is the identification with the paternal authority but this merely covers a deeper identification with the frustrating mother.

In both types of rigid male structures, the unconscious fear of punishment for genital activity is the key to the neurosis. In the face of this fear, the phallic male is defiant, rebellious, aggressive. The aggression, of course, is over-determined and has the function of seeing how much he can get away with before provoking retaliation. In this sense the aggression has the psychological meaning of defense and is the counterpart of the aggression of the hysterical female. The compulsive individual, on the other hand, submits and adapts his behavior to the demands of authority. He withdraws from genital activity but he does not relinquish the genital position. His submission is never complete for he has not surrendered, he has only stiffened and become hard. When the aggression does break through in the anal compulsive character it is sadistic and directed against the female. The true phallic male is capable of some tender feeling for the female.

Bioenergetic therapy is particularly rewarding in the treatment of the rigid character structures. Since these are individuals with a highly developed ego structure, considerable resistance is encountered in ordinary psychoanalytic work. As long as they are free from disturbing symptoms, they can resist pressure to an amazing degree. On the other hand, if one analyzes their physical spasms and rigidities, one can elicit considerable cooperation in the physical work needed to release the tensions. The analytic work should always proceed in such a way that insight and awareness accompany movement. The movement of the body will evoke dreams and memories from which the past can be reconstructed. Interpretation moves back and forth between the psychic realm and the somatic realm as each aspect of the personality presents itself to the analyst. To overcome any tendency to dichotomy, all manifestations, psychic and somatic, are viewed as expressions of unitary bioenergetic processes.

Under the heading of the phallic-narcissistic character, we discussed some of the basic bioenergetic problems of the rigid male character structure. The rigidity may vary in degree and kind. Variations in degree vary from healthy individuals, characterized by their warmth and spontaneity, to compulsives who are cold and machine-like. Since these are genital structures, genitality too will range from full orgastic potency to its almost complete absence (in the anal compulsive). None of these individuals will show erective failure, that is, the erection will not collapse as it may in the masochist. Characterologically, the anal compulsive must be considered a genital structure, however reduced the genital charge may be. In kind, the rigidity is either tubelike or solid. This is the basis for the division into two groups, phallic-narcissistic and compulsive. The former is based upon an identification with the male parent while the latter has an underlying identification with the female. This identification is related to the parental authority who represented the most frustrating force in the genital phase of the child's development. Thus rigid types may be active or passive within the limits of their structure. Then, too, the rigid type is further complicated by the admixture of elements from earlier periods. These appear as oral or masochistic traits which give the rigid character his pathological individuality.

In the discussion of the character types so far presented we have assumed that the neurotic pattern can be diagnosed and categorized. This assumption is made even though in practice difficulty may be encountered in any specific case. For one thing, the individual who does not have in his character structure some traits derived from deprivation at the oral level, masochistic tenderness stemming from suppression of his ego, some pathological rigidity, or all of these would be rare indeed. The characterological diagnosis depends upon the factor which dominates the personality and determines its pattern of behavior.

Nevertheless, character problems exist which pose great difficulty in classification. A mixture of neurotic tendencies may develop which defies classification because no dominant single factor can be discerned. Actually, this very situation creates a pattern of behavior which differs qualitatively from those already discussed. Psychoanalytic literature has recognized such a clinical type, which is a mixture of tendencies. This is the passive-feminine male character structure and it merits special consideration. We shall devote the next chapter to a discussion of this structure and to a consideration of its female counterpart.

15

The Passive-Feminine Character

When the character structure is determined by feelings of dependency, of inner emptiness and of depression which alternates with elation, we label it the oral character. Bioenergetically, it is characterized by a weakness of the aggressive function, by a lack of strength in the legs, and by an ego structure which is not securely anchored in reality or genitality. The masochistic character is seemingly aggressive but close observation shows that the behavior is provocative rather than aggressive. The dominant pattern is not elation and depression but attempt and failure, self-assertion and collapse ending in a morass-like condition. Bioenergetically, the masochistic structure is highly charged, but the muscle tensions are so severe that it is physically impossible to sustain a prolonged action. Both types may be described as pregenital structures— ego deficient, impulsive and anxiety laden.

In contrast, what I have described as the rigid type of character structure is based upon aggression in work and, on the genital level, upon the presence of an armor which is evident both emotionally and muscularly. The ego is securely anchored; its strength, however, is inversely proportionate to the degree of rigidity. Behavior is subject to control and is rigidly subject to the reality function. Anxiety is generally absent, but the rigid type of character is very rarely a pure type. Certainly the patients who present this structure frequently show both masochistic and oral traits to varying degrees. Nevertheless the characterological diagnosis is justified if the total pattern of behavior is clearly dominated by the rigidity and aggression. The practical character analyst will assess in each case the relative proportion of orality, masochism and rigidity, and will evaluate the role played by each of these factors in the total personality.

It is possible to have a mixture of character traits which defies easy classification. This is of no great importance if one is dealing with the combination of orality and masochism, that is, an oral character with masochistic traits or a masochistic character with oral traits. It is not possible for both elements to be equally strong for the simple reason that one is based upon an undercharged system and the other upon a highly charged system. Both are pregenital structures and the character analysis proceeds by the interpretation and resolution of specific problems on the appropriate level. Both come to therapy with the presenting complaint of anxiety. The analytic and bioenergetic work is oriented to effect an alleviation of the anxiety and a better relation to reality.

When an individual presents a structure in which pregenital and genital drives are fairly equally balanced, the picture is confusing. Such a situation exists in the character structure which is called the passive-feminine character. The problem posed to the analytic therapist is a difficult one and it merits a detailed discussion here.

In the article entitled "The Economic Problem of Masochism," Freud suggests three categories of masochistic disturbance: masochism with a perversion, moral masochism, and feminine masochism. The latter is not further explored by Freud and so we must turn our attention to other analytic writers for some knowledge of this condition.

Fenichel, in *The Psychoanalytic Theory of the Neuroses*, mentions this problem in his discussion of the perversions. A partial pregenital instinct competes with the genital primacy. Yet since the completion of the perverse act leads to a genital discharge, he recognized that these individuals do not lack genital primacy. The passive-feminine male is an individual in whom certain feminine traits are so evident that they determine one aspect of the personality. But it should be emphasized that we are not discussing here the problem of homosexuality.

What are the characteristics which incline one to the diagnosis of passive-feminine character? A man about forty years old came to see me after he had been under analytic therapy for many years. He had a soft, modulated voice and a gentle manner. There were no hard lines on his face, especially absent were the deep grooves from nose to mouth. By profession he was a designer of furniture. The big problems of his life stemmed from a determined opposition to authority and an inability to achieve a satisfactory love relationship.

In another case, a young man in his early thirties complained about his inability to speak when in a group. In addition, he had difficulty in establishing a satisfactory work function and in forming a love relationship. He, too, had a gentle, considerate manner, a soft, modulated voice, and a good-looking face without strong lines.

Reich described certain qualities as characterizing this type, "exaggerated politeness and compliance, softness and tendency to cunning." In discussing a specific case history, Reich (1949, p. 83) wrote: "Phenomenologically, he was a typical passive-feminine character: he was always over friendly and humble; he kept apologizing for the most trifling things. In addition he was awkward, shy and circumstantial."

Other writers place their emphasis upon the "passive-receptive" attitude, or upon the submissiveness. It is difficult to unearth from a study of the literature the specific personality traits as distinguished from the characterological passivity which would justify the description of feminine as applied to a man. I propose, therefore, to list the features which I have observed in the cases under my treatment. Then we can discuss them in the context of a specific case.

The most important physical characteristic which distinguishes this type is the soft, feminine-sounding voice. It impresses one as being feminine by its lack of deep resonance and sharpness. The facial expression tends also to be soft and plastic. The manner of movement is never brusque or self-assertive. The body type may be either rounded in outline with rather narrow shoulders or V-shaped with broad shoulders and narrow hips. The hands are characteristically soft and fairly weak. This is about as much as one could discern in the outward physical appearance of these patients. The manner was well described by Reich.

The analytic work or the bioenergetic work proceeds easily but soon runs into a typical resistance. On one side there is a wealth of material which the patient produces about his early childhood but without any affect, on the other the patient is anxious and willing to do anything asked of him, but again, without any active participation in the process. The resistance appears as just this lack of ego participation in the therapeutic endeavor covered by the guise of an "exaggerated positive transference." Yet this positive transference is just as real and valid an ego expression as the negative resistance which underlies it. The bioenergetic approach in these cases takes both aspects into consideration and if the proper therapeutic procedure is followed the results are satisfactory.

The first case was that of the man who was a furniture designer. He had the typical soft voice and manner and he was very polite and cooperative. The body outline was rounded off rather than angular and the shoulders were narrow. He had been in analysis and psychotherapy for many years before I undertook his treatment. While he felt that he had been helped, his deep-seated dissatisfaction and problems had not been touched.

At the time he began the therapy with me he had just

been married for the third time to a girl many years younger than himself. This relationship posed some problems for him. For the first few months he was very excited sexually, but soon thereafter his sexual desire for the girl decreased and she was forced to take the initiative in their sexual activities. His interest was drawn to other women and he found himself constantly looking at the breasts of every woman he saw. This interest in the female breast was an old preoccupation. In addition, he had had strong *voyeuristic* tendencies aimed at seeing women undress.

His family background and early environment are characteristic. He described his father as "of the old school, authoritarian, pedantic, easily irritated and usually pitching in and bringing up the children when he was at home." Of his mother he said, "As far back as I can remember she's been somewhat nervous and high strung, but with much charm and capable in certain ways. She was always interested in art—especially from the point of view of decoration." He had a younger sister who was his father's favorite. She was more aggressive than the patient. He had been jealous and envious of her but he also liked and admired her. He recalled having fought often with her. He felt that she had an advantage which he resented. On more than one occasion during the therapy he expressed his resentment against the seeming dominance of women in American society.

One memory from his early experiences stands out. He recalled that at the age of four or five he had "some little white worms" in his anus and they would cause an itching. He said, "It would give me quite a bit of pleasure when my mother took them out for me." Later childhood memories were full of fear and guilt over masturbation. He began to masturbate at about five years of age. He remembered that his mother warned him not to touch his penis. Masturbation continued throughout childhood and adolescence but always with great fear and guilt. He had a memory from the age of six or so which has remained vivid in his mind. He was going to bed one evening when he saw the pale face of a man outside in the dark looking into his window. It gave him a terrible shock.

His experience of the ejaculation of semen while masturbating one day upset him very much. He had not heard anything about it and he felt that something was seriously wrong with him. On another occasion, when he became faint at the sight of blood flowing from a cut in his hand, a teacher related it to his masturbatory activities. During adolescence he was obsessed with thoughts of death. On two occasions boys who were close friends of his were killed accidentally. He was sure that he, too, would die soon.

Fear of the dark plagued him during childhood. He was often scared for hours after going to bed. His parents used to go out for the evening while the maids slept at the other end of a large apartment. His interest in the female body goes far back into childhood. He said, "I can remember taking an interest in the female body even when I was very young and still had a nursemaid. I can remember being excited about the roundness of her arms and whatever I could see although she didn't undress in front of us children."

Adolescent sexual experiences were limited to occasional petting parties. Sexual intercourse was initiated at the age of seventeen with prostitutes "without much actual satisfaction." Prostitutes continued to be his source of sexual experience for many years. He also had a deep fear that he would catch a venereal disease from them. When he did succeed, later, in establishing a regular sex life, he was never sure that he loved the girl, and he would break off the relationship as soon as the girl made demands on him.

One of the most common complaints of this patient was that he was always tired and lacked enthusiasm. Despite this, he worked very hard at his occupation. On two occasions in his life, however, he was able to mobilize a great amount of energy and to be very active and aggressive. The first was a business venture, the promotion of a line of machines, in which he engaged for two years with considerable success. After it had become routine, he lost interest in it. This activity took place at the expense of all sexual contact with women, as he gave to it all his attention and energy. The second was an interest in an anti-war movement in which activity he showed great leadership. This interest, too, collapsed and he came down with a severe attack of spinal meningitis.

I should mention that in one affair, which lasted for two years, the patient played an aggressive sexual role and was very attached to the girl. For her part the girl was somewhat passive in the relationship and went out with other men. He felt his attachment to be "sticky" and despite a torturing jealousy, he refused to marry the girl.

The bioenergetic work with this patient lasted a little more than a year during which time I saw him about twice a week. The early sessions were marked by complaints of being tired and lacking energy. On the couch and in movement, the body looked heavy and weighted. Hitting was done mechanically. The eyes and face had a dull expression. The breathing was subdued. At the end of the session, some slight improvement was visible in the patient. His face and eyes brightened, there was a more alive attitude in his body and occasionally a deepening of his voice. Yet each session began with the same complaints. The improvement didn't hold. It was apparent from this attitude that there were strong masochistic traits in the patient.

Contrary to the masochistic character this patient never complained about anxiety. In contrast, too, with the phallic type, the superficial muscular tensions were not very marked. The skin was without turgor, and below the umbilicus it was white and cold and without life. Once, while moving his eyes, the patient remarked that they were "wooden" and "without life." The general impression I had from these early sessions was of a lack of motility in the organism. He got depressed only slightly and while he mentioned suicide, he thought rather that he would go on for many years to die eventually of a brain tumor as had his father. The patient had a physical symptom which disturbed him. He complained of an area of numbness in the scalp, about three inches in diameter, above the right forehead. He continually rubbed at it as if to bring it to life. Palpation showed an area of skin drier and more scaly than the corresponding area on the opposite side but nothing else.

I directed the therapy at mobilizing energy and promoting motility, but this was not easy to do. The only real reaction I could provoke was by the use of the gag reflex, but even here I ran into marked insensitivity in the throat. Only by depressing the pharyngeal constrictors sharply did I get a response. The patient could not support any manipulations which were painful. He withdrew from the situation. Persistent voluntary movements produced a nauseous feeling and he stopped them. It was then that I had recourse to the gag reflex. On one or two occasions with the gag reflex, the patient felt some energy move upward into his head and especially into the dead area of the scalp.

Continued therapy seemed to produce a gradual improvement; less fatigue and somewhat more energy. During one session the patient remarked that he felt feminine in his movements. When I had him stretch his body and extend his arms, this feeling disappeared. The patient remarked also that he was aware of a lack of energy in the pelvic region and in the genitals. To this he ascribed his lack of decisiveness and strength. In contrast with the phallic-narcissistic character in whom the pelvis is charged but spastic, this patient's pelvis was soft and rounded. The masculine thrust of the pelvis was missing which was in keeping with his general lack of aggression.

One should ask—Where was the energy of this organism bound? Since he was not an oral or a masochistic character, we should like to know what happened to his aggression. True, he showed certain masochistic traits in the constant complaining about his tiredness, in his collapse into spinal meningitis and in the heaviness of his body. His fixation on the anal function was revealed in the memory of his mother extracting the worms from his anus. But the true masochist is never passive nor feminine. The masochist strives to be fully aggressive though it ends in collapse and failure. What Freud called feminine masochism we should more properly call the passive-feminine character.

The passive-feminine character doesn't collapse but neither does he make any strong aggressive gestures. In this case, a collapse did occur after a very determined act of ego assertion that lasted for some time. I have in mind his anti-war activities which must be interpreted as a rebellion against authority and ultimately against his father. The true masochist never rises to such a sustained level of rebellion. This patient had enough rigidity to prevent a continual collapse but, unfortunately, this immobilized all his aggression. He could only plod on.

I had the strong impression that the energy was blocked in the thoracic region; his chest was tight and did not move with respiration. Since the abdominal muscles were also tight, respiration was greatly reduced. Manipulative work upon the chest wall produced strong anxiety. The tensions were located deep in the intercostal muscles. It should be noted that this patient complained of heart palpitations which he experienced from time to time during many years. But I did not push the work on the chest wall. This pressure was too painful and one had to know more about the dynamics of the structure. In view of the severe throat spasm and deep pelvic tensions in this patient it would have been unwise to build up the internal pressure without providing an adequate outlet for its release.

Continued work with the gag reflex, with the strong expression of negative feeling, and with the hitting, failed to produce the desired result. I could not mobilize sufficient aggression to effect a strong release of feeling.* Despite a gradual improvement, the same complaints were continually expressed. This complaining, as we saw, denoted the masochistic element in the character structure which required consistent and persistent work. However, I became aware of another expression in this patient which indicated the severity of the disturbance. With almost every effort, the patient uttered a groan. This had a physiological basis in the disturbance of the natural respiratory movements. But the psychological significance of the sound alarmed me. Implied in the utterance was an attitude of resignation. It is as if the patient said: "I am an old man, and life is too much of an effort for me." Generally, one groans when the effort is so great that it is maximum for the capacity of the organism. If, then, the groan appeared with each effort, one could surmise that the patient was working at close to his physiological limit. Since even this was not enough for success, hopelessness and despair were to be expected.

One should not underestimate the feelings of hopelessness and despair in the passive-feminine character who does not engage in homosexuality as a way out. Psychologically, aggression (forward movement) is blocked by the intense castration anxiety; regression is prevented by the equally strong fear of homosexuality. In the true homosexual the bioenergetic dynamics are different. Genitality has been surrendered, although one can postulate that it had never been firmly established. The passive-feminine structure, as distinguished from the homosexual, is anchored in genitality but immobilized by fear. In masochism and orality, the problem can be resolved on the pregenital level. In this character structure the situa-

* This case was treated several years ago, at a time when the techniques of the physical approach were first being elucidated. Our procedures today are different, and in line with the intervening years of experience more effective. I am reporting the case as it actually unfolded because it provided me with insight into the dynamics of this character structure.

tion is complicated by the fact that neither forward nor backward movement is possible. It is as if the passive-feminine character reached the genital stage of ego organization but became paralyzed with fear. The problem then is just this paralysis.

Characterological problems are always difficult to overcome. The weakness in the structure must be strengthened at the same time that the compensating rigidity is reduced. In this patient, the weakness was the masochistic element with its threat of collapse, against which the rigidity offered a feeling of security and support. Both of these disturbances must be carefully analyzed and appropriate means employed to overcome them. The masochistic problem is similar to that discussed earlier in the chapter on masochism. The rigidity of the passive-feminine character has a special twist since the normal genital aggression of the rigid structure is blocked.

We know that this patient had a very authoritarian father of whom he was afraid. As a child he had never dared to show any rebellion against his father or to go against his wishes. His mode of behavior was to undertake everything his father wanted him to do, then gradually to drift away from the activity and give it up entirely. His father rebuked him severely for his failures, calling him awkward, clumsy, stupid, etc. A younger sister, on the other hand, was quite favored. In his attitude towards this sister and towards women in general an important aspect of his character was revealed.

On many occasions the patient related to me his strong interest in the female breast. They fascinated him and he could not help looking at them. His tendency to voyeurism had its basis in this attraction. He wanted to see women undress. The sexual act as such did not interest him. He not only liked to look at the breast but also to fondle them. Then he made a gesture with his hands in which he took the breast and shook it. I asked him to give in to this gesture. As he intensified the movement, his jaw jutted out and his hands clutched as if he would like to tear the breast off. For the first time the patient spontaneously felt and expressed strong hatred.

Towards his sister the patient had strong ambivalent feelings. He was jealous and envious of her, but he also liked and admired her. He felt that she had an advantage which he resented. Now the inference from this was clear. The breast was a symbol for the penis but it didn't carry with it the anxiety which the patient felt with respect to his own penis. His envy and resentment could be explained by his feeling that the female had not been castrated as he felt he had been. The breast however, is also a source of life, and, it is therefore, a symbol of power in its own right.

The conflict with the authoritarian father was transferred to the sister and to other female figures. The woman became his rival and enemy and the identification with her took place on this basis. Why did this transference take place? We can only say that the conflict between genital impulse and castration anxiety which produced a complete paralysis must be resolved somehow. A sort of regression occurred back to the breast but not on an infantile level. The passive-feminine male does not want to be an infant, he wants to be a woman. At the same time, he displaces onto the female all the hatred which was brought into being by fear of the father. But he does not relinquish the genital position. On the ego level, he shows feminine tendencies. On the genital level, he is masculine but passive.

In the character analysis of this structure, one is struck by the fact that the patient will speak of the strict father but without any show of anger. And while the hatred can be expressed against the female it leads nowhere since it is a defense formation. The conflict with the male must be resolved first by analysis of the transference situation. The patient must be made to see that his politeness, his compliance with and eagerness to please the analyst covers a deep hatred of the superior male. But the problem is complicated by the fact that these patients will then agree with the analyst and nothing will change. They are so anxious to please that one can get them to agree intellectually, but they do not feel it. To achieve an affective response the pressure upon the patient will have to be as intense as was the original pressure from the father. This can be done character analytically or it can be done bioenergetically, but it will be no less painful one way or the other.

We said that, psychologically, there was displacement of the opposition from the father to a female figure. Dynamically, there is a withdrawal of energy from the genitals to the thorax. The genital position is not relinquished. All the energy is not withdrawn. Enough is withdrawn though to reduce the conflict and prevent the paralysis. If this energy is brought downward again in sufficient intensity, the oedipal conflict will be reactivated. Marked resistance will be manifest. The transference situation will become charged. To accomplish this, the work on the legs must be carried out to the point of pain. The aggression must be mobilized, and if it is done through hitting this should be carried on to the point of near collapse. The tensions preventing the forward movement of the pelvis and jaw must be released and this too will be painful. It goes without saying that these maneuvers must be coordinated with a deep character analysis so that the patient is fully aware of the necessity for such action.

In the passive-feminine male, severe tensions exist in the deep muscles while the surface muscles are relatively soft. This accounts for the soft movements which these men show. The immobilization of genital aggression interferes with the normal development of masculine muscularity unless this occurs as a secondary, compensating phenomenon. There are, thus, two factors which account for the feminine tendencies. First, there is the failure of the normal masculine development to occur, upon which there is superimposed a later identification with the female.

Therapy in the case under discussion was terminated

before I could apply the insights I had gained. They proved their validity in subsequent analyses.

The passive-feminine structure results also from the conflict between weakened genital impulses and severe genital frustration. Here, too, rigidity serves as an immobilizing force which ends in the almost complete suppression of masculine aggression. Let me illustrate with another case.

This second patient had also been in different kinds of analytic therapy for many years. Experience has confirmed that these are difficult cases to treat. Progress is invariably slow. He had several complaints: one was an inability to speak out when in a group, another was a feeling of dullness and cloudiness between the eyes which made concentration very difficult at times. He had great difficulty in establishing a satisfactory love relationship, and he suffered from a sinus condition.

The passive-feminine nature of this patient was clearly revealed in a soft voice which lacked the masculine tonality, in a manner which was extremely polite and gentle and in a facial expression which seemed boyish at times and ascetic at others. Lines of struggle and determination were absent from the face, the features of which were markedly regular. It should be mentioned that one thing which gives the voice this special quality is the soft rolling of the "r" sound.

There could be no question about the diagnosis. His history revealed the absence of aggressive behavior except for a period of war service and a prior period of college sports when he was a member of a team. It is interesting to note that despite this patient's inability to express himself before a group, it was only when he was part of a group that his aggression emerged. As an officer in the army he earned the respect both of his superiors and his men.

The body structure of this patient was very different from that of the preceding one. He was tall with very broad square shoulders from which the body tapered down to narrow hips and thin ankles. The feet were narrow with a tight, contracted arch. His arms and hands resembled the lower extremities. The patient told me that at the age of about four he had to wear braces on both legs to correct some deformity. Exactly what the deformity was he didn't know. However, he has never felt secure on his legs and feet.

Could there be anything more manly looking than those broad shoulders and narrow hips? Were they a compensation for the passive-feminine structure? Or were they the expression of this structure? I had once been inclined to the former view but the realization that raised shoulders are an expression of fear made me change that opinion. One reacts to fright by taking in the breath, pulling in the belly and raising the shoulders. The effect is to inflate the chest and immobilize the energy in the thorax. As we saw, this is the mark of the passive-feminine character, so that rather than being a secondary development, the broad, squared shoulders are an expression of the passivity. The narrow hips result from severe pelvic and thigh tensions which diminish the pelvic capacity and reduce genital potency.

In this case, one could presume the presence of a strong oral component from the body structure. The weakness of the legs, especially the thin, narrow feet with their lack of contact with the ground, is pathognomonic of an oral disturbance. So, too, are weak hands and wrists. Further, this patient had a narrow neck which was out of proportion with the broad shoulders. More significant was the lack of charge in the head which could be deduced from the feeling of dullness and cloudiness in the forehead.

The family history was typical. His father was a successful man who expected his sons to be strong and manly. The patient felt that he had never been able to measure up to this demand. Despite a strong identification with his mother, the patient never experienced a sense of closeness in his relation to her. He had an older brother and a younger sister. His closest family feeling was with this sister. I was able to analyze and bring out his identification with and hostility towards the female but it made little change in his character. This was equally true in the preceding case and, again, for the reason—that this was a defense formation. The important conflict is with the superior male or with the therapist.

In this type of passive-feminine character, the strong oral element in the structure greatly weakens the genital drive. This character type differs from the oral character by a better contact with reality, less tendency to periods of depression and elation, and a marked decrease in the typical verbosity. The energy swing is anchored in the genital function although the charge is weak. Many individuals with this type of structure suffer from premature ejaculation. Underlying the psychological problem is a severe castration anxiety.

The development of a structure of this kind is determined by the oral deprivation at an early age and the later genital frustration which paralyzes the aggression. These individuals, as children, reach the genital stage of ego organization, but with an inherent weakness due to the strong oral element. If, at this period, the child's genitality and aggression are encouraged, the oral disturbance will gradually diminish. In these matters, one must think quantitatively. The frustration which could block the aggression of such a child would not be severe enough to produce that effect in a healthier organism. The weaker organism does not give up its genitality, regression in this sense does not occur; it gives up its aggression and assumes a passive attitude. There is, as analytic writers have pointed out, a displacement from the penis to the breast, which is regarded as a substitute penis. Castration anxiety is thereby avoided. The mechanism is the same as in the first case cited. Feminine traits appear due to the inhibition of the natural masculine aggression and only secondarily by the subsequent identification with the female.

The passive-feminine individual is characterized by his paucity of emotional expression and by his relative physical immobility. On the one hand, the impulsiveness of the pregenital characters is lacking; on the other, he also lacks the aggression which marks the phallic male. The rigidity which guarantees his genital function immobilizes his aggression. On the surface, the psychological conflict centers around the attitude towards the female. Stemming from the oral disturbance is a deep need for contact, and this conflicts on the genital level with the desire for discharge and satisfaction. It is difficult, if not impossible, to play a double role at the same time. The passive-feminine character can function either as the infant in a sexual relationship with an older woman, or as the father figure towards a younger, more dependent female. He cannot be the "man" to a woman.

If one studies the case of the passive-feminine character presented by Reich in his book, *Character Analysis*, one realizes that the fundamental analytic procedure employed was to make the patient aware of his inhibited aggression. When this is accomplished, the whole disturbance is laid bare and the successive layers of the character structure can be worked through. The resistance encountered is formidable. It is not that the patient refuses to recognize his lack of aggression or passive-feminine behavior, the problem is how to mobilize the blocked affect. When one realizes that the aggression in these characters has been blocked or inhibited since the development of the genital phase, the magnitude of the task can be appreciated.

It is appropriate at this point to ask if there is a female character structure which corresponds to the passive-feminine type of male character. Or, what characterological picture would one find in the female if a similar combination of pregenital and genital disturbances existed? It is obvious that the structure in the female would not resemble the passive-feminine structure in the male because any disturbance in the female personality would tend to decrease her natural feminine qualities.

This problem has a double aspect as in the case of the male sex. The pregenital tendency could result either from a masochistic disturbance or from an oral disturbance. Let us consider the former condition first.

If the masochistic disturbance is not so severe that it prevents progression to the genital level, the final character structure will depend on the severity of the genital anxiety. Since both elements are quantitative factors it is impossible to assess in advance the resultant structure. Analysis necessarily proceeds from a given problem to the elucidation of its dynamic forces and historically determined components. Let us examine a specific case.

This patient came to therapy with a number of complaints: dissatisfaction with her sexual function, specifically the presence of disturbing fantasies; feelings of inferiority and insecurity; and attacks of anxiety. The patient was in her middle twenties, of medium height and with a clear concise manner of speaking. The outstanding feature of her physiognomy was a strong, aggressive jaw. The neck was average but the shoulders were exceptionally narrow and pulled forward. The chest was equally narrow with a protruding sternum. At the waist, the body broadened into rather full hips into which the legs were inserted like pegs. I had a very definite impression of these legs which I described as "stuffed doll's legs." There was a lot of flabbiness in the pelvic region which overlay a spastic condition in the deep-seated muscles.

The masochistic component in the character structure could not be overlooked. The sexual fantasies were frequently of a typical masochistic nature. Yet one must hesitate to characterize the total structure as masochistic. Missing were the provocative behavior, the customary whine and the uncertainty and confusion in expression. Similarly, the presence of an aggressive attitude, characterologically and bioenergetically, speaks against a diagnosis of masochism. True, the aggression lacked strength, and one can assume that it had a secondary function to compensate the fear and weakness of the deeper layer. However, the true masochist is incapable of such compensatory actions. But of even more importance is the fact that the marked rigidity clearly evident in the upper half of the body was sufficient to prevent the collapse to which the masochistic character is subject.

The body structure of this patient showed two contradictory aspects. The lower half of the body impressed one as being masochistic, the upper half belonged to the rigid type. To the former can be ascribed the masochistic sexual fantasies, to the latter the aggressive behavior. But what is significant in these structures is the presence of certain masculine signs and traits. Most common of these is the presence of hair on the face (along the jaw), sometimes a heavy growth on the legs and frequently the male type of pubic hair distribution. Some of these females are quite muscularly developed and will give a history of having competed equally with boys in their sports. This spirit of competition with the male may also be found in other activities. In the case under consideration the patient remarked to me that she often felt that she could do things better than her husband.

How are we to interpret the relation of these elements to each other in this structure? How is it that the combination of masochism and rigidity in the female produces an overaggressive behavior pattern rather than the passivity which results from the same problem in the male? How can we account for the disturbance in the secondary sexual characteristics? Masochism alone does not produce such changes, nor does rigidity if it involves the total structure. Why should the combination of these two tendencies produce this specific effect? To answer these questions, I believe that we must know more about the bioenergetic development of female sexuality.

When the female child reaches the genital stage of libido organization, she naturally turns to the male members of the family as love objects. I say naturally because the process seems inherent in the normal growth and development of female sexuality. This statement does not exclude the fact that there is also a growing sexual interest in the male children of her acquaintance. The distinction between sexuality and tender feelings is not made at this age. That the mechanism of this development is more complicated in the female child than in the male is recognized. The boy child does not have to change the love object as he develops from the oral stage to the genital stage. His relation to his mother takes on a new interest and meaning. The girl, on the other hand, must transfer a part of her object libido to another sex. But this is not a deliberate action. Bioenergetic processes occurring at this time focus the energy charge in the vagina while the clitoris gradually recedes in importance. To understand the disturbances in female sexuality the dynamic processes which produce this important development should be more thoroughly understood.

Freud (1931a, p. 252) studied the question of female sexuality as late as 1931. Let us examine some of his observations and conclusions. "We have long realized that in women the development of sexuality is complicated by the task of renouncing the genital zone which was originally the principal one, namely, the clitoris, in favor of a new zone—the vagina." In this statement we find an example of the error in thinking which comes from the interpretation of biological processes by psychological concepts. It is impossible to conceive of a child "renouncing" one activity in favor of another when it is a question of normal growth and development. When an infant learns to walk and stops crawling, is it correct to say that he renounces or gives up his previous form of locomotion? There is no question of choice involved. As the legs become stronger, a new function which is more highly charged supersedes one that gradually loses its meaning. But the child never renounces his crawling, he turns to that form of movement whenever it is appropriate. The same is true of nursing, or bottle feeding. They are not renounced by the child in the normal course of events. More adequate forms of satisfaction take their place.

So far as I know, no female has "renounced" the clitoris. If the development has proceeded normally, the vagina is the more highly charged organ and capable of yielding a much greater satisfaction. The clitoris, then, recedes into the background. Clinical experience has confirmed this observation that no female can "renounce" a clitoral orgasm for a vaginal orgasm. If this is accomplished therapeutically, it is only because sufficient feeling, charge or energy is concentrated in the vagina so that it becomes the main effector organ for discharge.

The fact remains that in some women this development in favor of the vagina does not occur. They do not have vaginal orgasms. The vagina is relatively undercharged while the clitoris retains its original sensitivity. What can cause this arrest of development?

Let us go back earlier. Freud (1931a, p. 255) is of the opinion that human beings have a "bisexual disposition" which is especially marked in the female. "The sexual life of the female is split into two phases, the first of which is of a masculine character, whilst only the second is specifically feminine." Freud must base this masculine quality upon the clitoral charge. But this view is open to serious objection. If one looks at infants in the first year of life it is often very difficult to distinguish the sexes without recourse to the clothes or the genitals. Is it not more accurate to say that in the pregenital phase the sex is relatively undifferentiated. One may also recall that pregenital character structures are also sexually undifferentiated. The oral activities and even the play of young children does not show any sexual distinctions. Yet at this early age infants have already made some contact with the genital by touch. But since this organ system is not functioning in a specifically sexual way, that is, for discharge, we can infer that the sensations experienced are approximately similar in both sexes. At this stage, then, the clitoris is not a masculine organ, it is simply the most accessible part of the rather nebulous genital zone. The charge is distributed over the whole region of the vulva and the touch of the child is not focused on any specific part. We can say, then, that there is nothing specifically phallic about the clitoris at this time.

Freud (1931a, p. 256) admits that he "[does] not know what are the biological roots of these specific characteristics of the woman." Yet it is these roots which determine the natural course of the sexual evolution of the individual while the psychological interaction with the environment plays a secondary role. The latter may provide a favorable medium for this evolution or it may interfere with the natural process. The tadpole and the young fish evolve differently in the same pond. The oak and the fern grow in the same soil.

Can we elucidate some of these biological roots or factors? We know that the female will evolve in a direction which will bring into function the mammary glands and the reproductive system, especially the uterus and, of course, the vagina. Full function of these structures only occurs after puberty but maturation proceeds from the onset of the genital phase. When the apple first appears on the tree it is a long way from the ripened fruit, but we know it is not a pear or a plum. When the bioenergetic charge invades the vagina from the vulva inward, the basis is provided for the self-perception of sex. Gradually, the normal female child becomes aware that she is a girl and not that she is not a boy. I venture to suggest that the specific quality is the turning inward of the bioenergetic current or stream of excitation; in contrast to the boy in whom the flow proceeds more and more outward to cause extension.

This inward turning which is the specific quality of vaginal excitation is supplemented by the function of the other female organs to produce femininity. Whereas the male discharges all sexual energy through the penis, this is not true of the female. Some, the proportion being unknown, is stored and discharged in the mammary glands and uterus. The man has no counterpart to the flow and ebb of the menstrual cycle. One other important distinction is the role of the male sexual organ in initiating the sexual act. It is the more aggressive organ and the male is the more aggressive organism, and this quality accounts for his greater muscular development. It is not a question of mechanics but of relative bioenergetic charge. The failure to understand this accounts for a common psychoanalytic fallacy.

Is the relation between the nipple and the mouth of the infant analogous to that between penis and vagina? Certainly! We have two erectile organs and two receptive cavities. But where the mechanics of the two systems are similar, the bioenergetic relationship within each system is different. Where the penis is the dominant aggressive organ in the sexual act, that function belongs to the mouth in the act of nursing. The infant's mouth is a powerful sucking organ—the vagina is not. It is not the nipple which seeks the mouth but the mouth which seeks the nipple. If there is any doubt about this, simply observe the actions of the young of any mammal. Put your finger into the mouth of a day old pup and you will be amazed at the strength of its pull. That the human infant cannot move towards the nipple as easily as other newborn mammals is not due to any lack of charge in the mouth. Bioenergetically, the nipple is the passive organ in this relationship. Without the suck of the mouth the milk would not squirt whereas the genital system of the adult male is capable of independent rhythmic discharge of semen as in a nocturnal emission.

Let us now return to the developing female child. We assume that all children reach the genital level for this marks their contact with reality. The question is—How strong is this contact or how securely anchored in genitality is the personality? Our characterological classification depends on the answer. In the oral character genitality is dominated by oral strivings. This is the significance of Freud's (1931a, p. 253) observation that "where the attachment to the father was peculiarly strong it had been preceded by a phase of equally strong and passionate attachment exclusively to the mother." The masochistic character transfers the marked ambivalence of the pregenital phase to the genital function. In both of these types genitality as a function of discharge is relatively weak.

The child with a masochistic disturbance approaches the genital phase hesitantly. The masochistic disturbance at the anus prevents the build-up of sufficient charge to complete the movement inward. Bioenergetically, the charge at the genitals is weak; the energy tends to remain at the root of the penis in the male, in the female it does not extend beyond the vulva and clitoris. The vagina remains undercharged. The child's attitude toward her father is likewise ambivalent and hesitant. If she meets with a favorable response and is accepted in her femininity, the masochistic problem will become a trait in a hysterical character structure. It should be borne in mind that such children need a greater reassurance on the genital level than a child who reaches this level without serious prior disturbance. Generally, in such families, the reverse happens.

In the case we have been discussing, the father's attitude towards the patient ignored her femaleness. His approval of her depended on the accomplishment of certain goals he set: good marks at school, achievement in music, etc. And her achievements could never equal the standards he set. I ignore the fact that it is a personality disturbance in an adult male not to respond to the charm of the young female child. Under such circumstances there arises a conflict in the child between the aggressive behavior demanded of her on an ego level and the receptive quality which emerges with the development of vaginal charge and sensation. This, then, becomes generalized into a conflict between the ego and sexuality in which the ego is the winner. Energy is withdrawn upward into the thorax and head, as in the passive-feminine character, and a severe rigidity of this region develops. The effect of this rigidity is to immobilize the tender feelings while aggression and determination are favored.

The split in the personality is manifested as a split in the body structure. The upper half of the body is highly charged, rigid and aggressive. The lower half is weak, masochistic and passive. These girls develop very strong feelings of pride which in adult life make submission to the male difficult.

The dominant conflict is with the father and this is later transferred to the male therapist and to all men. Even the masochistic problem is transferred to the male.

This leads to a secondary identification with the male which is favored by the dominance of the aggressive tendencies. The block against the moving of the energy inward into the vagina keeps the energy in the region of the vulva. As the identification with the male proceeds, the clitoris takes on a real phallic quality and may enlarge. There is a tendency toward muscular development. Such women are aggressive in the sexual act but this must be considered as a defense against submission. In their attitude towards men there are many contradictory feelings. Superficially, they compete and attempt to dominate. If they prove stronger than their partner, they become very contemptuous and castrating. The male is the recipient of all their hatred derived from their early frustration on the genital level. On a deeper level, these women want to be forced to submit. This stems from the strong masochistic layer in the personality. If this layer and its accompanying emotions are worked through, it becomes possible to create the conditions which would permit the normal development of vaginal charge and orgasm to take place.

How much masculinity will these women show? Two factors play a role. One is the loss of femininity which of itself will allow certain masculine traits to appear. The other is the extent of active masculine identification. The presence of brothers in the family constellation who are favored will further the masculine identification, which may take the form of an exaggerated muscular development. Apropos of this, it should be added that excessive hair tends to appear wherever this exaggerated muscular development occurs.

When the total pattern of behavior is dominated by this aggressive attitude, which tends toward competition with the male on his level, one is justified in describing the character structure as masculine-aggressive. Although it has a different aspect, it is bioenergetically related to the passive-feminine character structure in men. We can describe the difference as follows: since aggression is the natural genital characteristic of the male animal, its inhibition produces a passive character. In the female the genital quality can be described as aggressive receptivity. This is in line with the turning inward of the stream of excitation. The failure of the receptive function to mature leaves a desexualized aggression as the outstanding quality, that is, the aggression is only in the service of the ego. The seeming sexual aggression of these women is an ego drive and not a genital drive.

A few points remain to be cleared up. Does the female suffer from castration anxiety? Is penis envy a natural feeling for the female or is it the result of pathological processes? I firmly believe that no woman would ever feel penis envy if she has the perception of a full functioning vagina. Bioenergetically, the vagina is fully adequate for the sexual needs of the female. If, however, the vagina is undercharged relative to the clitoris, perception will be focused on the relatively more highly charged organ. The female, then, is forced to become aware of its inferiority as compared with the male organ. Such women will suffer from penis envy and show a strong castration anxiety. This, however, has its basis in a real traumatic situation.

I am in disagreement with Freud on the motives for the girl child turning from the mother as an object of her libido to the father. To my mind this is a natural event in the course of the normal development of female genitality. What requires explanation are (1) any delay in this change of love object, (2) the development of masculine tendencies, and (3) the loss of equality in the genital relationship. Definitive femininity is not the result of a "very circuitous path" which has as its point of origin the "negative Oedipus complex" and the acceptance of castration.

We have not discussed the problem posed by the combination of oral deprivation and genital frustration in the female. This combination would produce a character structure composed of oral dependency covered over by a rigid pride. When a girl child who has suffered from a feeling of deprivation on the oral level turns to the father as a love object she transfers to him the unsatisfied oral longing for contact and support plus the need for sexual love. These are the patients in whose analysis we find that the change in love object took place late and carried an excessive charge. Freud had commented on this problem without recognizing its cause. When they meet with frustration on the genital level, the hurt is very severe for it amounts to a rejection on both levels. The rigidity which ensues is equally severe and the later feelings of hurt pride which develop seem very exaggerated. The characterological picture differs from the masculine-aggressive structure we studied earlier. The conflict between oral needs and genital desire will manifest itself in terms of a struggle over dependence versus independence. There will be a characterological ambivalence between submission and holding back. What is lacking is an aggressive attitude towards life and towards sexuality. The body structure will show both the oral weakness and the later rigidity, the latter more obvious in the upper half of the body. There is no identification with the male since a strong charge is lacking in the clitoris. The behavior pattern is one of dependence, passivity and sensitivity with a strong childlike quality which alternates with independence, rebellion and pride. Much remains to be said about this character structure and the problems it poses but it must be reserved for another study.

In the preceding clinical chapters (9–14) we have studied the more common neurotic personalities in terms of the main neurotic character types. But this book would be incomplete without a discussion of the schizoid character, which is essentially a problem belonging to the psychoses. Many individuals who are borderline schizophrenics are capable of maintaining a contact with reality which permits them to function in the outside world and be treated in the analyst's office. While the subject is immense, some statement of the bioenergetic principles involved in this problem is necessary.

16

The Schizophrenic Character

In the preceding chapters we studied the disturbances of
ego development which are described as neuroses. A
"neurosis" may be defined as a distortion or defect in the
relation of an individual to reality. A neurotic has contact
with reality, though his attitude may amount to a rejection of its demands, as in the oral character, to distrust
and suspicion or to an overdetermined aggression. His
contact is never immediate and direct otherwise we would
have no justification for calling it neurotic. But it is also
never completely lost or broken. The neurosis may be compared to a defect in vision such as myopia, or astigmatism,
or to the narrowing of the visual fields. In contrast, the
psychosis is a form of blindness. The individual who is
schizophrenic has lost contact with reality.

If this statement seems an oversimplification of a very
complex problem, we should realize that it merely poses
the problem. We are faced with the necessity of defining
reality and of establishing the nature of the organism's
contact with it. Actually, the differences which exist
between the neurotic and the psychotic, while qualitative
by psychiatric standards, can be reduced to a lowest common denominator and viewed as quantitative phenomena.
Are there not borderline cases in which it is difficult to
decide if a given pattern of behavior should be described

339

as neurotic or psychotic? Has it not been said that all individuals in civilized cultures show some manifestation of schizophrenic processes?

It is not my intent now to explore this problem in all its details. On the other hand, the analytic therapist should be familiar with the dynamics of the schizoid character structure since it is commonly met with in office practice. And we shall find that the bioenergetic concepts elaborated upon earlier make possible a better conception of this disturbance while they provide new methods for the treatment of this difficult condition.

The term "schizophrenic" was introduced by Bleuler to describe a syndrome which had previously been called dementia praecox. The word, "schizophrenia," which means a splitting of the mind and, by extension, a splitting of the personality, is so apt a description that it has become identified with the very nature of the disorder. In contrast to this basic concept, the present attitude, largely influenced by psychoanalytic thinking, regards schizophrenia as a regressive phenomenon in which the withdrawal from reality is carried to an extreme. Thus, we have two points of view from which to study the schizophrenic process: In one the splitting occurs within the personality so that the unity of its elements is destroyed. In the other, the important schism is between personality and reality. It shall be our purpose to show that both points of view are valid and represent two aspects of one phenomenon.

In this discussion, we can dispense with detailed case histories. The text books of psychiatry are full of them. It is recognized that the schizophrenic comes from a troubled and disturbed home environment. We shall inquire into the etiological factors responsible for this condition later. For the moment, the big problem is to understand the mechanism of the important symptom formations and thereby gain some insight into the nature of the underlying pathological process.

One of the most striking symptoms which the schizophrenic individual presents is the phenomenon of depersonalization. In this loss of contact with the total body or with any part of it there is a loss of contact with reality. Naturally, one important aspect of reality for the individual is the feeling of his own body. The other aspect is the feeling for material objects and processes in the external world. Since these are really the two sides of the function of perception, if we can explain the former we shall be in a good position to comprehend the latter and to deepen our knowledge of the ego and its disturbances.

All writers agree that in depersonalization the individual reports a loss of contact with the body or with significant parts of it. There are accompanying sensations of strangeness and of unreality. Sometimes the person has the feeling that he is looking at himself from outside of the body or from a distance. More frequently, the depersonalization is limited to a part of the body which is felt as an alien structure (not part of the self), and even as under the control of another will. In an attack of depersonalization, a split occurs; the material body or some part of it no longer belongs to the individual, it isn't his body as he has customarily experienced it. Obviously something has happened to break up the unity of the organismic feeling. What happens? How can we explain this phenomenon?

I should like to report the description of such an acute attack which, while extreme, is nevertheless very revealing. "I would sometimes get the strange feeling that I had no control over my breathing. The thought came that if I should suddenly stop breathing I could not start it again. I seemed to be outside of my body, looking at it as if it wasn't me. I had feelings of weakness and dizziness, and I felt I was going to die. Then I would scream and collapse and the feelings would slowly pass away. It was awfully frightening." This patient was hospitalized following a series of such attacks.

In the analysis of a reaction such as the above, we face the necessity of deciding whether the report of the patient is an accurate description of the event or merely the product of a disturbed imagination. Certainly one cannot dispute a statement of feeling for the observer can only be aware of its external manifestation. Whether the patient was outside of her body or not, no one can know.* We must accept her statement of the feeling and attempt to comprehend it. We do not simplify the problem by describing it as due to a disturbed imagination. To explain this disturbance we would still have to account for the original feeling. In this problem of depersonalization we face a phenomenon which transcends psychology and physiology.

Let me supplement this patient's statement with another observation. Several years ago my wife became very excited at the prospect of going abroad. As the excitement mounted she suddenly became aware that there were two of her. This feeling of doubleness was uncomfortable but it did not upset her much. She was literally "beside herself" with joy. One of the doubles was the body, fully alive and functioning normally. The other was a spirit-body. (The so-called ethereal double.) The experience lasted several hours then it disappeared as the excitement slowly subsided. I was present during this occurrence but I did not see or feel the doubleness. Then, I recall several occasions from my own childhood when my excitement in a pleasurable situation became so strong that everything had an air of unreality. It was like a dream state, a situation in which one pinches one's self to see if one is awake. Some time ago I met a famous medium who said she was able to get outside of herself which had the advantage, as she put it, that she could see if her slip was showing from behind.

---

* Compare this with Paul Schilder's comments on depersonalization. "He observes his actions and behavior from the point of view of a spectator." Also, "when one tries to imagine oneself according to the *second* instruction, there is very often a spiritual eye which is in front of the subject and looks all over the body." Again, "The emanation of the substance of the head out of its frame is of special importance. This emanating substance is the carrier of the localization of the ego." *The Image and Appearance of the Human Body.* New York, International Universities Press, 1950, pp. 138, 84, 96.

Bioenergetic analysis enables us to advance an explanation for these phenomena which, while it cannot be experimentally confirmed at present, offers a good working hypothesis. Excitement manifests itself by increased motility but we must also assume that the increased motility is the result of an increase in the bioenergetic charge of the organism. This increased charge prevades all the tissues and shows in the warmth and color of the skin and in the sparkle of the eyes. As the charge grows stronger its effects transcend the body proper. The atmosphere in the immediate vicinity of the organism becomes charged and the organism loses the sense of its customary boundary. Once this limiting barrier has been transcended, the ego is overwhelmed and flooded. Psychologically speaking, the id is in immediate contact with the universe. One's feelings confirm this insight. It is as if one is in the grip of forces mightier than the self, like a mote in the air or a piece of driftwood in the ocean. Bioenergetically, the interaction is between the core and the cosmos.

In the intense pleasurable states reality dims but does not vanish. Dreamlike though it may be, we know we are awake or there is sufficient ego left to test reality by the proverbial pinch. Since the ego is a derivative of the id, the latter, in re-asserting its domination, re-establishes its innate function of self-perception. This follows a basic scientific law which Freud recognized. A differentiated function must be present as a tendency in the unstructured state from which it evolved. So long as the tissues are highly charged energetically there is no loss of the self but simply a loss of the boundaries of the self. Reality, as we know it, ordinarily, is a product of the ego function. As the ego is overwhelmed it is this reality which weakens.

This reality of the ego, a material reality, is not the only reality. The id function has its own reality which is as valid as that of the ego although it is incapable of coping with the material needs of the higher animal organism. It is a reality dominated by the pleasure principle much as is that of the infant, but it is as valid and desirable in its own right as that other reality which is under the aegis of the reality principle. It is the reality of the deepest and fullest sexual orgasm, of great religious experience and of the wonder of spring and of birth. It is the reality which touches the mysteries of life but does not become mystical. It is not the experience of the schizophrenic reaction.

The process whereby a double self is created is more complicated. When the atmosphere about the highly excited organism becomes strongly charged, cohesive forces seem to develop in it. Ordinarily, all living organisms show an aura about the body which is a natural field phenomenon existing about all charged systems. My associate, Dr. John C. Pierrakos, has made an intensive study of the energy field about the human organism in both health and disease. I hope that he will publish his observations soon. It seems that, in very highly charged states, the organism can move out of its aura or field, which then remains behind in the form of the body, and follow the body as a shadow. Once set up as a nucleus it will retain its form and cohesion so long as energy streams from the body into it. By virtue of the energy bridge between the two systems, the perception of the self is doubled. The field phenomenon collapses and disappears as soon as the subsidence of the excitation withdraws the energy into the body proper. Here, again, there is no loss of the self, no psychotic splitting of the personality.

I know as I write this that many readers will become skeptical. Some will question while others will turn against all bioenergetic interpretations. This was a reaction which greeted many of Freud's most valuable contributions. They will ask if I have seen these "ethereal doubles," if I believe in spirits? I can only say that it is not a question of belief, of spiritualism of parapsychological phenomena. We are attempting to understand an illness, the symptoms of which, if they are taken seriously, are incomprehensible from the viewpoint of the reality of our everyday lives. The hypotheses I offer will find their validity in the crucible of therapeutic endeavor.

Let us return to the question of depersonalization in the

schizophrenic. Before we do so, however, one question is to be answered. What holds the average adult so tenaciously to the everyday reality of life? Why are we so afraid of insanity? These questions bring to mind another. Why do so many people have a secret fear that they can lose their minds?

Psychiatrists recognize in this problem a great fear of the unknown. Civilized man clings to accepted patterns and resists new ideas so forcibly that it is, at times, dangerous to advance them. If one strives all through life for security it must reflect a deep-seated insecurity. It is also part of our cultural neurosis that too frequently security is measured in terms of material possessions. But even when we achieve some sort of material security in our lives, inner security and peace eludes us. In contrast, the wild animal in nature has this inner security but no guaranty for his material welfare. It does seem as if one cannot have both.

In Chapter 2 we discussed the antithesis between inner and outer, between the id and the ego, between the material and the spiritual. We can conclude that the average adult is bound to external reality by the drive for material goods. Material needs—food, clothing, shelter, the means of transportation, etc.—exert a tremendous force to keep the individual in contact with everyday reality. This is not neurotic unless it is overdetermined as it tends to be in our civilization. Today one has no time to dream. The realm of the exotic, of the spiritual, of the involuntary disturbs established routines and threatens our security. Fortunately, outlets are provided for the expression and satisfaction of our spiritual needs in love and sex, in religion and art. But even in these activities civilized man is bound by too strong a consciousness of reality, preventing his escape or release into the great unknown, the world of the spirit.*

---

* Paul Schilder comments on some observations of Linderman to the same effect: "Our tendency to live in the world of

If we analyze this further, we can see that it is the aggressive drive, which functions basically to satisfy material needs, that limits the spiritual expression. We could have foreseen this antagonism from our concept of the instinctual drives. In Figure 16, the shaded line represents the material, aggressive, earthly quality of man which

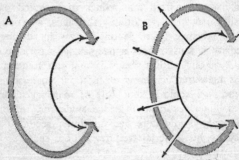

FIG. 16. Instinctual drives: A, Normal; B, Psychotic escape.

envelops and holds in the single line representing the spirit—eros or love. In the adult, as compared with the child, the greater development of the muscular system favors the aggressive component. Too frequently the aggressive drive turns inward against the spiritual feelings as a masochistic phenomenon and further depresses the spiritual function.

In states of intense excitement, the charge is so great that the aggressive component is powerless to restrain the feeling. It overwhelms the muscular system and the skin and reaches far out. The outlets are insufficient to discharge the flood which overflows the banks: On the other hand, the depersonalization of the psychotic is due to a failure of the aggressive drive to contain the normal charge. This is no flood but the breakdown of normal bar-

---

reality leads us to neglect what is going on in the field of sensations." *The Image and Appearance of the Human Body.* New York, International Universities Press, 1950, p. 86.

riers. For this to occur, the aggressive drive must be very greatly reduced. This is what we find in the schizophrenic personality. He is anti-material, anti-everyday reality. We can describe it as a withdrawal but it is tantamount to material death. I could, therefore, agree with another schizophrenic patient who told me that her body was dying. When this happens, the spirit or free energy tends to leave the body. This is experienced as "dying" as the first patient reported. Of course, they never die this way. The fright is sufficient to reawaken the aggressive, self-preservative tendencies and integration occurs. It must be that enough energy leaves the body to create a center self-perception outside of the body.

Complete depersonalization is less common than the feeling of depersonalization in part of the body. The temporary cessation of function in a part, generally a peripheral part, results in a loss of energy from that part. It then becomes alien, strange and unrelated to the self.

Faced with this problem, psychoanalysts have recourse to Freud's statement that the ego is primarily a body ego. Fenichel adds that it is "the perception of one's own body." But psychoanalysis is confused as to how to work with the concept. I quote from Fenichel (1945, p. 419) on the subject of depersonalization: "When the normal body feeling disappears from consciousness, this does not necessarily mean that the corresponding amount of body ego has been withdrawn from the organ in question. It may mean that the organ has become charged with a large amount of libido which is concealed by an intense counter-cachexis." This observation is valid for the hysterical paralysis or the hysterical amnesias, but no such patient would describe this feeling as strange. In the hysterical reaction, the part of the body split off from consciousness is warm-blooded and pink colored. In the schizophrenic reaction, the split off part is white or livid and cold. To work with body concepts one must observe the body. Hysteria is an ego defense reaction. Schizophrenia is the result of the disorganization of the ego. They do not look alike, they are not similar, and they cannot be explained in the same psychoanalytic language.

What I wish to suggest is that the most fundamental split in the schizophrenic personality is that between the aggressive instincts and eros, the spiritual force. The psychosis differs from the neurosis in that in the psychosis instinctual defusion is total whereas it is only partial in the neurosis.

I describe as "schizoid" a character structure which shows schizophrenic tendencies but in whom a serious break with reality has not taken place. The schizoid character will also show this basic antipathy to material reality and the tendency to complete instinctual defusion. In them, the aggressive instinct is not merely weak, as it is in the oral character, it is dissociated. The schizoid character identifies consciously with his spiritual feelings. The need for aggressive action is accepted only as a matter of survival and on this basis a pattern of behavior is set up which includes an aggressive attitude. Despite its apparent strength one can find occasions in his history when the aggression failed completely.

I recall a young woman from whose history alone one could diagnose the schizoid character. Her body structure also showed in its organization those splits which are characteristic of this condition. When I spoke with her I noticed that she looked me right in the eyes, and I then became aware that she had her eyes fixed on mine all the time. I thought this strange so I asked her if she could speak with me without looking at me. She could not turn her eyes away. It made her anxious. This is contrary to the neurotic tendency which is not to look at the person. I had the strong feeling that she maintained her contact with me through her eyes. When she turned them aside, the contact was broken and she became frightened. Other aspects of her behavior showed this same effort to maintain contact with the world of material reality.

I don't believe that I need prove the great insecurity that underlies such behavior. To clutch at an object so desperately is to betray the deep inner fear of its loss.

The weakness of the normal barrier is translated psychologically as a weakness of the ego. The loss of the limiting membrance is a loss of ego. In this respect, we recall Freud's statement that the ego is a surface and the projection of a surface. Biologically speaking, the true surface of the body is the skin; energetically the muscular system under the skin serves as the more important restraining membrane. The problem of the schizoid character and of schizophrenia lies in the lack of ego identification with and in the weakness of the muscular system.

If this is correct, an important modification must be made in Freud's formulations. It is not eros, the bearer of life, which is the unifying agent or binding element in the organism. Rather, the much maligned aggressive instinct holds body and soul together. Eros favors the return of the spirit to the universal, the godhead. This is the Nirvana principle, as it is also the aim of the great Oriental mystic religions. Return it does, eventually. But during the life of the organism, this striving for union with the universal is channelled into the sexual function by the self-preserving aggressive instincts.

The weakness of the muscular system in the schizoid character and in the psychotic is not due to a lack of muscular development as we ordinarily understand that expression. Very frequently, the schizoid character has great muscular strength and will show strong muscles. In this he differs from the oral character in whom the muscular system is underdeveloped. In the schizoid, the musculature is tense, the deep muscles are very spastic and the whole muscular system is uncoordinated and segmented. One does not get a feeling of unity from the body structure.* The head does not look as if it is securely joined to

* The same lack of unity has been observed on the psychological level. R. G. Hoskins writes, "More impressive is the common feature that is detectable in the members of all groups, namely, a loss of the inner cohesion of the personality. Whether this be designated as 'weakness of the ego,' 'intrapsychic taxia,' or what not, it is the break-up of the individuality into disjunctive fragments that is most striking." *The Biology of Schizophrenia*. New York, Norton, 1946, p. 92.

the trunk, there is marked splitting of the body at the diaphragm and the lower limbs are not functionally integrated into the body.* One of my patients explained her feeling of being disjointed by saying that the ligaments of the joints were too loose. She showed me that she was "double-jointed" at her knees.

Whether this statement is generally true or not, long study has convinced me that the energy flow in the muscular system of the schizoid character is interrupted or broken at the joints. One finds, for example, that the ankle is frozen and unbending. Coordination and grace in movement are lacking unless the movement has been consciously mastered. Many schizoid characters become dancers or athletes in order to develop a feeling of coordination and unity in their body. The lack of coordination and grace shows itself most clearly in the natural aggressive movements—those involved in anger and sexuality. The strong individual muscles are the result of an effort to compensate the basic defect. We shall return to the body structure and movement of the schizoid character again. I should like, first, to discuss another common schizophrenic symptom—hallucination and projection.

In the following analysis it would be well to distinguish between these terms. Projection can occur without hallucination. It is sometimes seen in the neurosis. A patient complained to me that he could make no contact with his wife. He described her as being withdrawn, cold and like a ghoul. I saw his wife the next hour. She was warm, alert and in contact with me at every moment. It was my patient who was withdrawn and ghoulish. He had projected onto his wife his perception of himself. But this is not psychotic. The interpersonal relationships of this patient were disturbed. He correctly perceived the quality of the disturbance, but since he could not accept the fact that it was due to his neurosis, the only other alternative was to believe that the other party was responsible. It is like looking at the world through dark glasses. This pa-

* See footnote on p. 349.

tient saw his wife through a pall cast by his own inner gloom. But even this common type of projection bears a qualitative resemblence to the schizophrenic process.

The schizophrenic hallucination is based upon a projection. This projection determines the form and content of the hallucination. The voice the schizophrenic hears is his own and, of course, the words he hears express his own thoughts. I, too, hear my inner voice while thinking. But this tells us little about the mechanism of projection. We can gain some insight through analysis of the phenomenon of the visual hallucination.

The schizophrenic will tell you that occasionally he "sees" forms and shapes which no one else observes. The form may be more or less distinct, as that of an angel or a devil, or it may be vague. In addition, the schizophrenic "sees" other phenomena—lines which traverse space, the aura about individuals, etc. One must differentiate among these phenomena. If one calls everything "crazy," one risks closing the avenue into the schizophrenic world. One must then "shock" him into reality, but such procedures do not guaranty that he will accept a reality so preferred.

The schizophrenic withdrawal from reality applies only to the material aspect of the world about us. We saw that it was based upon an inhibition of the aggressive instinct with the result that the spiritual and sensory component is abnormally active. There is a natural antithesis between movement and perception. We, too, reduce our motility when we wish to increase our auditory or visual acuity. The schizophrenic is in contact with a world of which the average person is unaware. We must admit that it exists otherwise we could not comprehend the schizophrenic problem. And we can, with special training, observe similar phenomena. This world consists of energy waves; energy field processes which surround us in the atmosphere. So far, the schizophrenic is not hallucinating. A certain degree of depersonalization has occurred. In this state, if projection develops an hallucination occurs. The form and content of the vision is not in the atmosphere, it is in the schizophrenic mind, but it can only be projected upon a screen of atmospheric forces. This screen is necessary for projection to take place. Can you form an image if a movie projector throws its light into space? Can you picture animal-like forms in the sky if there are no clouds? Given the screen, what is the mechanism which functions (as the movie projector does) to form an image?

I pose the thesis that the basic schizophrenic split is in the defusion or dissociation of the two instinctual drives. This dissociation is brought about by a block in the pathway of the aggressive impulses which prevents them from entering consciousness.* This implies a *secondary* split in the schizophrenic personality between the drive and the perception of the drive. Clinical observation places this block in the deep muscles at the base of the skull. Let us see how this block explains the phenomenon of projection (Fig. 17).

In the psychotic condition, the block at the base of the skull is so strong that very little of the aggressive, material impulses get into the brain. That little which does get in reaches only the subcortical centers. It does not reach the

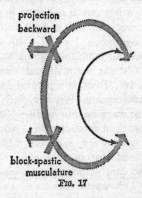

projection
backward

block-spastic
musculature
Fig. 17

* See Otto Fenichel: "It seems that the break with reality does not serve the purpose of gaining more instinctual pleasure but rather of combatting the instinctual drives directed towards objects." *The Psychoanalytic Theory of Neurosis*. New York, Norton, 1945, p. 440.

center of consciousness in the neopallidum. Sometimes even the charge in the subcortical centers is so reduced that the vital activities, such as eating, are reduced to less than the minimum. This is what we call "negativism" in the psychotic behavior. On the other hand, in the paranoid state of schizophrenia, impulse formation is strong and active. When the energy of these strong aggressive impulses meets the block at the base of the skull it is deflected. Most of the energy is deflected out backwards, some of it is deflected out through the ears and, occasionally, a part is deflected out through the eyes. This deflection outward through the eyes is the projection which accounts for the visual hallucination. However, it is the least common of the hallucinatory phenomena.

When the energy of these impulses is deflected backwards, it charges the atmospheric field surrounding the back of the head. Since we are dealing with a very heightened sensitivity in the schizophrenic, we can understand why they would have the feeling that "something is going on behind my back." It could also be interpreted as "someone is staring at the back of my head," or "I am being followed," etc.

Occasionally one meets with a nonpsychotic individual who feels this block. One patient told me, "When I get angry, I feel a commotion at the back of my neck and head. I get frustrated because I can't get the anger out. This makes me more angry and I get even more frustrated. Then I keep going on saying the most senseless things but I can no longer stop it."

Many people suffer from the fear that someone will attack them from behind. They sit in the last row of the theatre or lecture hall and turn around frequently to reassure themselves.

Since it is the aggressive impulse which is projected outward, it is easy to understand the feelings of persecution from which the schizophrenic suffers. The content of the delusion is to be interpreted in the light of the schizophrenic's life experiences, if these can be elucidated. The bioenergetic mechanism of schizophrenic projection and hallucination is not in itself a proper subject for psycoanalytic interpretation.

Corresponding to the block at the base of the head, one finds in schizophrenic individuals a severe block consisting of very spastic muscles at the junction of the pelvis and backbone. These are homologous points on the line of flow of the bioenergetic current. Since the flow of the energy current is pulsatile and pendular in nature, it is always equally disturbed at both ends of the trajectory. In the psychotic individual the aggressive drive is not in the service of sexuality any more than it is in the service of the ego. As a result the psychotic is without the ability to achieve a sexual discharge. Any sexual sensation he has is vague, diffuse and nonspecific. The drive needed to focus the charge in the genital apparatus has been deflected outwards. This statement also applies to the schizoid character structure but to a lesser extent and dependent upon the degree of integration in the personality.

Projection occurs at the pelvic block just as it does at the nuchal block. Again there is the perception of an activity just behind one. Only here the interpretation frequently has a sexual meaning. Fenichel (1945, p. 429) reports an observation by Bibring of a woman who "believed that she was persecuted by a man named 'Behind.' She attributed to this man characteristics which were in fact true of her own gluteal region." This mechanism explains the fear of homosexual attack in the male psychotic. But if the bioenergetic dynamics of the problem are not understood, the difficulty in trying to explain such fantasies psychologically is very great. Let me quote Fenichel again. "Freud's first finding that the persecutor represents the homosexual object certainly remains true; but the fact that the persecutor represents at the time the subject's own features shows that this object, in the patient's fantasy, had been incorporated and reprojected." Such analytic statements, while they may be true, do not help us to understand the mechanisms of these processes.

The lack of aggression coupled with the intense need of the schizophrenic for contact on the interpersonal level makes him an easy victim for the active, aggressive homosexual. I have never seen a schizophrenic or schizoid with the marked bodily characteristics of the opposite sex such as could be observed in true homosexuals or in passive-feminine men. Yet homosexual practices and fantasies are not uncommon among psychotics. The interpretation of this behavior must be made on another level.

Ideas of incorporation are another common symptom of the schizophrenic disturbance. These fantasies include all of the natural body orifices—oral, anal, respiratory, and others. If we take them literally, we fall prey to the schizophrenic delusion, in that a dissociated part is made to represent the whole. In this respect Rosen, who interprets all schizophrenic fantasies as oral phenomena, has made a significant contribution. Rosen's (1953, p. 7) comment on Schreiber's delusion, which has been analyzed by Freud, is worth quoting. "Furthermore I began to understand, and never lost sight of the fact, that the wish for the warm impregnating sun that was Schreiber's delusion would ultimately spring from the need to put the sun in place of the cold sun that made him insane."

The typical attitude of the oral character may be expressed as a feeling, conscious or unconscious, that "the world owes him something." He feels that he was cheated, that he didn't get enough or his fair share. But the oral character has no feeling of persecution, no fear that he will be attacked. The schizophrenic attitude can only be described as one of terror. This terror underlies the frozen immobility of catatonic stupor, the frenzy of catatonic excitement, the delusion of paranoia and the resignation of hebephrenia. Such a panic can arise only out of the experience of a situation in which the very existence of the individual was threatened.

Ideas of incorporation should be interpreted on the oral level and these interpretations would reach the schizophrenic or schizoid character. In addition to the deep-seated fright arising from a threat to existence, the schizophrenic has strong feelings of deprivation. Their homosexual activities must be regarded as an attempt to gain the warmth of intimate human contact. But their need far transcends the need of the neurotic patient. The therapeutic task is no easy one. It is not sufficient to bring the psychotic back to reality, to eliminate his hallucinations and to remove his delusions. The reconstituted ego must be strengthened so that it can cope with reality without too great a strain. In the therapy of schizophrenia, the most important therapeutic factor is the sincere warmth and affection of the therapist. Rosen (1953, p. 8) shows his appreciation of this requirement when he says that, "the therapist must be a loving, omnipotent protector and provider for the patient." Unlike the oral character, the schizophrenic is not the baby at the breast. While they are more dependent, they show little of the leeching or sucking tendencies which one finds in the oral character. The schizophrenic is the infant in the womb. He needs your life as the embryo needs that of its mother but he can make no demands upon you for it. If the therapist is afraid or has no vitality to spare, he cannot help a schizophrenic or schizoid structure. We can conclude that it is this basic foetal need which is expressed in the ideas of incorporation.

The suggestion that the schizophrenic behavior has this foetal quality of attachment and dependence points to the possible etiological factors in the disturbance. Before we consider them, however, we must understand more about the schizonphrenic disturbance. Much has been written about the resemblance between the thought processes of the schizophrenic and those of the infant or primitive man. No doubt regression, in the behavior of the schizophrenic, is frequently observed. Sometimes they have to be treated and cared for as if they were infants. But this resemblance can be greatly over-stressed. The bioenergetic dynamics of the ego structure is different in each case. Their psychology is also very different. Robbins calls schizophrenia a dehumanizing process. The schizophrenic is a dehumanized being, a description we would not apply to the infant or the primitive. But in what way are they alike and how do they differ?

Infant, primitive and schizophrenic lack the ability to deal with reality as we understand it in our world today. All three face experiences which are beyond their comprehension and for which they must invent special systems of thought. The young child does not understand its parent's inability to satisfy its needs. It creates two categories of forces in the external world, the good ones which satisfy and the bad ones which deprive or frustrate. Given such a division it is easy to comprehend the child's belief in witches, Santa Claus, etc. The primitive, too, is forced into such a dualistic, even pluralistic, concept of forces in the universe: good gods which further the life interests and threatening gods who would thwart life. The schizophrenic, also, has this basic antithesis of good and bad, frequently related to God versus the devil, love versus hate, warmth versus cold. In such a rigid, simple framework of reference, thought processes will show the condensation, the displacement, and the symbolic quality which Freud showed to be characteristic of dream life. But the difference!

The infant functions on the pleasure principle which knows only tension or the release from it. Reality in terms of the forces which operate in the external world is unknown for lack of the necessary growth and development. Psychotic functioning is not based on the pleasure principle; in fact, it is the inability of the psychotic organism to move towards pleasurable excitation which is the core of the problem. The omnipotence of the infant is real. He is the future, the legatee of everything the past has produced, the creator of tomorrow. If this turns out to be an illusion, I can only say that we have failed in our obligation to the child. The delusions of grandeur so typical of schizophrenia are truly delusions.

The primitive functions on a reality principle, but one

which is limited by the lack of accumulated experience.
Within the limits of his knowledge he shows the ability
to adapt his behavior to the exigencies of the external
situation. He has the sense of motility and coordination
which would permit those fine adjustments of movement
and which would make his actions accord with reality as
he knows it. This the psychotic lacks. The actions of the
schizophrenic are not motivated by the pleasure principle
and he has not the muscular control to function adequately in reality. Under the circumstances, he begins by
denying himself and ends by denying the world of reality.
It is this denial of the material reality which dehumanizes
the schizophrenic even as an angel is not human. The
crash of his ego causes the destruction of the material
world.

In the schizophrenic reaction there is one symptom
which portrays the physical process underlying the disease.
Catatonia is not only a pathogomonic sign of the schizophrenic illness, it is also a criterion for classifying the
severity of the pathological process. Generally, patients
who are catatonic have a more favorable prognosis than
those who show the other forms of this illness. Some of
the manifestations of this illness must be understood as
attempts at the restoration of the ego function. The destructive outbreaks can be so construed. They represent
the release of aggressive impulses which while irrational
and dangerous to the environment tend to promote both
ego strength and integration in the schizophrenic. I have
always believed that much could be accomplished if the
schizophrenic could be allowed to smash some old furniture in a carefully controlled setting. Many schizophrenics
relate that following such an outbreak they feel much
better. Of course, such measures must be part of a broader
therapeutic program.

In this connection Fenichel (1945, pp. 437, 438) states:
"A restitutional striving toward the lost objective world is
the root of many catatonic symptoms." Specifically pertinent is the statement that "catatonic rigidity reflects a

conflict between the impulse to act and the defense against it." Ferenczi had the idea that catatonia was the result of a high frequency alternation of activating and inhibiting impulses. The muscular spasm of the neurosis differ from catatonic rigidity only in degree and localization. These differences are essentially quantitative.

I had occasion recently to treat a patient who had just been released from an institution following a series of electric shock treatments. His appearance when I first saw him was shocking. His face had a cadaverous expression, the skin was drawn tight on the bones and the mouth drawn in as in death. His voice was barely audible and he could only say "yes" or "no" to a question. All movements were extremely slow, yet he could hit the couch with some degree of force. I used the gag reflex on him twice. Some tears came to his eyes and his face softened and brightened immediately. His legs went into a strong involuntary tremor.

When he returned for the next session, I repeated the procedure. I had him bend his legs several times then hit the couch. When he lay down on the couch, his legs began to tremble rather violently. I used the gag reflex again but this time his expression did not brighten. This surprised me a little because he had come into this treatment looking a little more alive than on the previous occasion. I asked him to strike the couch lying down. His movements were very mechanical. Then, when I stopped his arm in mid-air, it remained in that position. Watching him carefully, I observed that his eyes were becoming more glassy, his expression lifeless and his voice barely audible. I felt that he was receding into himself, falling back into a catatonic stupor. What had happened? One had to deduce that the excitement produced by the aggressive movements was too strong. He was evidently frightened by the strong tremor in his legs. Since he could not control or stop this movement voluntarily, he dissociated his perception from his body. His legs continued to tremble but it was a mechanical action. He was aware that they were moving but it had no significance for him. He was not there.

Where was the self in this state of catatonic stupor? When I asked him if he could hear me, his voice said "yes." I had stopped the trembling in his legs and he lay quiet, motionless. Yet all senses were awake. Light could penetrate those glassy eyes, which were somewhat rolled up, but nothing came out. The aggressive, motor, material side of his being was dormant. The tender, sensory, spiritual component was alive and alert. This aspect of his personality could be reached, the other was withdrawn; he was dissociated. One half of his personality was awake, one half was asleep—a sleep that resembled death. This recalls that feeling expressed by other schizophrenics that it is their body that dies, not the spirit or the mind. I made him sit up and I talked to him, explaining what had happened. Gradually his eyes brightened and his face became alive. Then a sad expression came over it. When we finished the session, he was more normal looking than at the end of the preceding hour.

This is an observation of a state of catatonic stupor which bears some resemblance to sleep. We could understand more about this state if we knew more about the dynamic, bioenergetic mechanism of normal sleep. In catatonic rigidity we find the same dissociation but the muscular system is frozen rather than stuporous. In both cases, the motility of the organism is very much reduced, but in catatonia sensory perception is alert. What is of prime importance in the study of these phenomena is the relation of the ego to the motor process. While the latter is purely a psychic phenomenon, it is dependent upon the underlying bioenergetic process in the soma. The ego can be compared to a cork riding on the waves. Its upward or downward movement is the result of the wave motion. At the same time it is the most vivid manifestation of that motion. Or it can be compared to the electric light bulb which will manifest the flow of current in the circuit.

If the ego is dependent upon the body current, the latter itself can be independent of the perceptual process. If an important split occurs between perception and movement, if the current is prevented from reaching the perceptual organ, we have the manifestation of projection and hallucination. In catatonia, the unity of perception and impulse exists to some degree. Just because of this unity, the ego, in self-defense, will subdue the impulse even at the expense of temporary cessation of its function. This is not a willed and conscious process. This function of repression belongs to that part of the ego which we designate as the superego.

We know that the ego has as part of its function as an organ of perception the power to inhibit or release action. This inhibitory function derives from its position of control in the reality principle. It controls, as Freud expressed it, the approaches to motility. It gives the command for action or it can withhold that command. The ego is the captain to whose orders the soldiers are subject. In spinal shock, the inability of the lower neurones to function can be compared to the loss of the captain. Only gradually do the lower echelons recover their autonomous ability to move, but higher coordination is lacking. Bioenergetically, the ego triggers the muscles to discharge. However, it can only trigger that which is charged. The impulse charges the muscles, sets up the action, loads the guns. Then it awaits the order.

Why does the ego withhold its assent? We can well understand the refusal of the ego to permit an action if that action could lead into a foreseeable dangerous situation. We would, then, describe such behavior as rational and not neurotic. The holding back of aggression under circumstances which demand action is the problem posed by all patients in therapy. The psychoanalytic answer is that there is an unconscious fear which makes the ego withhold the action. This fear can be traced back analytically to experiences in early life. But these fears can persist despite an awareness of these early traumas. The fear must be faced in the present. But what is the present fear?

Bioenergetic work with these problems has forced the realization that the fear is related to the spasticity of the tissues. When a strong impulse reaches a spastic muscle a danger situation arises. A possible analogy is the comparison with a small balloon into which one attempts to blow a large volume of air. One risks having it explode in their face. A better analogy is the passage of a large, hard fecal mass through a contracted anus. The resulting pain is a warning that something may tear. And not infrequently an anal fissure does result.

I treated a patient who had been in Freudian analysis for nine years. One of her main complaints was that she suffered from intense pain in the lumbosacral region. She told me that this pain dated from early in the analysis and coincided with the loss of genital feeling. The deep muscles at the junction of the pelvis and backbone were very tense. I could release some of this tension by special movements and manipulation, but the pain would come and go, and at times it was as severe as ever. I then pointed out to the patient that the tension served to prevent any energy from getting into the genital apparatus. In the early sessions, every mention of genitality made the patient frightened and confused. I had to proceed slowly and depend upon my ability to reduce the deep spasticity. Working this way, verbally to allay her genital anxiety and physically to reduce the tension, I reduced the pain gradually to a point where she was free from it for considerable periods and its severity was considerably less than its former intensity. It was interesting to note that the first strong breakthrough of genital sensation was accompanied by pain in the vagina.

From this brief discussion, we can see that pain is the perception of an intense conflict. The somatic components of this conflict are an energy force which meets a barrier. If the barrier consists of spastic tissues, we can try to elucidate the etiological factors responsible for this condition. It is like a functional scar, which resulted from the original traumatic situation and is the present day basis for the unconscious fear. It must be conceded that no permanent improvement will occur unless the early history is analytically worked through. But can it be denied that direct work upon the spasticity will reduce the fear and enable the conflict to be more readily apprehended in consciousness? It is not our task to force the barrier of pain although the tolerance of pain is part of the reality principle. Only to the degree that the spastic condition is improved and better motility established is the dead hand of the past removed from present day functioning.

In the third edition of *Character Analysis*, Reich reported on a case of schizophrenia which he treated with bioenergetic methods. I should like to comment on his observations, first, because they formed the starting point of my own thinking, and, second, because my experience has placed me in a position to elaborate on his concepts. Reich's study of schizophrenia had the great merit of attempting to comprehend the mechanisms of the schizophrenic problem in terms of the basic bioenergetic functions. Its weakness lay in the fact that Reich's point of reference was the pleasure principle and not the reality principle.

In place of the reality principle, Reich introduced the concept of the development of coordination. One must agree that the growth of consciousness of self is related to the increasing ability of the organism to coordinate or fuse its various muscular activities into purposeful movements in relation to reality. Reich's (1949, p. 446) statement on this point is basic to any comprehension of the dynamics of the schizophrenic problem. "With the growing coordination of the movements, their perceptions are also coordinated one by one with each other, until, gradually, the point is reached when the organism moves in a coordinated fashion as a whole and, therefore, the many different perceptions of the self are united into one total perception of the moving self. Not until then, we must conclude, can we speak of a duly developed consciousness." This coordination doesn't take place in a vacuum.

It occurs as a reaction to the continued stimulation from a warm and loving environment. Coordination represents, therefore, a better, and more effective orientation towards the environment and this, in term, becomes the reality function.

It is Reich's contention that the schizophrenic, in contrast to the armored neurotic, is strongly charged emotionally. On the surface this may seem true for they belong to the category of impulsive character structures. This appearance can be explained by the fact that they lack ego defenses, which is related to their lack of a strong ego. Actually what we find is that they are more sensitive than the neurotic and less aggressive. We must not be misled by their destructive outbursts. It is easy to break things or destroy them. Aggression, however, implies a constructive goal. The sensory function is overdeveloped while the coordination and unity of the motor function is greatly disturbed. It is the lack of unity and coordination in motor activity which explains the phenomena that puzzled Reich. The schizophrenic has a soft chest and reduced respiration while the neurotic, with a rigid chest, has a better respiratory function. Why this is so we shall see later. In general, Reich (1949, p. 459) correctly stated the problem when he wrote that in the schizophrenic, "The biosystem has a very low tolerance for sudden increases of the emotional, i.e., bioenergetic, level of functioning."

In his analysis of one case, Reich (1949, p. 415) recognized that the schizophrenic split, however expressed, such as between Good and Evil, represented the dissociation of the personality into two "diametrically opposite situations in her character structure which were mutually exclusive and incompatible." These opposite situations are nothing other than the two basic instinctual tendencies, aggression and tenderness, material and spiritual, "this world" and "that other world." Since the patient identified with the spiritual aspect and lived in "that other world," the aggressive, real world of material needs and feelings was felt as strange, alien and the "forces which influence" one. The "forces" in this patient must be interpreted as the energy of the material aggressive drive. Since this drive is the expression of the life force in the tissues of the body, no one can fully repress it. If it is not perceived and accepted as part of the personality; some contact with it will be established indirectly via projection and introjection.

Loss of contact with the aggressive, material, driving power manifests itself as total depersonalization. Reich's patient experienced this total depersonalization as being "outside of myself; I felt double, a body here and a soul there." We have already studied the mechanism of this total depersonalization. This patient, as all individuals, desired the unification but she rejected the body, through which that unification is alone possible.

In many schizophrenic experiences we find that the walls of a room play an important role. Hearing voices and seeing things at the walls is a common schizophrenic experience. The most vivid statement by the schizophrenic is that the "walls are alive." To understand this remark we must bear in mind that the schizophrenic perceives movement outside of himself while his perception of internal motility is blocked; that is, the schizophrenic perceives the effect of his projection as a reflection from the walls without being aware that he is its source. What makes the walls seem alive is the energy movement in the space. When we look at an object through a charged space, the vibration of the space is projected onto the object which then seems to be independently alive. That space itself is alive in the sense of movement and vibration under all conditions is a fact which the impressionist painters so vividly portrayed and which, today, few artists would deny. The schizophrenic is much more sensitive to phenomena such as these than the average person.

The property some individuals have to excite and charge the atmosphere about them is recognized. Many strong individuals have such a powerful personality that it seems to radiate from them. We say that "we feel their presence."

Or it is sometimes described as "animal magnetism." The strongest manifestation of this property is reserved for the eyes. In some persons, the eyes seem to shine or glow. When such eyes are turned upon one, one can feel the radiation emanating from them. Sometimes the eyes can have a radiation which is cold and evil, so strong that one can feel a shudder of terror when in contact with them. If we take seriously the common expression that the "eyes are the mirrors of the soul" we can have a better appreciation of these phenomena.

The eyes transmit feeling more vividly than any spoken word. In my career as an analytic psychiatrist I have always relied upon the expression in the eyes of patients. I have seen their sadness and their fear, their rebuke and their anger; their appeal, their love and their hate. But it was outside of my therapeutic work that I had my most striking experience with the look in another person's eyes. The incident occurred while riding in a subway train. A young woman who sat opposite to my wife and myself suddenly turned her eyes upon us. I felt a chill go through me as I found myself looking into the most hateful eyes I have ever seen. My wife reported the same reaction; we could not look at them. It was an uncanny experience.

It is in his eyes that the schizophrenic shows most clearly his illness. One can make the diagnosis, at times, from the eyes alone. Reich described it as "a typical far-away look of remoteness." They seem to look through you and not at you. When you look at their eyes you feel that you do not make contact with them. What is wrong with these eyes? How do they "go off"? In my catatonic patient, his eyes were so glassy that he looked like a cadaver. Yet, and this is astonishing, he saw everything about him. The only possible interpretation was that light could enter his eyes, the mechanical function of vision was intact, but *nothing* came out. It is as if the internal fire was extinguished or dampened. When my patient came out of his catatonic stupor, his eyes immediately came to life and looked friendly. What troubles the observer about the eyes of the schizophrenic is their lack of expression. Just as the face is masklike, so are the eyes expressionless. The schizophrenic is not without feeling, what he lacks is the ability to focus that feeling upon another person. Here, again, we see the lack of motor coordination manifested in the difficulty of body expression.

There is a difference between seeing and looking. The dictionary tells as that the former is a passive function. The definition of the verb "look" is interesting. I quote: "to direct the eye toward anything, to direct the vision with a certain manner or feeling."* The schizophrenic sees but he doesn't look. He hasn't available in the head segment the motor impulse necessary to "direct" his regard. It is the same lack which accounts for the flat, dull, lifeless expression in the region of the forehead between the eyes and for the empty feeling in the front of the head. The energy is blocked in the back of the neck and sometimes in the back of the head. It does not come through to the front part of the brain or head.

It is not an easy task to bring this energy through and to hold it in the eyes. To achieve this it is also necessary to increase the charge at the genital region and to hold it there. In one of my most favorable cases this took six months of sustained bioenergetic therapy. But we seek even more. We seek to strengthen the energy swing and to anchor it in the functions of reality so that it can withstand the pressures and vicissitudes which life in a social milieu entails.

Psychiatry is familiar enough with the schizophrenic problem to reach a correct diagnosis from a careful history or through the use of such tests as the Rorschach. Borderline cases, however, are more difficult to diagnose, although easier to treat. In the next chapter we will study the dynamics of the schizoid character structure as it is revealed in the analyst's office.

* *The Winston Dictionary (College Edition).* New York, Collier & Son, 1943.

17

The Schizoid Character

I suggested in the preceding chapter that the distinction between the schizophrenic and the schizoid character structure was one of degree. This is not to say that qualitative differences cannot be found. Certainly, at the extremes, one may hesitate to compare the institutionalized schizophrenic with the well functioning schizoid character. Yet basic similarities in the underlying dynamic processes of the personality structure compel the comparison for both theoretical and therapeutic reasons.

If an individual has never made an acute break with reality are we justified in describing the structure as schizoid? Such a diagnosis depends upon tendencies and not events. One hesitates to act on this basis in internal medicine. Few physicians will diagnose a patient as a potential cardiac if no structural damage can be proved. But one risks the attack which can and has happened as the patient leaves the doctor's office. If tendencies can be clearly established as criteria for diagnosis, preventive medicine will be greatly advanced. Depth analysis, either psychologically or bioenergetically, offers such a means to this end.

Fenichel (1945, p. 443) defines the schizoid problem in different terms: "Persons who without having a true psychosis yet show single traits or mechanisms of a schizophrenic type have been designated " 'schizoid' or 'schizo-phreniainitis' or 'ambulatory schizophrenia' or the like." Such individuals will show evidence of pathogenic mechanisms of a neurotic kind and of a psychotic kind. Then Fenichel adds a remark which is dynamically important. "Circumstances will decide whether the psychotic disposition will be provoked further or soothed." It is just this presence of a "psychotic disposition" as opposed to psychotic behavior which distinguishes the schizoid character from the schizophrenic. But what exactly is this "psychotic disposition"? While it may be helpful to point to "single traits" or "mechanisms" as evidence of such a disposition, it is fundamentally dangerous to base a diagnosis upon their presence or absence. One may recall the case presented in Chapter 10 on masochism in which the patient described a real hallucination; the vision of a face which he called "the devil." I had no hesitation in classifying the character structure as masochistic and not schizoid. He lacked a "psychotic disposition." On the other hand, I have seen cases in which this basic disposition could be discerned without a manifest single psychotic trait or mechanism.

All authors are agreed that in the schizoid character there is an important affective disturbance. Fenichel (1945, p. 445) specifically states that, "The emotions of these persons generally appear to be inadequate. . . . They behave 'as if' they had feeling relations with people." While such statements are basically true, it is difficult to use them as distinguishing characteristics. Neurotics show inadequate emotional responses, exhibit an "as if" behavior and use mechanisms of "pseudo contact" in their relations to other people. But I, too, am forced to say that the aggression of the schizoid is an "as if" aggression, it is "put on" as a matter of survival and bears the same relation to the personality as clothes. One senses that it is not an integral part of the real being.

The psychotic disposition must first be understood in terms of ego psychology. Let us compare it with the other character types. The rigid character structure is dominantly aggressive, determined and insensitive. His attitude may be characterized by the expression, "I will." Now, the will may be weak or strong depending on the physical strength and vitality of the body. The strength of the "I" or ego depends on the freedom from pregenital drives which may be intermixed in the structure. We have thus a quantitative factor and a qualitative factor. The masochistic structure is doubtful, hesitant and ambivalent. His basic attitude is reflected in the expression, "I won't," although on the surface he may make every effort to be positive. He invariably fails. The aggression of the masochist is turned inward, it is self-destructive. Regardless of the physical strength of the masochist, his "I" (ego) is weaker than that of the rigid character. His genital function is less secure and his attitude towards reality vacillates. The oral character has a weak aggressive drive. His attitude may be subsumed as an "I can't." This inability to cope with the demands of reality leads him to reject them. He carries a deep resentment against the injustice and unfairness of the social system. His ego is weak, for it is still tied to his oral needs and sense of deprivation, but it is real. The oral character identifies strongly with this ego attitude for he feels it to be the basis of his personality. To give it up is to lose his identity as he has always know it.

Now what of the ego structure in the schizoid personality? It shows none of these basic attitudes and all of them. Sometimes the schizoid acts with strong determination, but it doesn't last. The aggression doesn't collapse into a morass feeling, it disappears. When it surges there is a feeling of omnipotence because it has not been tested by reality. The function of reality testing is relatively undeveloped. This omnipotence of aggression differs from the inflated ego and elation of the oral character in that it is a true material drive. It is experienced as a power to do things and not as a power of thought. Where the oral character cannot accomplish anything with his inflated ego, the schizoid may and can be constructively creative. The very lack of ego restraint may make possible a breakthrough of the barriers of reality as they are ordinarily known into new ways of feeling and acting. We owe much to just such achievements by artists like Van Gogh, Gaugin and others. It is a will without an "I."

Ingrained characterological attitudes of "I won't" and "I can't" are missing from the schizoid personality. Since his basic attitude derives from a denial of the values of material reality he has no need to fight this reality. On the surface, though, one may find masochistic attitudes and oral tendencies which derive from specific experiences in his life history. These, however, are not related to the ego. They do not manifest themselves in the transference situation and are not found as deep resistances. In fact it is characteristic of the schizoid that he has few if any real ego defense mechanisms. For this reason, too, once a good contact has been established with him, the therapy may advance at a surprising rate. This explains Fenichel's (1945, p. 451) observation that, "Sometimes schizoid personalities react more favorably to analysis than one expects."

The schizoid character functions in reality as a matter of survival but without the inner conviction that its values are real. He lacks the control over his reactions which the neurotic has, neurotic though that control may be. He is more at the mercy of external forces than the neurotic. He responds to affection immediately and directly but just as immediately will he freeze in a situation which he feels is negative.

Where the schizophrenic in his break with reality completely loses his ego, the schizoid character can avoid the break and retain his ego. But it is a weak ego, weaker than the ego of the oral character. It is not that the schizoid character doesn't feel himself, he does. It is his feeling of himself in relation to material reality that is weak. On the other hand, his capacity for spiritual feeling, for tenderness, for sympathy is great. The schizoid perceives himself as a spiritual person, full of deep feeling, tenderness, sympathy, etc. Unfortunately, it is difficult for him to focus this upon an object in the material world; his lack of ego identification with and control over his motor coordination is an obstacle. Actually, the schizoid character can focus tender feelings upon another individual briefly. The tension created by the attempt to maintain contact forces a break. The concept of motor coordination must be understood as describing movement which is integrated with appropriate feeling. Dissociated movement is possible; the schizoid character may be an excellent ballet dancer. Dissociated feeling is typical, expressive movement is difficult. The tendency to instinctual defusion, to the dissociation of movement and feeling is characteristic of this condition.

Where the schizophrenic in his break with reality will suffer from depersonalization, the schizoid character maintains the body-mind unity by a tenuous thread. He uses his body as I use my automobile. He has no feeling that he is his body, but rather that the body is the abode of his feeling and thinking self. This is not infantile for it in no way reflects the infant's identification with bodily pleasure. The body of an individual is his most immediate reality as it is also the bridge which connects his inner reality with the material reality of the outer world. Here, then, we have the key to the therapeutic treatment of the schizoid personality. First, to bring about some identification with or to increase an identification with kinaesthetic body sensation. Second, to increase the depth and range of expressive movement. Third, to develop the body relationship to objects: food, love object, work objects, clothes, etc. The effect of this approach is to strengthen and develop the ego which, as Freud reminds us, "is first and foremost a body ego."

Let us study the dynamics of the body structure as we see it in schizoid characters. Frequently we are first impressed by the appearance of the head. It never looks as if it were firmly attached to the neck. Not uncommonly it is held at a slight angle in such a way that one feels it could roll to either side. Other character types sometimes carry the head inclined to one side in an expression of hopelessness. In these cases, the total body structure has the same expression. The schizoid or schizophrenic attitude is one of detachment, as if the head were pulled out of the main line of energy flow in the body.

Palpation of the neck muscles in the schizoid individual reveals strong isolated tensions but no generalized rigidity. The deep tension at the base of the skull is significant. The head itself is contracted and tight which may give the whole head a gaunt expression. Outside of this expression, the face is commonly masklike. The scalp across the top of the head is tight and there is a strong tendency to frontal baldness in the male. We have mentioned the flatness of the forehead and the lack of expression in the eyes. The mouth is never full or sensuous. After a time one is struck by the continued absence of joy, fullness or brightness in the expression. It is not gloomy, it is cold.

The shoulder segment in the schizoid character shows a characteristic disturbance. The arms have power but the movement of hitting is split. The body does not take part in the action. This is a different quality than the disturbance found in the oral character. There the arms appear disjointed and one senses that the evident muscular weakness is the responsible factor. In the oral character, the movement looks impotent; in the schizoid character it looks mechanical. The best way to describe the motion is to say that the arms move on a stiff, non-participating body which makes one think of them as the arms of a windmill. Regardless of the amount of physical strength in the schizoid, this quality cannot be missed. Masochistic movements are characterized by the sense of effort, but not of will. The very nature of the shoulder block is different. In the masochist, the shoulders have a muscle-bound look. The deltoid, trapezius and superficial muscles are overdeveloped. In the schizoid character structure, the muscle tensions are deep and based upon the immobility of the scapula.

I mentioned the quality of the neck tensions. The spasticity deep at the base of the skull is reflected in a corresponding block in the small of the back at the junction of pelvis and spine. This tension is so severe in some schizoid individuals that it may produce acute pain. It differs from the chronic low backache found in the rigid structures. The legs show the same relation to the pelvis that the arms do to the shoulder girdle, that is, there is no freedom at the hip joint. The result is an immobility of the pelvis which is more severe than that seen in any neurotic structure. The muscles of the thighs and legs may be flabby or markedly overdeveloped. In either case, one notes a lack of contact with the legs and with the ground. The feet are invariably weak especially the metatarsal arch. The joints are stiff and immovable and this is most clearly evident in the ankles. I have never seen a schizoid structure in which the ankle joint was flexible; it seems as if the joints are frozen. The importance of this will be evident later.

Fenichel (1945, p. 446) describes two characteristic muscular attitudes. "Usually an extreme internal tenseness makes itself felt by hypermotility or hypertonic rigidity behind an external mask of quietness; at other times the opposite takes place—an extreme hypotonic apathy." The former is a state of hypermotility dissociated from any emotional content. The body is tense and charged but movement is mechanical. In the second case, motility is reduced, but there is less affective dissociation. The hypotonicity is limited to the superficial muscles. Palpation always confirms that the deep muscles are spastic. Two female patients who had a schizoid character structure reported that they tended to retain fluid when they became somewhat apathetic. One patient said that she gained up to sixteen pounds by fluid retention. The increased motility induced by the bioenergetic therapy overcame this tendency.

We noted the observation that the respiration of the schizoid character and of the schizophrenic shows a characteristic disturbance. Reich described the low air intake in spite of the soft chest and seeming large excursion of the rib cage. There is another factor involved in this paradox. In the Schizoid structure the expansion of the chest cavity is accompanied by a contraction of the abdominal cavity. This prevents the diaphragm from descending or we may say that the diaphagm also contracts so that the downward movement of the lungs cannot occur. Under such a condition, the schizoid or schizophrenic makes an effort to breathe in the upper part of his chest in order to get sufficient air.

Further observation of the respiratory movements made me aware that the diaphragm is relatively immobile; it is frozen in a contracted condition. The lower ribs flare outward. Since the diaphragm is inactive, a strong expansion of the chest cavity tends to pull the diaphragm upward by suction. This same suction seems responsible for the collapse of the belly. One observes that the belly is sucked in during inspiration then pushed out during expiration. This is not the normal type of respiration. In the average individual chest and belly tend to make the same movement. This unity of the respiratory movement, one in which the wall of the thorax and abdomen move as one piece, is very evident in animals and children.

This kind of schizophrenic respiration has an emotional sign. If you duplicate it in yourself (inflate your chest and pull in your belly), you will hear a gasp as air enters your lungs. It is not difficult to recognize this as an expression of fright. The schizophrenic breathes as if he were in a state of terror. Occasionally this terror can be discerned in the expression of the eyes and face.

One immediate result of the immobility of the diaphragm is a division of the body into two halves, upper and lower. This is not a reflection of the antithetical relationship of ego and sexuality based upon the pendular energy swing which maintains the basic unity. The schizophrenic split represents the collapse and dissociation of the ego and of sexuality. The sexual behavior of the psychotic in the institution and of the schizophrenic outside may be regarded as an attempt to maintain or establish some function in reality. The use of sex as a means to establish contact with another human characterizes the sexual behavior of the schizoid character.

We can explain all these observations by the bioenergetic concept of lack of unity in the body structure. The various segments of the body are functionally split off from each other. But this is a quantitative phenomenon. In the severe case, the chronic schizophrenic, this splitting of the body structure is clearly evident from their figure drawings and in their body image (see Fig. 18). The schizoid character shows the splitting only as a tendency. Machover (1949, pp. 62, 75, 137) has observed this phenomenon in her study of the drawings of the human figure. "Schizophrenic or extremely depressed subjects may omit the arms as indication of positive withdrawal from people and things." Here is how Machover interprets another schizophrenic drawing. "The broken line further permits a fluidity of environmental exchange with an unintegrated and insecure body image. It would allow for the escape and evaporation of body impulses, while not offering protection against the hazards of the environment." Again, she shows good insight into the problem in this observation. "Individuals who indicate the joints may be suspected of a faulty and uncertain sense of body integrity. . . . The schizoid, the frankly schizophrenic individual . . . will lean on joint emphasis to stave off feelings of body disorganization."

Figure drawings will inform us how the subject perceives his own body. It may astonish some to realize that each individual, neurotic or psychotic, perceives it as it is; that is, the body image reflects the functional body. Since function is also expressed in structure and movement, we can use body structure and movement as diagnostic tools and therapeutic agents. In bioenergetic analysis, the interpretation is made from the body itself rather than from the drawing.

The major segmentations in the schizoid and schizophrenic structures are the separation of the head from the body, the splitting of the body in two at the diaphragm, the disunity of trunk and pelvis and the dissociation of the extremities. The separation of the head from the body is

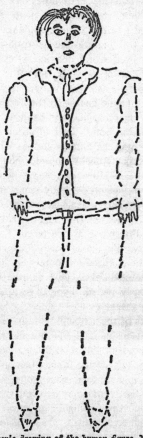

FIG. 18. Schizophrenic drawing of the human figure. Note the accentuation of the head, the dissociation of the hands from the forearms and the broken outline of the body contour. From Machover, Karen, *Personality Projection in the Drawing of the Human Figure,* 1949. Courtesy of Charles C Thomas, Springfield, Ill.

the bioenergetic basis for the split between perception and excitation. The similar separation in the lower half between pelvis and trunk implies a dissociation of the genital sensation from the total body feeling. In addition, the head, the pelvis and the extremities are contracted and undercharged which I would interpret not as a withdrawal from reality but as a failure in development.

In contrast to this picture, the neurotic structure shows a definite unity. In the oral character this unity is manifest in the withdrawal upward from the earth. This is very clear in the tall, asthenic individual. We can deduce it from the fact that the energy in the oral character tends to flow upward, overcharging the head at the expense of the lower part of the body. We find a dominance of those activities which may be interpreted as oral. The masochistic structure is typically muscle bound. Frequently the body structure is short and heavy with considerable muscular strength. The whole body seems to be holding in or holding back. The masochist struggles continuously against this total holding. The rigid structures, to the extent of their rigidity, move as one piece. There is no question of their unity. We can say of the schizoid body structure that it is held together loosely as if by the skin. Movements look mechanical. One has the impression that they are consciously willed. Typical gestures which stamp an individual are absent.

Where the eyes of the schizophrenic have the "far away" look which indicates a lack of contact with reality, the eyes of the schizoid patient seek the eyes of the therapist. One is struck by this desire for contact as if it were the dominating principle of their personality. While the voice is generally flat, the words may be clearly enunciated, and this also gives one the feeling of an effort being made. I recall another schizoid patient whose history was one of immense effort against terrible handicaps. In her early therapy, many of the movements were too strong for her. She became confused and frightened. I asked her to stop but she said, "I can take it." In no other type of character structure have I found such sincere effort to overcome problems.

We are in a position now to venture an hypothesis on the etiology of schizophrenia and of the schizoid character structure. We are forced necessarily to proceed inferentially from known bioenergetic principles, but we can confirm our ideas with clinical data and by the observation of infants.

We must begin with the assumption that at conception the organism is a unity. This means that we eliminate heredity as an important factor in the etiology of emotional illness. It may or may not play a role in determining the predisposition to functional pathology, but we must be cognizant of the fact that the importance of heredity as a factor in disease processes is constantly being reduced with the advance of medical knowledge. In previous chapters we studied the main neurotic disturbances in the emotional life of the individual and we elucidated many of the responsible factors. Not one of them nor all of them could produce the psychotic condition without the operation of a different kind of traumatic experience. So far as I know there is only one experience which is so traumatic that it could split the unit of the growing organism. The operative agent could only be described as the hatred of the mother for the child, a hatred which is mostly on the unconscious level.

One must understand the bioenergetic nature of hatred in order to comprehend its etiological role in this disturbance. First, however, let me point up the difference between this factor and those operative in the neuroses. The oral character develops in response to inner feelings of deprivation. The masochistic structure is formed in the process of suppression by a mother who is overprotective and oversolicitous of the child. Rigidity is a product of frustration, and development of the oedipal period. Is it possible that these children have not experienced any hatred from their parents? It is highly unlikely. If one observes the behavior of parents in the various crises which beset them, one will see and hear many expressions of hatred directed towards their children. But these are conscious reactions which pass with the situation. The damaging hatred is unconscious, deep-seated and persistent. It is operative in the very earliest history of the organism.

In ascertaining the nature of hatred we should begin by making an important distinction. Hatred and anger are not the same thing. Anger is a hot feeling which has as its object the removal of an obstacle to the flow of libido. Hatred is cold and unmoving. While anger may be destructive in its manifest action, its aim is basically constructive. Anger does not aim to destroy the object of libidinal attachment, hatred does. Anger is the flood of aggression unmixed with any tender feelings. Yet as soon as the flood recedes, the feelings of tenderness flow again. Anger is the thunderstorm on a summer day which is followed by the sunshine. Hatred may be compared with the unremitting cold and bleakness of a frozen wasteland. Freud pointed out that hatred is related antithetically to love. We all know that one can turn into the other. But how?

To understand a relationship we must define all terms in it. Can we define hate? It might be easier to attempt to define love. This is not so difficult in bioenergetic terms for the basic ingredients are known. We saw that the fundamental instincts were feelings of tenderness and movements of aggression. Love in the strictest sense can be described as the deepest feeling of tenderness expressed with the strongest aggression. Such a statement implies that it is the fullest expression of an organism. We can identify the deepest feeling of tenderness as one that stems directly from the heart and in which the heart is fully involved. The strongest aggressive action involves the total body musculature and expresses in action the full intensity of the heart feeling. It is obvious that such a strict definition does not fit all the manifestations which are described as love. The definition can be extended, then, as we wish, to include expressions in which the heart feelings are appropriately expressed in aggressive action although the intensity of the feeling and the strength of the aggression vary. Let us study some specific cases.

The love of a mother for the nursing infant is heartfelt and deep. Yet while the intensity of the tender feelings is at a maximum, the aggression is considerably reduced. At most it involves the upper half of the woman's body with emphasis upon the action of the mammary glands. We mentioned earlier that tender feelings which do not involve the aggressive tendencies can be described as sympathy, pity, etc. For that reason, those who need the physical warmth of body contact reject these feelings. If no tenderness is involved in the physical action its emotional quality can be described as sadism. Many women sense the sadism in an act of intercourse which lacks a tender feeling. Love, in every one of its expressions, seeks the union of two organisms on both the spiritual and physical levels. In the sexual act which is an expression of love the most complete union and identity of two organisms is possible.

What about hatred? Hate is frozen love. This explains why, as love cools, there is always the danger that it may turn into hate. On the other hand it is also possible that hate can be thawed out again into love. The mechanism whereby this freezing takes place is complicated. Two factors are involved in the process which depends upon a special predisposition. That special predisposition is a rigid structure, the two factors are cold and pressure.

In hate, the heart is cold and hard, the tender feelings are turned to ice. For this to happen, tremendous pressure must be exerted, the process being analogous to that whereby air is converted into a liquid. The pressure is exerted by the individual whose love is rejected. We noted in Chapters 12 and 13 on the hysterical character structure that the child who is frustrated on the genital level stiffens up and becomes rigid. Among adults we describe such an individual as proud, for pathological pride is expressed by a stiff neck and back. In effect this pride says,

"I shall not love you, then you cannot hurt me." Once this pattern of stiffening up in response to frustration is established it becomes a set pattern of response which is operative in later life.

Only a rigid character can become truly hateful. The oral character lacks the muscular development and aggression to confine his tender feelings. His need is too great. The suffering of the masochist prevents his freezing up. Hate is frequently the end result of a severe frustration in later life, generally the culmination of a loveless marriage in which the rigid partner is caught by his own rigidity and inability to move. Unable to seek a new love object, the hurt spouse reacts to the partner's cold by stiffening and becoming more rigid until finally the heart is frozen. This is a picture of the hateful person: cold skin, hard and cold eyes, rigidity of the body, cold hands which hurt rather than caress, and a manner which is impersonal, cold, compulsive and tight. Now what is the effect of this hate upon the sensitive, dependent infant?

The child of a hateful woman is subjected to this cold long before it is born. If the heart is cold and hard, what can we expect of the womb?* The embryo growing and developing in a cold, hard womb will also freeze but in a way that is different from the freezing which takes place at an adult age. In the womb the freezing is due solely to the cold and not to the pressure. The embryo is also much more highly charged energetically than the adult and its energy resists the freeze much better than the energy system of the rigid adult.

The process of this freezing may be compared to what happens to a water solution of brown sugar when it is gradually frozen. After a time one notes that the brown color is concentrated in the center while the periphery of the solution is clear ice. The center retains its fluidity to the last since the cold penetrates from the outside inward.

* Cf. Wilhelm Reich in *Character Analysis*, ed. 3. New York, Orgone Institute Press, 1949, p. 447.

There is produced in this fashion a partial separation of the solute and the solvent. Quick freezing or freezing under pressure would trap the ions or molecules of the solute in the frozen solvent and immobilize them. This observation can be repeated with other colored solutions.

In the embryo within a cold, unloving womb, a similar separation occurs. The free energy of the organism withdraws to the center while the peripheral system is frozen; that is, the core is alive but the structural elements close to the surface become frozen. Without this analogy one cannot explain the tendency to complete defusion which is characteristic of schizophrenia. What is frozen, then, is the physical motility of the organism. I do not mean to say that the foetus is turned into a block of ice. The freezing process is not so intense as to destroy life. Actually, its effect is most intense at the natural constrictions of the body, those areas which do not contain big organs which have quite a strong independent charge. One should expect to find the frozen condition most evident in the neck and waist and at the joints. These are the places where schizophrenic and schizoid structures show the greatest disturbance of motility. This is not schizophrenia. It is, however, the indispensable predisposition to this illness.

Postnatal life may provide a sufficiently warm environment to thaw the frozen areas. However, since it is unlikely that the birth of the child will in itself transform the mother, the newborn infant is projected into an environment which is frequently more openly hostile than the one it experienced in the protected state of the womb. The danger now becomes more evident. It becomes the gradual experience of the infant and the child that reality, experienced as the cold and hateful mother, poses a threat to life. On no other basis can we understand the utter terror, the fear of persecution and of physical violence and death which torment the schizophrenic.

These remarks are not intended as a condemnation of the mothers of schizophrenic patients. Our sympathy must extend to them as victims of a disturbance which in its own way is more severe than that experienced by their unfortunate offspring. One recalls again Dostoevsky's remark that "Hell is the suffering of those unable to love." Their unconscious sense of guilt in later life is pitiable.

One of the best books on the psychoanalytic therapy of schizophrenia is L. B. Hill's *Psychotherapeutic Intervention in Schizophrenia*. In this valuable work, he discusses the mothers of schizophrenics in a warm personal way. Hill (1955, pp. 109, 112, 121) admits that many psychiatrists regard the mothers of schizophrenics as "utterly hostile, malicious, and in every way a misfortune," but he feels that this is not completely true. Hill regards these mothers as ambivalent. But this is not the ambivalence of to love or not to love. It is the ambivalence of to love or to hate. From the surface appearance they may want to love this child and they may try, but an underlying hate prevails. Witness this remark, "Psychiatrists interviewing the mothers of schizophrenic patients have reported feeling much as a schizophrenic seems to feel—that mother is superficially optimistic, cooperative, friendly, and yielding, but that not far beneath the surface she freezes when anything unpleasant is mentioned." Too bad we have no record of the look in her eyes. It is on this occasion that her eyes will show the hatred which froze the infant. One more quote from Hill to show how close good psychoanalytic thinking is to bioenergetic thinking: "The disappointments which these mothers have in reality throw them painfully back into their world of inner objects of love and hate. The child who is being carried at the time of great stress and who comes from within and has recently been a part of the mother is the natural heir to all of her frustrated object seeking."

There is no theoretical consideration which urges us to place the earliest etiology of the schizophrenic condition in the prenatal period. Deprivation of mother love is not an experience which so far can be identified as occurring prior to the birth of the child. Adults who suffer from this feeling of deprivation show an infantile pattern of behavior. If the trauma is more severe than this it must represent a negative attitude and not the absence of a positive one. Such a negative attitude in the mother must have an adverse effect upon the child she is carrying at the time. This time element is the reason why one child will show this disturbance while his siblings may be free from it.

If, in this discussion, I have oversimplified the problem my intention to do so was deliberate. I have desired to make a point from which more detailed studies and investigation can be undertaken.

We saw the effect of hate upon the bioenergetic system of the child. How does this translate itself in terms of his emotional development? What are the psychological correlates of this disturbed bioenergetic state?

The schizoid character and certainly the schizophrenic must struggle through life with a vital core of feeling and energy but with a crippled and bound motor system for discharge. Since he can rely very little upon his motor system, he depends upon his heightened sensitivity to avoid danger and achieve success in the material world. This is of course inadequate so that his frustration increases the sense of conflict. Basically the conflict is what to do with his aggressive tendencies. For, like in all conditions of traumatic injury, there is an unconscious struggle to restore the lost unity. What prevents this?

Difficult as is the adult world of reality in which the schizoid or schizophrenic finds himself, it is a world of physical warmth as compared to the environment of his infancy and childhood. But while this warmth offers promise it also poses danger. The thaw may produce a flood which will overflow the banks. The flood of aggression, dissociated from tender feelings, could only lead to one thing: murder, the destruction of the object who threatened and hurt him, the smashing of all reality. Hill (1955, p. 151) put it well when he wrote, "for the schizophrenic to gain that independence from his infantile superego which is one of the goals of psychoanalysis is in his feeling fully equivalent to his murder of his mother."

We come to the conclusion then that the schizophrenic

hates his mother unconsciously. But he is not a cold, hateful person. His hate does not involve his heart, only his muscles. It was not his heart that froze, only his muscular system. But this poses a real problem for the bioenergetic therapist since any attempt to thaw out the frozen state must be made very gradually and under control. The schizophrenic is so much afraid of his hatred that he will resist any attempt to mobilize his aggression. Once this fear is broken through great progress can be made. Rosen (1953, p. 150) understands this so well intuitively that he will take up the challenge of the patient's aggression directed against himself. "The aim of therapy is to direct this aggression toward the therapist rather than to have the patient dissipate it amorphously in his usual schizophrenic fashion." This may lead to an actual physical struggle with the patient in which the physician can prove that physical aggression can be controlled to constructive ends.

This latent hatred of the schizophrenic for his mother is the bond that ties him to her just as her latent hatred binds her to the patient. Hatred not only freezes the individual motility, it also freezes the relationship. It is as if the schizophrenic and his mother were frozen together in a mutual bond of hatred and repugnance.

The schizoid character, in contrast to the schizophrenic, has much greater motility and coordination, a better organized ego and a measure of independence. In his treatment we can count on a greater conscious participation. Nevertheless, the basic schizophrenic tendencies are present and the therapy must be oriented along the same line as if one were treating a schizophrenic.

The schizophrenic and the schizoid character have no ego defenses. Now this will be a tremendous positive factor in their therapy for they cannot and do not unconsciously resist. Not that resistance is a conscious phenomenon. The schizoid character is unaware of any real resistance, but it will take the form of distrust, of fear of the therapist, of fear of the therapy. He is aware of this. These are patients who have no defense in depth and so must be on guard. As against this kind of resistance the therapist can only offer his sincere effort, his humility and his honesty.

As part of this lack of ego defense, the schizophrenic and the schizoid character have great sensitivity—especially about people upon whom they feel dependent. It has been said by others that they respond directly to the unconscious and I would subscribe to this statement. They can see through the therapist as quickly as any therapist can see into them. And who of us is free from his neurotic problem? To help them, then, one must know one's self well, especially his limitations and weaknesses. Since we cannot offer our schizophrenic or schizoid patient a perfect human being, we must make no pretense of doing so. We offer reality, the reality of ourselves which is the sincerity of our effort, the humility of our attitude and the honesty of our conscience.

These are indispensable personal qualities which every therapist working with such patients must have. There is one more thing which is absolutely required. That is warmth. No amount of sincerity, humility or honesty can help a schizophrenic or schizoid patient without the real warmth of the therapist's feeling for the patient. This means that the therapist must be a warm person and that he must really like the patient. The therapist's warmth is the therapeutic agent by means of which he can bring the patient more deeply into reality. Now here is where the lack of ego defense proves its aid. The neurotic will question even a sincere expression of warmth and affection, and only when the neurotic defense is eliminated is it fully accepted. Not so the schizoid or schizophrenic. To the degree that it is freely given is it freely accepted. Despite the magnitude of the problem, it is a great pleasure to work with the schizoid personality. In the course of therapy, as the warmth pervades their being, they will give generously to their therapist.

The schizoid and the schizophrenic demand one more

quality in their therapist. They demand that the therapist understand them. Other patients want this, too, but their neurosis blinds them to its presence or absence. These are isolated individuals who live in a world which differs from ours but which is just as real to them. It must be real to the therapist too. I am not speaking of the world of hallucinations and delusions but the real world of spiritual feelings to which they have access. Further, one must have to some degree at least a sensitivity which parallels theirs. It is for this reason that the schizoid characters fully understand one another. It is also true that one who has overcome this illness or disturbance is, perhaps, the therapist who can make the closest contact with them. If, in addition to the understanding of their spiritual feelings, one also understands their body sensations and can speak intelligently about them, a close and important bond can be established with the patient. It is in this respect that the knowledge of the dynamics of the bioenergetic processes is so important. One schizoid patient told me that she was way ahead of the analysts who worked with her. She had to interpret everything for them. But it is not enough that we be with them in our understanding. We must be ahead of them. In the sphere of aggressive behavior, of material reality, of sexual functioning, the schizoid character is a novice. It is not a matter of repression of attitudes or feelings about this world. It is a world he never fully entered into, which he doesn't know and doesn't trust. It is a world of action in which the tender feelings are fused with an aggressive component.

It is one thing to bring a schizophrenic back to a reality he once knew, it is another to build his ego to function fully and adequately in a world he didn't know. This other world is the world of the body and bioenergetic therapy offers the means of giving the patient immediate experience in this world. This is not to say that this other world cannot be experienced except through bioenergetic therapy. It is experienced in the contact of a good transference relationship and, to some extent, in any physical activity the patient may engage in outside of the therapeutic situation. But how much better it is if this experience can be gained directly and increasingly in the therapeutic session. For the warmth that the patient needs is the heat produced by the energy flow in his own tissues and musculature. Few patients are more thrilled than when they find their body becoming alive, their extremities warm, their skin pink and rosy.

I recall one patient who in the early part of her therapy became confused, bewildered and frightened when I had her arch her body backward and hold the position. She had to stop after only a few seconds. She began to shake and tremble but she didn't know what she was afraid of. I could point out that she was afraid of the sensation in her back, that she was afraid she would be overwhelmed, or that she might fall apart. All she knew was that she was confused. Yet in repeating the procedure and in having her work with her body steadily, she began to lose the confusion and fear. After a time she told me that she was no longer confused or afraid and that periods of confusion which troubled her outside of therapy had likewise disappeared. She could do more things with her body as she gradually gained control. Then she began to free more energy in herself and to experience pleasure as a bodily sensation in movement. If one knows the difficulties these patients have in coming to tolerate body pleasure, one can appreciate this advance. In all these patients, their ability to experience pleasure as a body sensation is a criterion of their increasing health. In another patient, this experience of energy streaming pleasurably through his body, although on the surface, was one of the finest experiences of his life.

One might ask at this point, in what way do the bioenergetic movements differ from physical exercises or other forms of physical activity? This is a very pertinent question for the therapy of this problem. Many schizoid characters have studied dancing yet it did not solve their basic problem. And, in fact, the whole range of bioen-

ergetic therapy revolves around a limited range of movements. But these are movements or attitudes in which the
unity of the body is dynamically stressed. It is only when
the total organism partakes in a movement that that movement becomes emotionally expressive. It is precisely because of this inability to move in a unitary way that the
schizoid or schizophrenic character is emotionally dull.
The neurotic who has this unity, even if characterologically rigid or patterned, is capable of a limited degree of
emotional expression.

It is important to the whole question of bioenergetic
therapy that the therapist have a thorough knowledge of
the dynamics of body movement. In hitting the couch, for
example, different individuals will use different parts of
the body. Some will strike only with the arms, their backs
are not in it. Some will use their backs, but the arms move
only as mechanical appendages. Only when an effort is
made to involve the whole body in the action is there a
concomitant feeling of anger. It is necessary to observe
which parts of the body are held back in the action to understand the nature of the block to the release of the appropriate emotion.

Emotional health may be defined in terms of the ability
of an individual to involve all of himself in his actions and
behavior. It should not be surprising that this implies the
equal ability in appropriate situations to restrain actions.
On the psychological level this may be interpreted as a
statement of the integrity of the ego, one that is not
split into a conscious ego and an unconscious superego;
one that is not divided by the defusion, partial or complete, of its component instincts. On the physical level this
implies the absence of chronic spasticity and tension in
the muscular elements of the body. An increased motility provides a greater range of action and permits more
flexibility in response to situations.

But we are not unaware of the importance of the
body expression as a reflection of its internal qualities.
We reserve a physical term to designate this innate vir-

tue—grace, and we extend this term to honor our leaders. Difficult as such a term is to apply, we can nevertheless hold it out as our ideal of physical harmony in motion just as beauty expresses that ideal in form.

To be free of the physical restraints imposed by chronic spasticities, to be liberated from the fetters of unconscious fears—this and this alone would make man capable of that love in which his deepest heart feelings are expressed with his strongest aggression.

Bibliography

Abraham, Karl, 1921, "Contributions to the Theory of the Anal Character." *Selected Papers on Psychoanalysis I.* New York, Basic Books, 1953.

———, 1924, "The Influence of Oral Erotism on Character Formulation." *Selected Papers on Psychoanalysis I.* New York, Basic Books, 1953.

———, 1925, "Character Formation on the Genital Level of the Libido." *Selected Papers on Psychoanalysis I.* New York, Basic Books, 1953.

Darwin, Charles, 1872, *The Expression of Emotions in Man and Animals.* London, John Murray.

Fenichel, Otto, 1945, *The Psychoanalytic Theory of Neurosis.* New York, Norton.

Ferenczi, Sándor, 1919a, "Technical Difficulties in the Analysis of a Case of Hysteria." *The Theory and Technique of Psychoanalysis II.* New York, Basic Books, 1953.

———, 1919b, "Thinking and Muscle Innervation." *The Theory and Technique of Psychoanalysis II.* New York, Basic Books, 1953.

———, 1921, "The Further Development of an Active Therapy in Psychoanalysis." *The Theory and Technique of Psychoanalysis II.* New York, Basic Books, 1953.

———, 1925a, "Contra-indications to the 'Active' Psycho-analytical Technique." *The Theory and Technique of Psychoanalysis II.* New York, Basic Books, 1953.

———, 1925b, "Psycho-analysis of Sexual Habits." *The Theory and Technique of Psychoanalysis II.* New York, Basic Books, 1953.

———, 1950, *Sex in Psychoanalysis.* New York, Basic Books.

Freud, Sigmund, 1893, "On the Psychical Mechanisms of Hysterical Phenomena." *Collected Papers I.* London, Hogarth Press, 1953.

———, 1894a, "The Anxiety Neurosis." *Collected Papers I.* London, Hogarth Press, 1953.

———, 1894b, "The Defence Neuro-psychoses." *Collected Papers I.* London, Hogarth Press, 1953.

———, 1904a, "Freud's Psychoanalytic Method." *Collected Papers I.* London, Hogarth Press, 1953.

———, 1904b, "On Psychotherapy." *Collected Papers I.* London, Hogarth Press, 1953.

———, 1908, "Character and Anal Erotism." *Collected Papers II.* London, Hogarth Press, 1953.

———, 1910, "The Future Prospects of Psychoanalytic Therapy." *Collected Papers II.* London, Hogarth Press, 1953.

———, 1911, "Formulations Regarding the Two Principles in Mental Functioning." *Collected Papers II.* London, Hogarth Press, 1953.

———, 1912a, "The Dynamics of Transference." *Collected Papers II.* London, Hogarth Press, 1953.

———, 1912b, "The Employment of Dream Interpretation in Psychoanalysis." *Collected Papers II.* London, Hogarth Press, 1953.

———, 1914, "On the History of the Psychoanalytic Movement." *Collected Papers I.* London, Hogarth Press, 1953.

———, 1915a, "Further Recommendations in the Technique of Psychoanalysis." *Collected Papers II.* London, Hogarth Press, 1953.

———, 1915b, "Instincts and Their Vicissitudes." *Collected Papers IV.* London, Hogarth Press, 1953.

———, 1931a, "Female Sexuality." *Collected Papers V.* London, Hogarth Press, 1953.

———, 1931b, "Libidnal Types." *Collected Papers V.* London, Hogarth Press, 1953.

———, 1950a, *Beyond the Pleasure Principle.* New York, Liveright.

———, 1950b, *The Ego and the Id.* London, Hogarth Press.

———, 1953a, *Civilization and Its Discontents.* London, Hogarth Press.

———, 1953b, *New Introductory Lectures on Psychoanalysis.* New York, Norton.

Glueck, E., and Glueck, S., 1956, *Physique and Delinquency*. New York, Harper.

Hill, L. B., 1955, *Psychotherapeutic Intervention in Schizophrenia*. Chicago, University of Chicago Press.

Hoskins, R. G., 1946, *The Biology of Schizophrenia*. New York, Norton.

La Barre, Weston, 1954, *The Human Animal*. Chicago, University of Chicago Press.

Machover, Karen, 1949, *Personality Projection in the Drawing of the Human Figure*. Springfield, Ill., Charles C Thomas.

Maier, N. R. F., and Schneirla, T. C., 1935, *Principles of Animal Psychology*. New York, McGraw-Hill.

Neumann, E., 1954, *The Origins and History of Consciousness*. New York, The Bollingen Foundation.

Reich, Wilhelm, 1942, *The Function of the Orgasm*. New York, Orgone Institute Press.

———, 1949, *Character Analysis* (ed. 3). New York, Orgone Institute Press.

Rosen, J. N., 1953, *Direct Analysis*. New York, Grune & Stratton.

Schilder, Paul, 1950, *The Image and Appearance of the Human Body*. New York, International Universities Press.

Sheldon, W. H., 1940, *The Varieties of Human Physique*. New York, Harper Brothers.

———, 1942, *The Varieties of Temperament*. New York, Harper Brothers.

Szasz, T. S., 1957, *Pain and Pleasure*. New York, Basic Books.

Thompson, Clara, 1950, "Introduction" to Sándor Ferenczi, *Sex in Psychanalysis* (vol. 1). New York, Basic Books.

Weiner, Norbert, 1956, *The Human Use of Human Beings*. New York, Doubleday (Anchor).

Wolfe, T., 1949, "Translator's Preface" to the Second Edition in Wilhelm Reich, *Character Analysis* (ed. 3). New York, Orgone Institute Press.

Index

**If you liked this book
you'll also enjoy the following paperbacks
from COLLIER BOOKS**

ASK YOUR LOCAL BOOKSELLER!